The Intentional Teacher

Choosing the Best Strategies for Young Children's Learning

THIRD EDITION

Amy Schmidtke

Volume Editor

National Association for the Education of Young Children
Washington, DC

National Association for the Education of Young Children

1401 H Street NW, Suite 600
Washington, DC 20005
202-232-8777 • 800-424-2460
NAEYC.org

NAEYC Books

Senior Director, Publishing & Content Development
Susan Friedman

Director, Books
Dana Battaglia

Senior Editor
Holly Bohart

Editor II
Rossella Procopio

Senior Creative Design Manager
Charity Coleman

Creative Design Specialist
Ashley McGowan

Publishing Business Operations Manager
Francine Abdelmeguid

Through its publications program, the National Association for the Education of Young Children (NAEYC) provides a forum for discussion of major issues and ideas in the early childhood field, with the hope of provoking thought and promoting professional growth. The views expressed or implied in this book are not necessarily those of the Association.

The EEA authorised representative is Authorised Rep Compliance Ltd.

Ground Floor, 71 Baggot Street Lower, Dublin, DO2 P593, Ireland

www.arccompliance.com

Permissions

NAEYC accepts requests for limited use of our copyrighted material. For permission to reprint, adapt, translate, or otherwise reuse and repurpose content from this publication, review our guidelines at NAEYC.org/resources/permissions.

The vignette on pages 242–243 is adapted, by permission, from Julie Olsen Edwards, "How to Get Started with Anti-Bias Education in Your Classroom and Program," *Exchange* (January/February 2017): 78–79.

"Language-Rich Communication" on pages 130–131 is adapted from A. Schmidtke, "Language-Rich Communication," Lens of the Child series working paper, December 2022. Used by permission of Buffett Early Childhood Institute, University of Nebraska.

Photo Credits

Copyright © Getty Images: vi, 3, 6, 13, 19, 32, 36, 40, 55, 56, 70, 75, 82, 84, 101, 116, 126, 145, 158, 159, 161, 253, 276, 300; circular headshots in Chapters 3–10

Copyright © NAEYC: cover

Courtesy of Keely Benson: 108, 157, 187, 273

Courtesy of Anatasha Cruz: 216

Courtesy of Yazmín Colón Díaz: 48

Courtesy of Burt Granofsky: 214 (bottom), 218

Courtesy of Cindy Hoisington: 61, 200, 208, 209, 210, 214 (top), 226

Courtesy of Julia Luckenbill: 269

Courtesy of Shenell Samuels: 201

Courtesy of Melany Spiehs: 271

Courtesy of Yen Thieu: 191, 224

Library of Congress Control Number: 2025934508

ISBN: 978-1-952331-39-8

Item: 1174

Contents

Volume Editor and Contributors

Volume Editor

Amy Schmidtke, EdD, is an early childhood educator, instructional coach, and leader with 30 years of experience advancing high-quality early learning. She specializes in guided play, child-centered learning, school-family-community partnerships, and professional development. As director of educational practice at the Buffett Early Childhood Institute at the University of Nebraska, she collaborates with school leaders and educators to strengthen early learning programs and district systems, applying research to enhance leadership, instruction, and family engagement. She holds a doctorate in educational administration from the University of Nebraska at Omaha and drives innovation through leadership, publications, collaboration, and professional learning initiatives.

Chapter Contributors

Holland Banse, PhD
Senior Researcher and Evaluator
Magnolia Consulting
Charlottesville, VA

Susan Bennett-Armistead, PhD
Associate Professor Emerita of Language, Literacy and Culture
School of Learning and Teaching
College of Education and Human Development
University of Maine
Orono, ME

Keely Benson, PhD
Associate Director
Early Childhood Research Center
University at Buffalo
Buffalo, NY

Keri Giordano, PsyD
Associate Professor
Advanced Studies in Psychology
Kean University
Union, NJ

Anne-Lise Halvorsen, PhD
Professor
Teacher Education
College of Education
Michigan State University
East Lansing, MI

Cindy Hoisington
Project Director
Education Development Center (EDC)
Waltham, MA

Tonya Jolley, EdD
Program Administrator
Buffett Early Childhood Institute
University of Nebraska
Lincoln, NE

Julia Luckenbill, MAEd
Adult Educator/Director
Davis Parent Nursery School
Davis Joint Unified School District
Davis, CA

Marie L. Masterson, PhD
Manager, ECE Competence and Practice
Council for Professional Recognition
Washington, DC

Michèle M. Mazzocco, PhD
Professor, Institute of Child Development
Director, Math and Numeracy Lab
University of Minnesota
Minneapolis, MN

Lori E. Meyer, PhD

Associate Professor

University of Vermont

Burlington, VT

Betül Demiray Sandıraz,
MS

PhD Candidate

Teacher Education

College of Education

Michigan State University

East Lansing, MI

Amy Schmidtke

(see biography above)

Kimberlee Telford, MS

Early Childhood Specialist

Buffett Early Childhood Institute

University of Nebraska

Omaha, NE

Crystal N. Wise, PhD

Assistant Professor

College of Education and Human
Development

University of Minnesota

Minneapolis, MN

Additional Content Contributors

Carol Burk, MSEd

Early Childhood Education
Specialist

Nebraska Department of
Education

Omaha, NE

Darcy Heath, MEd

Research Manager

Teaching Strategies

Phoenix, AZ

Tonya Jolley

(see affiliation above)

Amy Schmidtke

(see biography above)

Melany Spiehs, MS

Early Childhood Teacher
Education Instructor

University of Nebraska at Omaha

Omaha, NE

Kimberlee Telford

(see affiliation above)

Other Acknowledgments

NAEYC acknowledges with great appreciation and respect the contributions of Ann S. Epstein, author of the first two editions of *The Intentional Teacher*. This third edition stands upon her extraordinary vision and scholarship.

Thanks go to Michèle Mazzocco (University of Minnesota) and Amy Scrinzi (Meredith College) for their comments on and contributions to drafts of Chapter 7.

Preface

When Ann Epstein first authored *The Intentional Teacher: Choosing the Best Strategies for Young Children's Learning*, she addressed a critical and timely question in early childhood education: How can educators purposefully and effectively teach content to young children in ways that respect their development, curiosity, and individuality? The result was a foundational text that has guided countless educators in their work, challenging us all to reflect on our practices and embrace the role of intentionality in teaching.

As a preschool teacher when the first two editions were published, I found Ann's vision deeply inspiring. Her thoughtful approach to balancing child-guided and adult-guided learning shaped my practice and helped me create environments where children's curiosity and wonder could flourish. Over time, her work became a cornerstone of my professional journey—from teaching young children to facilitating professional learning and guiding early childhood leaders. It is with immense gratitude for her foundational vision that I approached the task of editing this third edition.

So why a new edition of *The Intentional Teacher*? Since the revised edition was published in 2014, advances in education research have expanded our understanding of how children learn and develop, in particular how they engage in deeper content learning than previously thought possible. For example, they tackle higher-level thinking and problem solving in math. They engage in scientific inquiry and thoughtful storytelling as they develop their language and literacy skills. Alongside these developments, our understanding of developmentally appropriate practices has been enhanced by the increasing recognition of the influence of children's cultures on development and learning, inequities in educational opportunities, and the power of curriculum and practices that are meaningful to learners' social and cultural norms, values, and experiences to enable all children to succeed. This third edition reflects these changes while remaining true to the core principles and approach laid out by Ann Epstein.

In this edition, I have had the privilege of working with a team of contributing authors, all experts in their content areas, who bring unique perspectives and specialized knowledge to each chapter. Their contributions have enriched this text with updated strategies and practices that support higher-order thinking, engage children in meaningful and thought-provoking ways, and honor the cultural and linguistic diversity of the young learners in today's early childhood programs. Together, these contributors and I aimed to provide educators with tools to create joyful, inclusive, and curiosity-driven learning environments that offer content-rich experiences where all children can thrive.

The Origins of Intentional Teaching

Questions about the best ways to teach young children are hardly new. As Ann Epstein noted in previous editions of the book, the debate around early childhood instruction often contrasts the extremes of child-initiated learning (where the teacher has a passive role) with those of adult-directed instruction (where children have a passive role and teachers use scripted lessons). Her work offered an essential alternative: a *both/and* approach in which both children and adults play active roles in the learning process.

A guiding principle of this book is that child-guided and adult-guided experiences each "work best for different kinds of learning, and elements of both can be combined effectively" (NAEYC 2022, 7), creating rich, meaningful learning opportunities for young children. For example, children's self-directed play offers many opportunities for teachers to observe and promote learning, and teachers also set goals and plan instructional activities that are based not only on children's interests but also on other knowledge and skills that children need to develop, often articulated in early learning standards.

This book continues to advocate for a thoughtful, intentional approach that uses both child-guided and adult-guided learning experiences. As previous editions did, it supports teachers to consider current theory and research, their knowledge of each child and their context, and their own professional knowledge and expertise to discern when and how to provide each type of learning experience.

This Book's Objectives

The first objective of this edition of *The Intentional Teacher* is to reflect the evolving understanding of early curriculum content and effective teaching strategies since the previous edition. While this edition continues to highlight approaches to rigorous content learning with young children that are grounded in developmentally appropriate practices, it also reflects the field's deepened understanding of how young children learn specific concepts, what content seems to be the most meaningful in the preschool years, and how best to support early learning as a foundation for all future learning. For example, in areas such as science, research continues to refine our understanding of how children develop foundational skills and how educators can foster inquiry and conceptual understanding.

This edition emphasizes strategies that integrate children's prior knowledge, strengths, and curiosity while promoting higher-order thinking and meaningful connections across subject areas. In support of this focus on robust content learning, the book offers ideas and strategies for engaging children in key subject areas through intentional, research-informed interactions.

The second objective is to expand on the integration of principles of equity and practices that reflect the strengths and experiences of children as central to intentional teaching practice. When educators create inclusive environments that weave children's knowledge and experiences into the activities and daily routines of the program, they ensure that every child feels valued and empowered to learn.

Finally, this edition seeks to inspire educators to reflect on their own practice, discover or rediscover effective approaches for teaching subject matter, and embrace the rewards of intentional teaching. There is nothing more fulfilling than witnessing a child's excitement as they master a new skill or explore a new idea. By fostering this excitement and curiosity, we ensure that learning is not only meaningful but also joyful for both children and teachers.

Organization of the Book

The book is organized into two main parts. The first two chapters lay out the meaning of intentional teaching. Chapter 1 introduces the concept and explains the rationale for promoting children's learning of knowledge and skills through both child-guided and adult-guided experiences. Chapter 2 discusses evidence-based practices for creating developmentally appropriate learning environments that support teachers to engage children with content. It has been expanded to delve deeper into the important role of the social and cultural contexts of children, families, and educators in teaching and learning, emphasizing the importance of knowing and valuing each child.

The second part of the book delves into curriculum areas, addressing intentional teaching strategies in eight domains and content areas: approaches to learning, social and emotional learning, physical development and health, language and literacy, mathematics, science, social studies, and creative arts. Each of these chapters begins with an overview of the area and then identifies the knowledge and skills in that area that children seem to acquire primarily through child-guided or adult-guided learning experiences. Throughout the chapters, readers get practical strategies, illustrative examples, and reflective questions to encourage their professional growth and inspire new approaches to teaching. The book concludes with Chapter 11, which offers guiding principles for intentional teaching and reflects on the joy and fulfillment that come from fostering young children's learning. The reference list can be accessed online at NAEYC.org/intentional-teacher-third-edition.

New Features and Advancements in This Edition

This third edition introduces several new features that reflect the field's growing emphasis on equity, cultural responsiveness, and advancing evidence-based practices in early childhood education:

> Role of contributing authors: As mentioned, each chapter is enriched by the expertise of contributing authors who bring fresh perspectives and specialized knowledge to their respective areas. These authors ensure the book reflects the latest research and innovative practices.

> Connecting teaching to children's lives: A new feature embedded in Chapters 3–10 highlights practical examples of how educators incorporate strategies that are developmentally, linguistically, and culturally appropriate for children. These vignettes showcase ways to honor children's social and cultural contexts, integrate family and community values, and create inclusive learning environments.

> Advancements in each domain: While the structure of the curriculum chapters remains consistent with previous editions, the content has been updated to reflect new research. For example, strategies in mathematics focus on fostering problem solving and critical thinking, and updates in creative arts emphasize the role of cultural expression and representation.

> Integration of joy in teaching and learning: This edition intentionally celebrates the joy of teaching by emphasizing the rewards for both teachers and children of environments where children's excitement and curiosity flourish. I hope that this book reminds educators of the transformative power of intentional teaching to inspire lifelong learning.

● ● ●

It has been a privilege to edit this third edition of *The Intentional Teacher* and collaborate with the experienced professionals who have contributed their expertise to it. My hope is that this book inspires you to reflect on your practice, embrace new ideas, broaden your thinking about children's content learning, and find renewed joy in creating learning environments that encourage children to explore, question, and discover. By engaging intentionally and responsively with children to promote their learning, we not only help them grow but also remind ourselves of the transformative power of teaching.

—Amy Schmidtke

CHAPTER 1

Introducing Intentional Teaching

Amy Schmidtke

During choice time, Diego, age 5, stands at the sink, soaking a sponge in water and squeezing it out. His teacher, Miss Sam, kneels beside Diego and imitates his actions.

"It's really heavy!" says Diego after resoaking his sponge.

"I wonder what makes it so heavy," muses Miss Sam.

"I think it's the water," answers Diego.

"How can you tell?" asks Miss Sam.

Diego thinks for a moment, then squeezes out his sponge. "Hey! I squeezed the sponge, and it's lighter now!" he says. "The water! The water makes it heavy!" Diego fills and squeezes out his sponge again, as if to make sure. "Now you make yours lighter," he tells Miss Sam.

"How?"

"Squeeze out the water."

Miss Sam does so and hands the sponge to Diego, who weighs one sponge in each hand. "There you go," he says to Miss Sam. "Now your sponge is light like mine."

Miss Sam turns to Joon, who is 4 years old and has a visual impairment, and asks if he would like to try the sponge experiment that Diego has been describing. Recognizing that Joon relies on tactile manipulation and other means of gathering information to explore and understand new concepts, Miss Sam gently touches Joon's hands with two sponges, guiding him to feel the difference in weight between a wet and dry sponge.

"Can you feel these sponges, Joon?" Miss Sam asks.

Joon feels the two sponges and says, "This one is . . . big?"

"Hmm," Miss Sam replies. "It does feel different, doesn't it? What else do you notice?"

Joon squeezes the wet sponge and then the dry one. "This one is heavy," he says.

"Yes! That's like what Diego noticed," Miss Sam nods. "Why do you think it's heavy?"

Joon listens as Miss Sam pours water onto the wet sponge, making a splashing sound. Joon's face lights up. "It's the water!" he says. "The water makes it heavy!"

"That's right! The water makes it heavy," Miss Sam says enthusiastically.

This book is about how an *intentional teacher,* like Miss Sam, acts with knowledge and purpose to ensure that young children acquire the habits of mind (approaches to learning) and knowledge and skills (content) they need to succeed in school and in life. Intentional teaching does not happen by chance. It is planful, thoughtful, purposeful, and highly complex. Intentional teachers use their knowledge, judgment, and expertise to organize learning experiences for each child. When an unplanned situation arises (as it always does), they embrace it as a teaching opportunity to tap into children's innate curiosity and interest in how things work.

Intentional teaching means acting with specific outcomes or goals in mind for each child and for all domains of children's development and learning. Content areas of learning (literacy, mathematics, science, social studies, and creative arts), developmental or early learning domains (social and emotional, linguistic, cognitive, physical), and approaches to learning all consist of important knowledge and skills that young children want and need to master. Intentional teachers, therefore, integrate and promote learning in all these areas.

Teaching with intentionality means understanding that *how* children learn is as important as *what* they learn. It involves crafting experiences that embody six key characteristics, which neuroscience has shown to have positive impacts on learning: learning experiences should be active (minds-on), meaningful, engaging, socially interactive, iterative, and joyful (Zosh et al. 2022). Opportunities to explore new ideas and questions and figure things out support the development of an active thinking mindset. Engaging experiences draw children in and encourage them to deeply interact with ideas and materials. When learning is meaningful—that is, connected to their experiences and interests—children are more likely to retain information and apply it in new contexts. Iterative learning, where concepts are revisited and built on over time, reinforces understanding and long-term retention. Social interaction, such as occurs during group play, project work, discussions, and problem solving, not only enhances learning but also promotes language development and collaboration skills. When children experience learning as a joyful experience, their intrinsic motivation increases, and they spend more time in active thinking and engaged in learning.

Historically, many preschool teachers have viewed content such as math, science, social studies, and literacy as too academic and incompatible with the exploratory nature of young learners, and they have been reluctant or unsure how to teach it. However, teaching content is not an *either/or* approach but rather a *both/and*. This book examines ways to teach content in ways that align with how children learn and that tap into their natural excitement and interest in understanding the world around them. By embedding active, engaging, meaningful, socially interactive, iterative, and joyful experiences into their teaching, educators foster learning that is both developmentally appropriate and content rich. These characteristics allow children to construct understanding, revisit and deepen concepts, collaborate with peers, build on their curiosity, and forge a lasting love for learning.

Following are additional examples of intentional teaching that illustrate several of the six key characteristics:

Miss Priya often takes the children in her family child care program on walks around the neighborhood, and they talk about the buildings, plants, trees, and animals they see. Sometimes they see a gardener working in the yard and eagerly ask what the gardener is doing. After one of these walks, Katie, almost 5 years old, draws a picture of a garden with many different plants. She asks Miss Priya to write down the story that Katie will tell her about it. Katie hands Miss Priya a small index card and a pencil and dictates, "This is a picture about my mommy's garden." Miss Priya writes down exactly what Katie says.

"Now," says Katie, "I'm going to tell you the names of all the flowers and vegetables in my picture."

Miss Priya points to the index card and asks Katie, "Do you think they will all fit?"

"Yes," says Katie, who begins to enumerate them as Miss Priya carefully writes down each one. As she nears the bottom of the card, Miss Priya again asks Katie if she thinks all the names will fit. Katie reconsiders. "I think I need more room." She takes the card and turns it over.

"Should I continue writing on the back?" asks Miss Priya.

"But then my mommy won't see it," says Katie.

"Mmm, I wonder what else you could do so your mommy can see your whole story."

Katie thinks again, then gets another index card and tapes it to the bottom of the first one. "Will that be enough?" asks Miss Priya. "There are still lots of plants left to name in your picture."

Katie tapes one more card on the bottom and sets two more on the table "just in case." Katie continues to name the flowers and vegetables, and Miss Priya writes down each one.

● ● ●

At small group time, the children in a 4s classroom make patterns with squares of colored construction paper. Hakim makes a complex pattern of red-blue-yellow-yellow, red-blue-yellow-yellow, red-blue-yellow-yellow. "Make one like mine," he tells Ms. Maria. All the children stop to watch. Ms. Maria copies Hakim's pattern, but on the third repeat she deliberately sets out pieces of red, blue, yellow, and then blue paper and waits for the children to notice.

When no one comments, Ms. Maria says, "This doesn't look right. Can you help me?"

The children offer different solutions until Hakim replaces the last blue square with a yellow one.

"That's right!" the children chorus.

"Now you make one for me to copy," Hakim says.

Child-Guided and Adult-Guided Learning Experiences

Intentional teaching requires wide-ranging knowledge about how children develop and learn as well as an understanding of the factors that influence their development and learning, including their individual social and cultural contexts. At some times or for some content, children seem to learn best from *child-guided experiences*—that is, they acquire knowledge and skills mainly through their own exploration and experiences, including through interactions with peers, in self-directed play. At other times and for other content, children learn best from *adult-guided experiences*—that is, in planned, playful learning situations in which their teachers introduce information, model skills, and so forth but also provide children with choices and agency. (See "Child-Guided Experiences + Adult-Guided Experiences = Optimal Learning" on page 5.) "Children learn in a multiplicity of ways—through active exploration and play; through observation of others, notably older children and adults; and through adults' explicitly sharing knowledge with them" (NASEM 2024, 77). Teachers must have a repertoire of instructional strategies and know when to use a given strategy to accommodate the particular situation, the purpose for learning, the specific content children are learning, and the individual child (Masterson 2022).

In child-guided experiences, children's natural joy in play drives their curiosity and learning, enabling them to take ownership of their discoveries. In adult-guided experiences, teachers intentionally blend structured goals with the freedom of exploration by incorporating playful activities. The division between child-guided learning and adult-guided learning is not a rigid one. Rarely does learning come about entirely through a child's efforts or only from adult instruction; it is not *either/or* but *both/and*. Furthermore, in any given subject, how a child learns will vary over time. For example, young children begin crawling and walking through spontaneous and natural movement experiences (child-guided experiences). However, they also learn to hold and use a pencil from the adults around them, and teachers often make a point of modeling and providing guidance as they develop these skills (adult-guided experiences). Children also

Child-Guided Experiences + Adult-Guided Experiences = Optimal Learning

An effective early childhood program combines both child-guided and adult-guided educational experiences. These terms do not refer to extremes—that is, child-guided experiences are not highly child controlled, nor are adult-guided experiences highly adult controlled. Rather, adults play intentional roles in child-guided experiences, and children have significant, active roles in adult-guided experiences. Each type of experience takes advantage of planned as well as spontaneous, unexpected learning opportunities.

Child-guided experiences . . .

are **not** entirely child controlled (with the teacher passive)	proceed primarily along the lines of children's interests and actions, with strategic teacher support	are **not** entirely adult controlled (with the children passive)

Example: Two children want to divide a bowl of beads equally between themselves.

Child controlled: The teacher does not get involved, even when the children become frustrated and begin to get angry at each other over who has more.	**Child guided:** The children first try to make two equal piles by eyeballing them, but they are not satisfied. The teacher suggests they count their beads. They do so and then move beads between their piles, count again, and make adjustments until the piles are equal. The teacher provides a brief statement summarizing what they did using key vocabulary.	**Adult controlled:** The teacher counts the beads and divides by two, telling the children how many beads each should take.

Adult-guided experiences . . .

are **not** entirely child controlled (with the teacher passive)	proceed primarily along the lines of the teacher's goals but are also shaped by the children's active engagement	are **not** entirely adult controlled (with the children passive)

Example: The teacher wants the children to learn about shadows and their properties, which is addressed in the state early learning standards and is a topic that could build on the children's delight in being in the sunny outdoors after a rainy winter.

Child controlled: The teacher allows the children to deflect the focus from shadows to a discussion of what toys they like to play with in the sandbox.	**Adult guided:** The teacher plans the lesson and leads a small group in exploring shadows with flashlights and a sheet. The teacher encourages and uses the children's input—for example, when they want to make animal shadows.	**Adult controlled:** The teacher controls all aspects of the lesson and delivers it just as planned to the whole group. The children have little input.

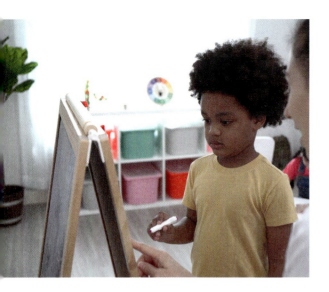

differ in how they typically approach learning due to their individual differences, cultures, experiences, and abilities. Some do a lot of exploring and thinking through problems on their own, whereas others readily ask adults for information or help. But every child learns in both ways. In the two vignettes on pages 3–4, the first one took place within a situation the child chose (child-guided experiences) and the second within a small group activity the adult organized (adult-guided experiences)—but in both experiences, the children and adults were actively involved in the exploration and learning, and the adults asked questions, made suggestions, provided interesting materials, and supported children to be active thinkers.

Similarly, the division of content into the knowledge and skills that seem to be best acquired primarily through child-guided experiences versus those acquired primarily through adult-guided experiences is not an exact process. For example, most children acquire basic language abilities largely through child-guided learning experiences (albeit with linguistic input from the adults around them); unless they have a hearing impairment, they are born with the capacity to hear and reproduce the sounds of speech and are inherently motivated, as social beings, to communicate with others. By contrast, identifying the letters of the alphabet is something that children cannot do intuitively; as arbitrary creations of a culture, letter forms and their names clearly are learned through adult-guided experiences. In other content areas, however, the division is not so clear. Yet even in cases where assignment to "primarily child guided" or "primarily adult guided" is more difficult, knowledgeable educators can make a determination that allows them to most effectively present content to a particular child or group of children.

Although these divisions are imprecise, they are still useful when you are considering when and how to support children's own discovery and construction of knowledge, and when and how to convey content in activities and instruction that you guide. That consideration is a major focus of this book. *The Intentional Teacher* explores which type of learning experience is likely to be most effective for which content areas and what you can do to optimize children's learning. It also emphasizes that regardless of whether children engage in child- or adult-guided experiences, teachers always play a vital educational role by building meaningful relationships with children; creating interesting, supportive environments and using instructional strategies to help advance children's thinking to the next level; using assessments to better understand children and inform their own plans and teaching; and making adjustments to support individual children.

In other words, both child-guided and adult-guided experiences have a place in the early childhood setting. It is not the case that one is good and the other bad, or that one is developmentally appropriate and the other not. Intentional teachers understand this and are prepared to make use of either or both in combination, choosing what works best for any given subject, situation, or child. They are flexible and responsive to the learning approaches and needs

Children with Developmental Delays or Disabilities

Like all children, those who have a developmental delay or disability benefit from both child-guided and adult-guided learning experiences and from personalized learning approaches tailored to their unique learning, physical, behavioral, and emotional needs. The level of support, strategies, and accommodations are often greater for children with a developmental delay or disability but vary for each child. While considerations and adaptations are suggested throughout this book, responsive adults adjust, modify, and apply a variety of approaches to nurture specific children's abilities and meet their needs. This child-centered approach helps ensure that the environment is as inclusive and supportive as possible.

of each child, including multilingual learners and those with developmental delays or disabilities. And whether in a child-guided or adult-guided situation, teachers build on what children already know and can do by connecting their experiences in their homes and communities to their learning experiences in the classroom. Playfulness can be woven into both child-guided and adult-guided experiences, sustaining children's natural joy and interest and enhancing engagement and retention.

Intentional Teaching Terms

At the top of the class's daily message board, Ms. Monica and Ms. Lyla write this sentence: "Who is here today?" Underneath it, they draw a column of stick figures, and next to each figure they write the name of a child or adult in the class. Each day Ms. Monica and Ms. Lyla indicate who is absent by making an erasable X in front of that name. They also draw a stick figure and write the name of any guest who will be visiting the classroom. If the guest is free to play with the children, the teachers draw a toy, such as a ball or block, in the stick figure's hand. If the guest is there only to observe, they draw a clipboard in the hand. By adding playful elements like drawings and symbols to represent visitors, the teachers create a sense of excitement and anticipation, turning the daily message board into a joyful ritual that children eagerly participate in each day.

Each morning the class begins by talking about who is present and who is absent. Then, together with their teachers, the children count the number of stick figures with no mark (those in school) and those with a mark (those not in school). They also discuss any guest who is coming and whether that person will be a "player" or a "watcher." Sometimes Ms. Monica and Ms. Lyla ask the children to predict whether a child who is absent will be back the next day. For example, after informing the class that Elijah left yesterday for a three-day vacation, Ms. Monica asks, "Do you think he will be here tomorrow?"

A few days before the class is expecting a guest who will share about her work as a book illustrator, Ms. Lyla draws a stick figure in a wheelchair holding a book, prompting questions from the children. Ms. Monica and Ms. Lyla offer simple explanations of the woman's disability, and they write down the children's questions they would like to ask about her work and how she gets around.

Later in the year, as the children's literacy skills begin to emerge, Ms. Monica and Ms. Lyla replace the stick figures with the children's names. Some children write their initial letters or their full names themselves. Children who are present make a mark (such as a dot, check, or plus sign) next to their names. Together with their teachers, they count how many names have a mark and how many are unmarked to determine how many children are in school and how many are absent. One day, when José's mother will be coming to show the class how to make tamales, José tells Ms. Lyla , "Escriba a 'mi madre.'"

"You want me to write that your mother is coming," she says, and draws a stick figure of a woman with a spoon in her hand.

José nods. "Mi madre!" he repeats, and smiles.

Ms. Monica and Ms. Lyla demonstrate intentional teaching throughout this daily activity. They balance both child-guided and adult-guided experiences. The children are naturally curious about the members of their classroom community, and using a daily message board helps to solidify their social awareness. The children know everyone's name and notice when a peer is missing. The children come to this awareness on their own—that is, through child-guided experiences. For adult-guided experiences, Ms. Monica and Ms. Lyla use the children's knowledge and interest to introduce literacy ideas and processes—writing each person's name on the message board, encouraging those who are able to write themselves, and helping children who are multilingual learners make connections between their home language and English.

Multilingual Learners

The term *multilingual learners* refers to young children who are acquiring one or more languages while continuing to develop their home language. Their language development differs in some respects from that of monolingual learners. For example, multilingual learners may take longer to acquire certain linguistic structures that vary across the languages they are learning (Espinosa 2018). In addition, although they may have a smaller vocabulary in each individual language, their combined vocabulary across all of their languages is generally equivalent to that of a monolingual learner (Hammer et al. 2014).

Intentional teachers recognize these differences and strive to understand the general process of learning multiple languages. They use this knowledge to provide appropriate support and create an inclusive environment. Research indicates that acquiring more than one language can enhance cognitive skills and improve academic outcomes (Espinosa 2018). Therefore, intentional teachers view multilingualism as a strength and adapt their teaching strategies and the environment to support children's learning in both English and their home languages (NAEYC 2020). Suggestions for supporting multilingual learners appear throughout this book and should be tailored to each child's unique needs.

They also embed mathematical concepts and processes into the activity. The children use classification (present vs. absent, players vs. watchers), counting (one-to-one correspondence of names and stick figures, tallying those with and without marks), and relational time concepts (yesterday, today, tomorrow). Ms. Monica and Ms. Lyla ask the children to predict, a process used in science; later, the children will discover whether their prediction is confirmed.

Throughout the activity, adults and children engage in conversation, which enhances language development. Using adult-guided strategies, Ms. Monica and Ms. Lyla intentionally introduce vocabulary words, such as *present* and *absent*. The natural flow of talk, in which adults capitalize on the child-guided desire to communicate, boosts fluency. Often Ms. Monica and Ms. Lyla remind the children of the class guideline about treating everyone with respect and kindness regardless of their abilities, and they discuss individual differences candidly rather than dismissing children's questions and curiosity as adults so often do out of embarrassment or not knowing what to say.

The concept of the intentional teacher and the organizing idea of child- versus adult-guided experiences has been discussed in this chapter using three terms that reappear throughout the book: *intentional, teaching,* and *content*. Because all these play such a key role in understanding the chapters that follow, let's clarify how these terms are used in this book and how they fit together.

The Meaning of Intentional

To be intentional is to act purposefully, with a goal in mind and a plan for accomplishing it. Intentional acts originate from careful thought and are accompanied by consideration of their potential effects. Thus an intentional teacher aims at clearly defined learning objectives (including in the social and emotional domains) for children, employs and individualizes instructional strategies that are likely to help children achieve the objectives, continually observes the children and assesses progress, and adjusts the strategies based on that assessment. Teachers who can explain *why* they are doing what they are doing are acting intentionally—whether they are using a strategy tentatively for the first time or automatically from long practice, and whether it is used as part of a deliberate plan or spontaneously in a teachable moment.

Effective teachers are intentional with respect to many facets of the learning environment, beginning with creating a nurturing and welcoming atmosphere and making decisions with the needs and wishes of children's families in mind. They deliberately select inviting equipment and materials that reflect children's individual interests, skills, needs, cultures, and home languages, and they put these in places where children will notice and want to use them. In planning the program day or week, intentional teachers choose which learning activities, contexts, and settings to use and when. They choose, within the context of program requirements, when to address specific content areas, how much time to spend on them, how to integrate them, and how to make them engaging so that children have plenty to discover and find enjoyment in. They understand that joy is an essential part of the learning environment. By fostering joyful experiences, teachers create a positive emotional climate where children feel safe to explore, take risks, and develop a lifelong love of learning. All these decisions and behaviors set the tone and substance of what happens in the classroom.

Intentionality refers especially to how teachers interact with children. Making connections with a child allows the teacher to support that child's sense of self, security, and self-regulation and to extend their learning. (See "Intentionality and Children's Learning" on page 11.)

A teacher's intentional decision making for supporting each child's unique learning needs and developmental stage is supported by the framework of principles and guidelines known as *developmentally appropriate practice* (NAEYC 2020). Developmentally appropriate practice requires teachers to think about what they are doing and how it will foster children's development and produce real and lasting learning—the definition of intentional teaching. Rooted in principles of child development, developmentally appropriate practice advocates balancing child-guided and adult-guided experiences to foster meaningful, lasting learning. It promotes the optimal development and learning of each child through a "strengths-based, play-based approach to joyful, engaged learning" (NAEYC 2020, 5).

The Meaning of Teaching

Teaching encompasses the knowledge, beliefs, attitudes, and especially the behaviors and skills teachers employ to enhance each child's learning. An effective teacher is competent in the following three areas:

> **Curriculum:** The knowledge and skills teachers are expected to teach and children are expected to learn, and the plans for experiences through which learning will take place. Effective teachers know the subject matter covered in their program's curriculum and how children typically develop with regard to each domain addressed. Efforts to specify the knowledge preschool children can gain and the skills they are able to develop have been made by states in their early learning standards and by specialized professional organizations. These are referred to in the focused content chapters in Section 2 of the book.

> **Pedagogy:** The ways teachers promote children's development and learning. Effective teachers ensure that children experience a meaningful learning environment that promotes their development in all areas of the curriculum. To begin, teachers establish a nurturing environment in which children feel valued for who they are and what they bring to the learning community. As stated by NAEYC (2020), "Educators design experiences that celebrate the diversity in the experiences and social identities of each group of children and counter the biases in society" (21). Beyond this basic responsibility, teachers honor differences in children's preferences, cultures, and home languages; are inclusive with respect to disabilities; partner with families; and use and adapt instructional approaches and strategies effectively to support each child's learning and thinking. The essential elements of pedagogy are highlighted in the standards for teaching and for teachers in NAEYC's "Early Learning Program Accreditation Standards and Assessment Items" (2019b), "Professional

Intentionality and Children's Learning

Children's learning outcomes are related to teacher intentionality in three core elements: teacher-child interactions, teacher practices, and exposure to academic content (Berliner 1987; Pianta et al. 2020).

Teacher-child interactions:

- Sensitivity and responsiveness: Teachers are attuned to children, enabling them to provide support, guidance, and interactions that are in line with children's interests and needs and unique abilities.

- Thoughtful questioning: Teachers pose questions that are meaningful to what a child is doing in the moment to get insight into children's thought processes and stimulate children's thinking.

- Effective feedback: Evaluative feedback from teachers focuses on facilitating children's learning rather than merely offering praise or disapproval.

Teacher practices:

- High expectations: When teachers provide responsive, individualized scaffolding and supports and expect children—all children—to learn, they do.

- Planning and management: While guiding children toward defined and sequenced learning objectives, teachers remain open to children's related interests.

- Learning-oriented classroom: Teachers share responsibility for the community with children, and through the environment and interactions help children value the educational setting as a place to learn.

Exposure to academic content:

- Engaging activities: Teachers connect activities to children's experiences, knowledge, cultures, and developmental levels.

- Developmentally appropriate curriculum content: Teachers consider children's current learning level, interests, and needs, gradually introducing more challenging content to promote discovery, understanding, and skill development. Intentionality involves finding the right balance, offering enough challenge to encourage learning and providing scaffolding as needed to ensure that the challenges are within the child's reach.

- Alignment with learning standards: Teachers intentionally align activities and content with program, state, or national learning standards to ensure children are meeting key developmental milestones while still incorporating play-based, engaging, and developmentally appropriate practices.

Standards and Competencies for Early Childhood Educators" (2019c), and the fourth edition of *Developmentally Appropriate Practice in Early Childhood Programs Serving Children from Birth Through Age 8* (2022). The report *The Power of Play: A Research Summary on Play and Learning* (White 2018) establishes that the quality of the classroom environment and of teacher-child interactions have been shown to predict long-term developmental outcomes for children. More than any other variable, teachers' instructional interactions define a program's quality and its impact on children's intellectual and social development (Cash et al. 2018; Dombro, Jablon, & Stetson 2020; Pianta et al. 2020).

› **Assessment:** The ongoing process of determining how children are progressing toward expected outcomes of learning and development, using multiple sources of information. Assessment takes many forms, from observational measures and portfolios of children's work to standardized tests and instruments, but it should always be "developmentally, culturally, and linguistically responsive to authentically assess children's learning" (NAEYC 2020). Effective teachers know how to collect, document, administer, interpret, and apply the results of assessment as they plan learning experiences for individual children and the class as a whole, and to monitor individual and group progress. By seeking to learn what families see children doing at home and sharing their own observations and assessment results with families, teachers partner with families to gain a more holistic picture of children's development and to ensure home and school work together to support children's early development. Some assessments are dictated by administrators or policymakers, and then the information is collected by teachers or outside specialists; other assessments are developed by individual teachers to fit their classroom needs and inform their plans. (Assessment also is commonly used for program and teacher accountability.) Guidelines for the appropriate assessment of early learning are defined in guideline 3 of NAEYC's position statement on developmentally appropriate practice (2020) and the assessment of child progress standard of NAEYC's "Early Learning Program Accreditation Standards and Accreditation Items" (2019b).

The Meaning of Content

Content is the substance or subject matter that teachers teach and is, therefore, the object of children's learning. In this book, *content* refers more specifically to the knowledge (certain vocabulary and concepts) and skills in an area of learning:

› **Vocabulary:** The language used in a content area. For example, vocabulary in the area of language and literacy includes the names of the letters in the alphabet as well as words such as *alphabet, book, author,* and *rhyme.* Social and emotional development vocabulary includes words for feelings *(angry, happy)* and the language used to invite someone to play or to politely tell someone you are not done playing with a toy yet. Visual arts vocabulary includes descriptors for color, shape, and texture as well as names of artists, genres, and techniques children are exploring.

> **Concepts:** The important ideas or principles within a content area, its "big ideas." For example, basic language and literacy concepts include that a relationship exists between spoken and written language; that in English, books are read from front to back; and that also in English, print on a page is read from top to bottom and left to right. In social and emotional development, basic conflict resolution concepts include that it is better to solve problems by talking than hitting and that solutions should be fair and agreeable to everyone. Visual arts concepts include understanding what makes something a realistic or abstract work of art and recognizing how art reflects people's cultural beliefs and values.

> **Skills:** The specific abilities needed within a domain of learning and development. In language and literacy, reading skills include recognizing the component sounds in words and the letters of the alphabet from their written shapes. In the area of social and emotional development, conflict resolution skills include expressing feelings, listening to others, and negotiating a compromise. Examples of visual arts skills are manipulating a paintbrush to make art and observing and comparing the work of different artists.

Although each content area has its own vocabulary, concepts, and skills for children to learn, some knowledge and skills connect across different areas. In the classroom, a well-rounded curriculum should help children build their vocabulary, understand the world around them, and develop a wide range of skills. Because many children are encountering these content areas for the first time in early learning settings, they need their teachers to "establish a foundation for lifelong learning and success" (NAEYC 2020, 36).

Although often celebrated for championing play-based learning, the preschool and pre-K segment of the early childhood education spectrum has sometimes been accused of being anti-content. If the accusation has some truth to it, it's partly because of carryover from a time when much of the emphasis in early education was on helping children learn to share, cooperate, and play nicely as they transitioned from their homes to a group setting. It's also partly due to misinterpretations of developmental appropriateness by well-meaning teachers who feel, for example, that they cannot display the alphabet because it pressures young children to memorize letters. Furthermore, some early childhood educators feel that "content" necessarily means teachers must use strategies that are not developmentally appropriate for young children. In truth, education can be *both* joyful and playful *and* also promote rich content learning for preschoolers when strategies align with the way young children learn, tapping into children's natural curiosity and enthusiasm to learn.

If preschool education has been criticized for neglecting content, primary-grade education, and particularly kindergarten, has been accused of going the opposite way and ignoring children's social and emotional development and the essentialness of play for learning (and, in response to academic pressures, of reducing support in other domains such as physical development and the arts). In answer to these issues in both segments of the birth through age 8 early childhood age spectrum,

> A growing body of work demonstrates relationships between social, emotional, executive function, and cognitive competencies (Immordino-Yang, Darling-Hammond, & Krone 2018) as well as the importance of movement and physical activity (Council on School Health 2013). . . . All are critical in educating young children across birth through age 8. Intentional teaching strategies, including, and particularly, play (both self-directed and guided), address each domain. (NAEYC 2020, 9)

The Broader Social Contexts of Intentional Teaching

All the decisions teachers make that have been discussed in this chapter—concerning curriculum, assessment, teaching strategies, relationships with children and families, and more—must be considered within children's social and cultural contexts, as these contexts shape children's development (Bredekamp & Willer 2022). Teachers act with intention when they seek to learn about and value the strengths and lived experiences children bring with them to the learning setting, appreciating differences in humans as normal and positive and celebrating the diversity represented by children's and families' social identities—including their race, ethnicity, home language, abilities, social and economic status, and family structure (NAEYC 2019a).

In addition, educators recognize that some children are consistently afforded opportunities to succeed without question, whereas others are judged and questioned by schools, community, and society due to their family income, race, disability, home language, or other factors (Bredekamp & Willer 2022). If teachers are to be effective at supporting each child's growth and learning, they must promote equity in learning opportunities, meaning that "all children and families receive necessary supports in a timely fashion so they can develop their full intellectual, social, and physical potential" (NAEYC 2019a, 17). Such supports are designed to eliminate differences in outcomes resulting from past and present inequities in society. Educators begin working toward providing equitable learning experiences by considering their own biases and any deficit perspectives they might hold toward particular children and families and then committing to helping each child thrive by building on their unique set of individual and family strengths.

Building on the principles of diversity and equity, inclusion emphasizes the importance of creating environments where all children and families, regardless of ability, are valued as full members of the learning community. Inclusive practices foster positive relationships and friendships while ensuring that every child feels a sense of belonging and has access to learning opportunities that support their full potential (NAEYC 2019a). Although inclusion is often associated with children with delays or disabilities, inclusion in this book applies to a wider context to ensure equitable participation by all children and families who have been historically marginalized in society, including in schools, because of race or ethnicity, gender, class, ability, and other social identities.

Early childhood teachers play a critical role in creating inclusive and equitable learning environments that reflect and embrace the diversity of children and families who are integral to the learning community. As they make intentional teaching decisions, educators

> Consider their own contexts, reflecting on the ways in which they themselves have experienced privilege and/or oppression

> Consider how they have absorbed messages of bias and consciously confront and strive to change them

> Reflect on how their decisions affirm and support each child and family through a strengths-based approach

> Actively work to counter the stereotypes and attitudes children absorb and construct from exposure to societal biases

> Join with others to work to change the larger systemic forces that perpetuate systems of inequity (NAEYC 2022, 19)

By embracing diversity, advancing equity, and practicing inclusion, teachers can create enriching and supportive environments that help all children thrive and reach their full potential.

The Synergy of Child-Guided and Adult-Guided Learning

This book advocates a purposeful and balanced approach to teaching content to young children, acknowledging that children learn through both child-guided and adult-guided experiences and that teachers are most effective when they are able to choose among and apply any of a range of teaching approaches without going to the extreme of either type of experience. As shown in the table on page X, that approach is neither laissez-faire, in which all learning is left to the child, nor entirely top-down, in which the child is seen as an empty vessel into which the teacher pours knowledge. Interactions between teacher and children are neither overly teacher directed and didactic nor overly child centered and left to chance. Instead, intentional teaching means systematically introducing content in all domains using a strengths-based, play-based, individualized approach. When child-guided and adult-guided experiences are infused with playfulness, learning becomes not only effective but also joyful. By balancing structured and free opportunities for meaningful exploration, teachers create a learning environment where curiosity and joy are at the heart of every experience.

Naturally there are individual differences in how children learn most effectively. Although all children require repeated and varied opportunities to learn a particular concept, what some children discover on their own or through interactions with peers, other children will encounter only through direct adult intervention. Therefore, the suggestions offered in this book cannot substitute for teachers' observing and knowing the experiences and developmental levels of the individual children in their programs.

The term *intentional teaching* indicates that teachers play a thoughtful role during both child- and adult-guided learning and conveys their commitment to child development and learning principles as well as to educational content. Defining and following such a balanced approach may help educators get past polarizing debates and arrive at more effective practice. Furthermore, this approach will inspire educators to continually update their knowledge and reflect on their practices—that is, to be intentional teachers whose methods ensure successful outcomes for young children.

● ● ●

Although teaching is an intellectual endeavor—requiring knowledge of subject areas, learning progressions in each area, and a balanced approach to teaching content—it is also a deeply emotional one. When teachers bring a contagious enthusiasm to the learning environment, each day becomes an adventure of discovery and growth for both the children and themselves. Infusing every interaction with the joy that makes learning a truly transformative and fulfilling experience for all is a hallmark of an intentional teacher.

For Further Consideration

1. In what contexts do child-guided experiences seem to predominate? In what contexts do adult-guided experiences seem to predominate? In what situations do adults themselves learn primarily through their own efforts, and in what situations is their learning primarily guided by others? How can understanding adult modes of learning inform how teachers intentionally teach children?

2. What do you believe about content learning in early childhood? How does your program approach the teaching of content? How can the early childhood field reverse a common perception that it is anti-content?

3. How can intentional teaching help to support all young learners, including children who are multilingual learners and those with developmental delays or disabilities?

4. What can you as a beginning or experienced teacher do to guarantee that intentionality has a place in your daily interactions with children?

Learning Objectives

1. To define key characteristics of positive teacher-child relationships and their impact on children's development

2. To identify teaching practices and components of a learning environment that support young children's content learning, creativity, and enjoyment of learning

3. To describe ways to foster inclusive, empowering learning environments that value and reflect the identities and perspectives of children and their families

CHAPTER 2

Effective Practices for Intentional Teaching

Amy Schmidtke, Tonya Jolley, and Kimberlee Telford

"The children are really enjoying running in the sunshine at outside time now that we're over the rainy winter," says Mr. Simon to his preschool coteacher. "I wonder if there's a way to also make them aware of light and shadow as the days get brighter and the trees leaf out." The next day, as the children chase one another around a wide oak tree, Mr. Simon comments that sometimes he sees their shadows and other times he doesn't. "Why do you suppose that is?" he asks.

"You have to move," suggests Vinod. "It won't make a shadow if you stand still."

"Uh, uh," says Natalie, standing in place. "I'm not moving, and I see my shadow."

"I know," says Mikhail, "You have to stand away from the tree."

Mr. Simon steps away from the tree and stands facing into the sunlight. The children comment that he doesn't have a shadow, but Sunil, who is facing Mr. Simon (with the sun behind him), says excitedly, "Look! I have a shadow."

Some children stand alongside Mr. Simon, others alongside Sunil. They observe which group does or does not have shadows but can't explain why. Then Mr. Simon points to the sky. "Maybe the sun has something to do with it," he muses.

Natalie says excitedly, "When you see the sun, you don't see your shadow."

Mikhail hides behind the tree. "I can't see the sun or my shadow," he observes.

The children stand in different positions relative to the sun, each time noting whether they make a shadow (except Vinod, who continues to experiment with moving and keeping still). Over the next several days, the children notice whether the tree trunk and its branches make shadows and how the shadows change as more leaves grow out. The following week, on a cloudy day, they comment that there are no shadows at all! Their growing interest in light and shadow leads Mr. Simon and his coteacher to plan a small group activity indoors using flashlights and a hanging sheet.

Mr. Simon is being an intentional teacher. He thinks about a content area in his state's early learning standards (the natural world and its processes—an aspect of science) and how he can build on the children's spontaneous delight in being outdoors on a sunny day to focus their attention on light and shadow in the environment. He makes casual observations, in the context of their play, to draw the children's attention to the topic. His questions about why shadows appear encourage the children to make careful observations and try different ideas, and they evaluate—and sometimes contradict—one another's ideas while their teacher listens with interest but does not correct them. When the children are still puzzled, he doesn't give them an answer but gently guides them to consider another line of reasoning (the position of the sun) as they continue to make sense of what they observe and attempt to explain their reasoning for their ideas. Mr. Simon takes advantage of the many opportunities the outdoor learning environment provides for learning about light and shadow (trees, the sun, clouds, and movement). He also plans a small group experience so the children can explore other materials (flashlights and sheets) as he builds on their curiosity and extends their learning about a scientific phenomenon.

Mr. Simon's teaching exemplifies several high-quality practices in early childhood education:

> Understanding that preschool-age children are naturally interested and excited to learn content

> Having a goal in mind for children's learning, based on their interests and on his state's early learning standards

> Identifying interesting and open-ended materials (outdoors and in the classroom) that support learning

> Fostering a joyful environment for children that is rich with engaging materials and positive learning interactions between peers and adults

> Encouraging children to explore the materials and concepts at their own developmental levels

> Interacting with children to refine and extend their discoveries

> Encouraging children to interact with and learn from each other

> Providing opportunities for children to generalize their ideas across different situations and with varied materials

These practices are based in child development theory, educational research, and the reflections of generations of teachers. Educators use these practices because they know they work. They value them because they reflect common ideals and beliefs about human development, and they advocate their use in every classroom, regardless of the curriculum.

Through the years, some policymakers have called for "teacher-proof" methods of instruction, and some curriculum developers have responded with scripted lessons teachers can implement with little training and almost robotic consistency. Understandably, many educators resist the idea that good teaching can be so mechanical or superficial. Well-designed, ready-to-use resources should not be dismissed out of hand, however, if the curriculum is designed with an understanding of how young children learn and provides opportunities for both child and teacher input. Such materials can offer a welcome and useful starting point for the novice teacher or even for an experienced teacher approaching an unfamiliar subject area, but they do not relieve teachers of the need to be intentional. Teachers must still decide how to apply the curriculum to individuals and groups of children. With time and experience, most teachers will bring more of their own creativity to teaching.

An Overview of Effective Teaching Practice

The essence of intentional teaching is thinking about what you are doing in the classroom and how it will foster children's development and produce real and lasting learning. Much has been said about what constitutes effective, high-quality practice in early childhood education, the principles underlying it, and how to measure the implementation of it (Bredekamp 2019). These discussions constitute too much material to be covered thoroughly here. What this chapter does provide, however, is an overview of how intentional teachers use these practices in the classroom: knowing and valuing children as individuals, using play as a central learning tool, structuring the physical learning environment thoughtfully, designing a balanced daily schedule, interacting with children, building relationships with families, and assessing children's development.

Knowing and Valuing Each Child

At the very core of intentional teaching is a commitment to recognizing and cherishing the unique qualities of every child. An intentional teacher possesses a strong knowledge of child development and subject areas. By combining this knowledge with an understanding of children's individuality and their social and cultural contexts, teachers can integrate their pedagogical knowledge and teaching skills in ways that are responsive to each child's learning interests and needs. The synergy between these elements ensures that teaching practices and classroom environments are tailored to the highest standards, that learning opportunities are equitable for every child, and that the most effective strategies are employed to support each child's development and learning.

Develop Supportive Relationships with Children

Building stable, supportive relationships with children promotes their healthy brain development, boosting their motivation, engagement, academic outcomes, and overall development (Center on the Developing Child 2016). Characteristics of strong teacher-child relationships include the following (Hammond 2015; Jeon et al. 2021; Mapp et al. 2022; Pianta et al. 2020):

> Warmth and support: Teachers create a safe, nurturing environment where each child feels secure, comfortable, and ready to learn. This emotional safety encourages exploration and risk-taking—essential parts of learning.

> High expectations with high support: Teachers who set and convey high expectations *and* provide ample support can help children reach their full potential. This balanced approach fosters a sense of accomplishment and motivation. For children with developmental delays or disabilities, individualized supports help ensure that they can participate fully and gain confidence.

> Trust and respect: Trust and respect form the foundation of teacher-child relationships. When children trust their teachers, they feel comfortable seeking guidance, expressing themselves, and taking risks in their learning.

> Consistency and predictability: Children thrive in environments with consistent and predictable routines, which help them feel safe and understand what is expected.

> Responsive interactions: Teachers who actively listen and respond to children's needs foster belonging and engagement. They display empathy and tailor strategies to each child's needs.

> Positive communication: Positive, encouraging communication helps build each child's self-esteem and confidence.

Cultivate a Sense of Belonging and Respect for All Children

An inclusive classroom fosters a sense of belonging, dignity, and justice. Teachers recognize each child's background and abilities and work to make every child feel safe, respected, and valued (Cobb & Krownapple 2019). They create a positive learning environment by honoring each child's voice and encouraging self-expression (Souto-Manning, Ghim, & Madu 2021). For children with developmental delays or disabilities, this means recognizing their strengths and supporting their autonomy so that they feel included and capable within the classroom community.

Equity in the classroom means ensuring that each child has what they need to thrive. Rather than treat everyone the same, intentional teachers adjust their approach (Ezzani 2020; Iruka et al. 2020) and "provide different levels of support to different children depending on what they need" (NAEYC 2019a, 7). For example, one child might be better able to fully participate in learning experiences and engage with peers at group time when allowed to sit on a special seat for sensory needs; a multilingual learner might benefit from being paired with a peer who speaks that child's home language and is more fluent in English. By meeting children where they are, teachers foster an environment that is both equitable and supportive (Souto-Manning & Rabadi-Raol 2018).

Build an Inclusive, Culturally Responsive Classroom

Intentional teaching celebrates each child's culture, integrating diverse perspectives and traditions into learning to build a welcoming, empowering classroom (Gay 2018). Intentional teachers recognize and appreciate their students' cultural diversity, using these insights to make learning more engaging and meaningful. When children see their cultures reflected in the classroom, they feel valued, which can build a sense of belonging and pride in their cultural heritage (Hammond 2015).

Teachers create this inclusivity by getting to know each child's background, including family traditions, values, and beliefs and the skills and knowledge individuals and communities possess from their cultural, social, and historical experiences—what is known as *funds of knowledge*. Incorporating children's funds of knowledge into teaching creates connections that honor children's identities and make learning feel relevant and personal (Maitra 2017; Reyes et al. 2016; Whyte & Karabon 2016). Utilizing a child's funds of knowledge might include helping children set up a culturally relevant dramatic play theme, such as a panaderia (bakery) (Salinas-Gonzalez, Arreguin-Anderson, & Alanis 2017). Similarly, families of children with developmental delays or disabilities bring unique insights and strengths that can support their child's learning. These include knowledge of successful home routines and the types of activities the child prefers to engage with.

> Miss Gena, a preschool teacher, is passionate about integrating children's funds of knowledge into their learning experiences. During a conversation with Noah's father at pickup time, she learns that their family is Lakota and that they regularly share stories that have been passed down for generations. Miss Gena decides to create a storytelling corner in her classroom.
>
> She invites Noah's grandfather, whom Noah calls Grandpa White Eagle, to visit and share a traditional story with the class. When Grandpa White Eagle arrives, he sits with the children in a circle and tells the story of Iktomi the spider, a well-known trickster character in Lakota culture. He uses a calm and expressive voice, drawing the children in as he shares how Iktomi's cleverness and mistakes offer lessons about respect and kindness. The children listen intently and ask questions about the story and Lakota life. Noah is proud to see his grandfather share their family's heritage with his friends.

Supports for Children with Developmental Delays or Disabilities to Participate Successfully with Their Peers

Every child belongs and can learn. Design your space, routines, and activities so they are adaptable. This proactive, universal approach supports children's strengths. Many children with developmental delays or disabilities benefit from simple accommodations and modifications. Although some children need specialized supports from special education professionals, you can still make learning and the physical environment accessible and appropriate for all children.

Begin with looking beyond a child's disability, label, or delay, and get to know them as a person. Observe, talk, and play with them so you learn their interests, abilities, needs, and personality. Build relationships with their families. This will help you select strategies that will best help that child learn and socialize.

Consider the following strategies to support children with developmental delays or disabilities.

Environment: Arrange the classroom furnishings so that children can maneuver around the room by themselves. Make sure materials are within reach. Watch for classroom clutter and unstable flooring (throw rugs that move easily) that make the classroom space inaccessible. Reducing clutter also helps minimize distractions. Establish a safe, quiet space (for example, a calming corner) children can use when they need some time to themselves. Avoid placing children who use wheelchairs in the back or on the outer spots of a gathering space.

Routines: Keep routines predictable. Use visual supports, such as pictures or props, to teach children routines, help them stay engaged, and aid them in transitioning between different activities. For example, offer a child a picture or symbol of two areas for them to choose one to indicate where they will go next.

Interests: Incorporate something a child enjoys into an activity or interest area. If they love music, use songs and rhythms during routines and activities.

Peers: Peers can model positive prosocial and communication skills and demonstrate everyday routines. Plan activities that require more than one child's participation to accomplish a task. Instead of an adult always working with a child with a developmental delay or disability, pair the child with a peer buddy who can carry materials, help the child clean up, or model what to do during a game or activity. Provide guidance to help a child who needs support interact with their peers; for example, offer a toy or other object, like a popular book, they can use to initiate interaction or conversation with a peer.

Noise: Managing noise in the classroom plays an important role in both learning and behavior. Loud classrooms affect a child's ability to understand increasingly complex language. Carpets and other sound-absorbing materials, like wall hangings, heavy drapes, felt, and chairs with tennis balls on the bottom of metal legs, help reduce classroom noise.

Materials: Modifying materials in the classroom can have a big impact on independence. Add pencil grips to crayons and markers to make them easier for children with motor difficulties to hold. Glue small knobs to puzzle pieces to make them easier to pick up. Attach jumbo paper clips to book pages to make them easier to turn. Provide dress-up items with multiple ways to fasten them.

Individualized support: Consider what you expect children to do and learn during typical routines and activities, then think about the supports you can provide to help a particular child be more independent and successful. Here are some examples:

- Break down activities into smaller, more manageable tasks and teach the tasks one by one. For example, help a child put on their coat and get the zipper started, then have the child pull the zipper up so they finish the task with success.

- If a child uses a nonverbal mode of communication (picture symbols, sign language), teach all the children to use it.

- Give assistance only as needed, such as prompting a child navigating an obstacle course about the next action.

- Provide wait time for children to respond. Allow several ways for them to do so, such as through gestures, actions, verbal responses, or picture cues.

- Provide opportunities and varied situations for repeated practice throughout the day.

Whatever the needs of the children in your classroom, learn to rely on your professional expertise and judgment. Collaborate with and seek input from others who have valuable experience and knowledge to share with you, including families and specialists. Remember that regardless of individual needs, children are first and foremost children—and effective practices for young children are effective practices for *all* young children.

Adapted from P. Brillante, "Every Child Belongs: Welcoming a Child with a Disability," *Teaching Young Children* 10 (5): 18–21. Tonya Jolley also contributed.

After the visit, Miss Gena incorporates storytelling into their daily routines. During large group time, she encourages the children to share stories from their own families. She includes books and materials that feature characters and themes from all the children's cultures, ensuring that they can see themselves and their classmates represented in the classroom.

Through these activities, the children feel valued, and their cultural identities are celebrated. This approach helps each child feel connected to their classmates and take pride in their heritage, building a classroom community where everyone feels included.

Examine Preconceived Ideas

Teachers must be aware of any preconceived notions they may hold and work to support each child fully (Alvarez 2024). Preconceived notions include implicit biases, which are subconscious stereotypes and assumptions that can influence an individual's behavior and decision making without their awareness. Intentional teachers understand that these biases can impact their interactions with children, so they thoughtfully examine their beliefs, attitudes, and practices related to children and families and actively work to provide equitable learning experiences for all

Culturally Responsive Strategies for Engaging Children in Learning

Throughout this book, vignettes illustrate how teachers can engage children in content learning through culturally responsive practices in early learning programs. Strategies include the following:

- **Culturally relevant materials:** Include books, toys, and art supplies that reflect students' backgrounds. For example, provide bilingual books and toys as well as materials that represent the children's cultures.

- **Family partnerships:** Invite parents to share their cultural traditions, foods, stories, or other things that are important to them.

- **Personalized learning:** Connect learning experiences to students' home experiences. For instance, nursery rhymes or songs from children's own cultures can support language and literacy in a meaningful way.

- **Inclusive storytelling:** Include stories and books with characters from a variety of cultures and identities to help children see themselves and their communities represented and to learn about people and places that they would not otherwise encounter.

- **Language support:** Provide support in students' home languages, such as labeling objects and using bilingual materials, to help children feel included and valued and to support their learning in both their home languages and English.

children. This includes addressing implicit biases against children with developmental delays or disabilities, which may affect how teachers view their potential. By addressing their own biases, teachers can help build a more inclusive classroom.

Anti-racism requires teachers to actively challenge racism and promote fairness. For example, teachers might reflect on classroom materials and make sure they represent a wide range of cultures and identities (Allen et al. 2021; Elisa 2020) and evaluate their discipline practices to ensure that no child is treated unfairly due to race or background (Gilliam et al. 2016).

Building anti-bias and anti-racist practices means teachers listen openly, seek to understand each family's background, and make sure each voice is heard (Utt & Tochluk 2020). (See "Building Partnerships with Families" on pages 38–39.) Insights gained allow teachers to better support the needs of each child and collaborate effectively with their families. By practicing anti-racism and addressing implicit biases, teachers create a more inclusive and equitable learning environment where each child can thrive.

Centering Play in the Classroom

Play in all its forms has immense value for young children's learning and development. It is naturally active (minds-on), joyful, meaningful, engaging, iterative, and socially interactive (Zosh et al. 2018). Play is characterized as freely chosen and process oriented, with the focus on exploration rather than specific outcomes. In addition, play often includes make-believe and imagination (White 2018).

An intentional teaching approach includes a continuum of playful learning, including self-directed play (where children independently explore their own interests), guided play (where teachers introduce a learning goal, select materials, and support children as they lead the activity; Zosh et al. 2022), and games. In all types of playful learning, children explore their environment, develop social skills, and enhance their cognitive abilities (Silverman 2019). Play provides practice for decision making, problem solving, and communication skills in a safe and supportive environment. It also promotes creativity and imagination, fostering a sense of curiosity and wonder (Cavanaugh et al. 2017).

Viewing play as a continuum allows teachers to see how different play types contribute to learning. For example, self-directed play experiences, with no set goal, can enhance social development and encourage exploration. Guided play experiences, with more adult support, help develop specific skills and knowledge (Zosh et al. 2018). Like guided play, games can be designed in ways that support learning goals, either by the adult or naturally through the game itself.

Intentional teachers play a crucial role in facilitating these varied play experiences. They create environments that support and encourage play, providing materials and opportunities for rich and meaningful play activities. Teachers understand how different types of play serve different developmental goals and integrate both types to support learning. By recognizing the importance of play in children's development, teachers support holistic learning and foster a love of learning that can last a lifetime.

In particular, guided play is an effective approach to content learning for young children because it provides a balance in learning experiences that are both playful and supported by teacher guidance. What sets guided play apart from other types of play is its focus on specific standards-based learning outcomes and intentional design for promoting children's development and content learning. The intentional design ensures that children engage in meaningful learning experiences around the content areas described in Chapters 3 through 10. Although teachers initiate a guided play activity, provide specific materials, and pose thoughtful questions, children choose how they participate in the activity. Teachers play a critical role in adult-guided play by scaffolding content learning—that is, they provide "just right" support, or just enough assistance for children to achieve their learning goals. The scaffolding helps children deepen their understanding, make connections, and develop new skills.

Structuring the Physical Learning Environment

The first thing an intentional teacher does, even before the children arrive, is set up the classroom. Teachers create this setting with careful consideration of children's development, curriculum goals, teaching strategies, and characteristics of the families and community (for example, the families' cultures and languages and whether the community is urban, suburban, or

Facilitating Guided Play

Enhance children's play and development with these strategies (Hassinger-Das, Hirsh-Pasek, & Golinkoff 2017; Jensen et al. 2019; Schmidtke 2022c; Zosh et al. 2022):

- Use knowledge of curriculum content, academic standards, and children's individual interests and learning needs to plan activities that support a learning goal.

- Integrate curriculum content into play areas and playful learning into adult-guided experiences.

- Set up the environment and curate materials so children lead in the discovery related to the learning goals.

- Take an active role by listening actively and responding to children's actions, ideas, and wonderings.

- Ask probing questions that guide children to the next level in their exploration.

rural). The setting must promote not only children's learning but also their pleasure in learning and the motivation to pursue it. Because the classroom is a teacher's main work space, it should be welcoming and inspiring to the teacher, too.

Provide a Safe and Healthy Indoor and Outdoor Environment

To be licensed by a county, state, or other authorized body, a program must comply with applicable standards for sanitation, ventilation, lighting, and temperature control. This is a primary responsibility of the teacher as well as the program (NAEYC 2019b). In particular, children's safety depends on teachers being able to see and hear what is happening from anywhere in the room.

The classroom and outdoor play area should have adequate space to move freely and incorporate elements of Universal Design for Learning. Programs commonly consider the children's need for space and mobility, but teachers also must have space to move with children, join their play, and take advantage of learning opportunities as they arise.

Organize the Space in Interest Areas or Centers

Distinctive areas encourage different types of activity and expand the range of content children are enticed to pursue. They also promote thoughtful decision making, as children survey the room and choose where, with what, and with whom they want to engage. Taken together, a program's indoor and outdoor areas should address all aspects of children's development and allow groups of various sizes to play in each area. They should accommodate activities of different noise and physical energy levels, including offering places where children can find quiet and solitude during the day. Relative position should also be considered—for example, locate the art area near a sink and separate the quiet and noisy areas.

Typical indoor areas might include the following:

> **Library:** A quiet area filled with books and comfortable seating for children to explore and enjoy reading

> **Blocks:** An area with various types of blocks for children to build structures and engage in spatial and mathematical thinking

> **Dramatic play:** A space equipped with props and costumes where children can role-play and act out scenarios, promoting social and emotional development

> **Art:** An area with a variety of art materials and tools for children to express themselves creatively through painting, drawing, and crafting

> **Music and movement:** An area for children to explore rhythm and movement through music, dance, and simple musical instruments

> **Toys and games:** A space with a variety of toys and games that promote cooperative play, problem solving, and fine motor skills

> **Discovery:** An area with hands-on materials and objects for children to explore scientific concepts through observation and experimentation

> **Sand and water:** An area with sand, water, and various tools for sensory exploration and imaginative play

> **Cooking:** A space for children to participate in simple cooking and food preparation activities, promoting math, science, and life skills.

Outdoor spaces might include the following:

> **Gross motor equipment:** Space with equipment designed to promote physical activity and gross motor skills development (climbers, slides, tricycles)

> **Open areas:** Spacious areas that allow children to run, jump, skip, and engage in other forms of active play

> **Natural and sensory:** Spaces that encourage exploration of the natural world through gardening, observing wildlife, creating art with natural materials, and playing with sand and water

Your program may not have access (or at least not regular access) to some of these indoor and/ or outdoor spaces. You can still provide meaningful experiences by creatively adapting what resources you do have available. For example, if you do not have a designated outdoor play area and walks are not feasible, create a safe area in the room or building where children can move their bodies freely and use small equipment like a balance beam. You could also bring in plants, an aquarium, and natural items for children to care for and explore.

Supply a Variety of Plentiful Equipment and Materials

Indoors and outdoors, intentional teachers provide sturdy, open-ended materials that reflect the diversity of children's homes and communities. Although most materials are available daily to encourage in-depth exploration, some are rotated periodically to expand children's experiences and respond to new skills and interests. Reintroducing familiar materials can also inspire new uses. These items should offer different textures, smells, sounds, and tastes. Manipulative materials like blocks, beads, shells, puzzles, and playdough allow children to explore with all their senses, transform (change), and combine (put together and take apart). Labeling and storing equipment and materials visibly and accessibly encourages children's initiative and independence in finding, using, and returning supplies on their own.

Having fewer types of items but more of the same or similar things is often better. This approach reduces wait times, which can be challenging for young children, even for preschoolers who are beginning to share and understand turn taking. It capitalizes on children's excitement and initiative, allowing them to put their ideas into immediate action. When children work with the same or comparable materials, such as varied types of blocks, they are more likely to compare and share observations about their experiences, promoting social interaction and providing insights into what their peers do, see, and say. Duplicates of dress-up clothes and props promote higher-level play and communication, as there are multiple roles available for children to assume—two firefighters or two chefs, for example.

Display Work Created by and of Interest to Children

Documenting and displaying children's work prompts children to recall and reflect on their experiences, expand on their ideas, and talk with others about their ideas, processes, and choices. Use walls, shelves, and pedestals to showcase artwork, emergent writing, science projects, photographs of activities, rules they create for a game they invent, family photographs, mementos of field trips, turn-taking lists for distributing snacks or choosing a song, and so on. Adding brief captions or descriptions can highlight the learning behind each piece, such as what children observed, created, or shared during an activity.

Change displays regularly to keep children's recent work in focus. Displays that have been up too long cease to attract attention. Photos of current projects with short explanations can also keep the display dynamic. Focus displays on children's activities and achievements rather than adult information, which should be posted separately or in a small designated area. This approach showcases children's learning to parents, administrators, and visitors, connecting them to the classroom environment.

Use Technology Intentionally

Children are surrounded by interactive media in their homes and community spaces. Media exposure includes software programs, applications, broadcast and streaming media, children's television programming, ebooks, the internet, and other forms of content; the best are designed to facilitate active and creative use by young children and to encourage social engagement with other children and adults, but discernment is needed. According to the NAEYC & Fred Rogers Center technology and interactive media position statement (2012), when used intentionally and appropriately, technology and media can support children's learning and relationships with both adults and peers. Priorities when integrating technology in children's learning include the following:

> Use digital tools in ways that match young children's development. For example, choose apps that encourage exploration and creativity rather than those with a lot of rules or complex instructions.

> Support learning with evidence-based uses of technology. Choose technology that aligns with how young children learn best, such as ebooks with interactive story elements that build language skills.

> Help families use technology as a positive learning tool. For families with limited access or experience, provide simple guidance or, if possible, loan devices. As with all topics you discuss with families, conversations around technology and media should be reciprocal. If families are interested in how to use technology to support their child's learning without adding stress, offer suggestions or resources (Donohue & Schomburg 2017).

Reflecting Children's Experiences in Classroom Materials

Reflecting children's lives and experiences in the classroom involves more than displaying objects or media that showcase the practices or celebrations of particular groups. Diversity applies to who and what we are every day. Here are some ideas for materials that will acknowledge and respect the cultural diversity of the children and families in your program. For all areas, labels and other written materials should appear in English and children's home languages.

Art area: Crayons in different skin tone colors; materials that showcase and encourage children to make the arts and crafts found in their culture and community (for example, ceramic bowls and statues, clay to make pottery, woven wall hangings and placemats, and yarn and frame looms)

Block/construction area: Animal figures representing both typical and unusual pets (such as dogs, cats, snakes, and pigs); toy vehicles representing different types of jobs (such as construction equipment, farm tractors, and taxicabs); diverse building materials used locally (such as wood, bricks, ceramic tiles, and boards made of recycled plastic)

Book area: Books in English and children's home languages; books depicting a variety of family structures, races, ethnicities, cultures, and ages (including older adults); books showing people of all genders engaged in a variety of activities at home, work, and leisure; books depicting children and adults with various ability levels

Dramatic play area: Dolls representing different races, ethnic groups, and genders; kitchen utensils and food packages like those found in children's homes; dress-up clothing with items from different cultures and occupations; child-size disability aids (for example, walkers, crutches, and eyeglasses with lenses removed)

Music area: Recordings with songs reflective of children's cultures; musical instruments from a variety of cultures

Science area: Real examples and/or photos of plant and animal wildlife native to the area; tools and other items related to local weather patterns (such as for snow removal, sun protection, rainy season, or hurricane preparedness)

Scheduling the Program Day

The intentional teacher's goal is to offer children a rich and varied mix of learning opportunities within a supportive framework of routine. A well-considered schedule that meets the needs of all children creates an inclusive environment where everyone can thrive (Lesperance 2021).

Establish a Consistent yet Flexible Daily Routine

Routine provides young children with emotional stability and security by establishing predictability and expectations. For instance, morning greetings from teachers can help ease the transition from home to school for children and reassure families entrusting their child to someone outside their home. Including greetings in their home languages provides a sense of safety and respect for multilingual learners and their families.

Give careful consideration to the number and nature of daily activities to strike a balance between too many and too few. Avoid overly frequent transitions, which can be disruptive for young children. The sequence and length of activities provide important experiences in temporal relationships and support the development of early mathematics concepts. Flexibility in routines allows teachers to capitalize on spontaneous teaching opportunities and extend children's interests. Further, recurring routines enable children to revisit materials and repeat activities, deepening their understanding of familiar concepts.

Consistency in routines also provides teachers a framework for planning and integrating content into each component of the day. For example, numerical concepts can be explored during various activities, such as counting the number of children present during greeting time or tallying how many children are playing in each area during choice time. In addition, offering children choices within the schedule empowers them and fosters a sense of shared control with teachers, even during adult-led activities.

Allow for a Variety of Types of Activities

Structure each day to provide balance of activities that cater to different aspects of children's development:

> Self-directed play

> Guided play

> Cleaning up and taking care of individual needs

> Group activities for introducing concepts, reading aloud, discussing events or problems that are meaningful to the children, and sharing rituals that build community

> Small group experiences for peer learning and exploring higher-level content in more depth

> Indoor and outdoor play, including movement

> Socializing with adults and peers

> Problem solving with materials and people

> Sharing snacks or meals

> Rest time (depending on children's ages and the length of the program day)

> Transitions

> Consolidating and reflecting on learning

This range of learning activities enables children to learn content using all their senses, abilities, and interests and to make meaningful connections. Although the schedule maintains a predictable sequence, the specific activities within each component vary daily based on children's interests and teachers' goals. This balance of consistency and variety ensures that children can find engaging things to do while sharing control with adults. Too much variety can overwhelm young children, so the daily routine should provide variation, repetition, and extension of learning experiences over time.

Use a Variety of Groupings

Children benefit from a variety of groupings, including working alone, alongside each other, in pairs, and in small and large groups. Although some groupings occur naturally, teachers create others, especially small and large groups, to include a variety of learning experiences. Group settings provide opportunities for social learning as children observe, listen, play, solve problems, and share ideas with peers. These interactions also support language development, as children hear and use new words and refine their communication skills. Group times are particularly beneficial for multilingual learners, who are often motivated to learn their peers' language so they can be part of the group. Effective teachers carefully observe individual and group dynamics to ensure each child feels secure and supported. They may strategically place children together for small group activities based on comfort levels, language skills, or cultural backgrounds to facilitate positive and rewarding experiences for all.

Allow Just Enough Time for Each Type of Activity

The duration of each activity should suit children's abilities and interests, neither frustrating them nor boring them. Allow flexibility in timing to accommodate individual differences. For example, one child might need a few extra minutes to finish an art activity while the other children wash up for snack time. Quick eaters could clean up and go outside with one teacher while slower eaters linger and chat with a second teacher.

This flexibility helps smooth transitions and avoids upsetting young children. Often when teachers see an increased need for behavior supports, adjusting the schedule or a particular activity can help.

Connecting Teaching to Children's Lives

By Melany Spiehs and Carol Burk

In a large group discussion with 3-, 4-, and 5-year-olds, Ms. Sarah shows the class a tortilla press that Eduardo's mom brought to help them make tortillas.

Ms. Sarah: (*Holds up the tortilla press.*) Do you know what this is for?

Liam: It's a thing for . . . (*Makes smashing motion with his hand.*)

Ms. Sarah: So you put something in it and press down, like this? (*Imitates Liam's motion.*)

Liam: (*Nods.*)

Margaret: My mom has that!

Ms. Sarah: That's right! It is a tortilla press, and today we are going to make tortillas using masa.

The children move to tables, and Ms. Sarah hands them a small bit of masa (dough made from ground corn). The children roll the masa and push it down as flat as it can go, talking about their motions and actions. Ms. Sarah says, "When you are done, you can take your masa to Eduardo's mom. She will press your tortilla for you."

Once the masa is pressed, the children take it to Miss Alice, another teacher, and she puts it on a griddle.

Miss Alice: The griddle must be hot to cook the tortilla fast.

Margaret: My mom says "Be careful" when she makes it. It can burn me!

Miss Alice: Yes, your mom is right to be careful.

Margaret: I love tortilla! My mom puts cheese on mine.

This experience was a result of the teachers responding to a curriculum lesson from the previous year. As part of a farm study, the suggested lesson was to make bread with the children and discuss where food comes from. The teachers noticed that the children weren't interested in bread and butter, and they later learned that these were not typical foods eaten in most of the children's homes. But many families shared stories about making tortillas together, and this inspired the teachers to rethink the lesson for the following year's group of children, who also had funds of knowledge about tortilla making.

When teachers integrate children's knowledge and their family and cultural practices into the curriculum, there is an increase in learning and engagement. It also provides important mirrors in the classroom where children are seen and valued. The activity of tortilla making connected home and school life while still enabling children to achieve the fine motor, language, sequencing, and science goals of the lesson.

Interacting with Children

Children's interactions with teachers and peers, more than any other program feature, can determine what children learn and how they feel about learning (Cash et al. 2019; Dombro, Jablon, & Stetson 2020). In the early years, learning is largely a social process. Connecting with young children means recognizing that relationships are the basis of instruction and learning (NAEYC 2022). Even children's encounters with materials are often mediated by others. It is, therefore, critical to understand how children develop and offer them the kinds of support and encouragement that promote growth and progress.

The following sections outline core strategies for establishing and maintaining an interactive environment that supports children's learning and development. (See also "Core Strategies for Interacting with Children" on page 35.)

Meet Children's Basic Physical Needs

All children have basic physical needs regarding food and nutrition, toileting, physical and psychological comfort, and safety and health. Having one's essential needs met, beginning in infancy, forms the basis for the fundamental trust all humans need to grow and develop. Attending to children's needs for physical care also helps meet their psychological need to feel safe and secure.

Children's needs change through their early years, but adults maintain an important role in helping to meet those needs. Infants need someone to feed, change, cuddle, and play with them; toddlers venture out to explore on their own but check back frequently to verify that their trusted caregiver is still there and available. At 3 and 4 years old, children can function independently or with peers for longer periods of time if they have established this basic trust early on. The security of knowing that caring adults will meet their basic needs prepares young children to venture beyond the familiar, setting the stage for all future educational experiences.

Create a Warm and Caring Atmosphere

Children feel secure and successful when teachers interact positively with them, both verbally (listening, conversing with interest and respect, using a calm voice to problem-solve) and nonverbally (smiling, hugging, nodding, making eye contact, getting down to children's eye level).

Warm, sensitive, and nurturing interactions are beneficial for children's developmental and academic outcomes. In comparison, harsh, critical, or detached adult behavior can reduce children's engagement and motivation and limit their potential (Rucinski, Brown, & Downer 2018). Effective teachers "contribute to a climate of mutual respect by showing interest in children's ideas, experiences, and work or creative products" (NAEYC 2019b, 42) and "develop individual relationships with children by providing care that is responsive, attentive, consistent, comforting, supportive, and culturally sensitive" (NAEYC 2019b, 41). Such behaviors promote children's positive development and learning.

Core Strategies for Interacting with Children

- Meet children's basic physical needs.

- Create a warm and caring atmosphere.

- Encourage and support language and communication.

- Encourage initiative.

- Introduce information and model skills.

- Acknowledge children's activities and accomplishments.

- Support peer interactions.

- Encourage independent problem solving.

Encourage and Support Language and Communication

Teachers support children's language development by taking conversational turns, allowing time for children to express thoughts, and using questions judiciously. Interesting materials and experiences encourage children to talk. A positive classroom climate and peer interactions also promote language development. Intentional teachers engage with all children, including those who are quiet or exhibit behaviors the teacher perceives as challenging. (For other suggestions on encouraging language and communication, refer to Chapter 6.)

Encourage Initiative

Children are naturally curious, independent, and self-directed learners. They signal their intentions from an early age, such as reaching for a toy or asking for more juice. Preschoolers often develop elaborate plans, like building a whole city in the block area. When given freedom to choose, make mistakes, and try again or try another way, children gain confidence to continue learning under their own initiative. Encourage this initiative by respecting children's interests, being enthusiastic about their activities, following their lead, offering suggestions when they seem stuck, and participating as partners in their play. (For other suggestions on encouraging initiative, refer to Chapter 3.)

Using a Collaborative Approach to Classroom Rules

A powerful way to make rules meaningful is to create them collaboratively with the children. When children are part of the rulemaking process, they feel a sense of ownership and are more likely to follow the rules because they understand the reasons behind them. Sometimes a problem that arises in the classroom might lead to a group conversation, and the benefit of creating a rule becomes apparent. For example, if disagreements over the use of toys or materials are recurring, you might bring the problem to the class at group time by using puppets to act out a similar

incident, then invite the children to discuss how the puppets could solve their problem. This conversation might lead to a classroom rule such as "We take turns with toys so everyone gets a chance to play."

Once rules are set, reinforce them by modeling the behaviors and referring children back to the rules they helped create. For instance, if "listen to each other" is a class rule, the teacher might say, "I'm listening carefully to what you're saying because I want to understand your idea. We decided this is important in our room." This approach shows children that rules are not just words but actions that everyone, including adults, follows to create a caring classroom. (See Chapter 9 for more on rulemaking with children as part of a community.)

Children's understanding of rules is shaped by their cultural context and their age, so creating fair, or just, rules means being mindful of these differences (Rasminsky & Kaiser 2016). For example, in some cultures children are encouraged to speak up and express their opinions, whereas others may be taught to follow the rules adults set. By recognizing these differences, teachers can approach rule setting and expectations in ways that reflect children's home settings and that feel fair and respectful to everyone (Garrity & Longstreth 2020). Frequent discussions with families as well as professional development about cultural practices and values can help teachers create a classroom that respects and includes every child's culture (Gilliam et al. 2016).

Introduce Information and Model Skills

Although content has always been part of early childhood education, many teachers remain unsure about how to incorporate content in a developmentally appropriate way. Young children construct knowledge by combining their own experiences with instruction and examples from peers and adults. This book seeks to help teachers recognize that even content that can be taught only by telling and showing things to children (direct instruction) can be included in the curriculum by using teacher-guided strategies appropriate to young children's developmental levels. Rather than quash children's initiative and spirit of inquiry, teaching with intention gives them the tools to spark further discovery and mastery.

Acknowledge Children's Activities and Accomplishments

It is preferable for teachers to show they value children's work through interest and encouragement rather than praise, which can have negative effects. Praise invites comparison and competition, raises anxiety, and limits children's ability to evaluate their own work. Encouragement, in contrast, promotes initiative and self-confidence and helps children evaluate their work objectively rather than depend on adults' approval. When you offer acknowledgment and encouragement, be specific and focus on the child rather than give your opinion. Comment on their actions, ask authentic questions to learn more, record their ideas, help them draw connections, and support them in sharing their work with others. (See further discussion on praise versus specific feedback on page 274.)

Support Peer Interactions

In general, preschoolers eagerly build relationships with peers and adults. These relationships offer numerous benefits. Peers can become play partners, allowing children to explore leadership roles and learn from one another. They also provide information, entertainment, and emotional support. These relationships can help children develop a sense of identity and learn about different languages and cultures.

Teachers play a crucial role in fostering relationships between peers by building their own authentic, supportive, and reciprocal relationships with children. They set the tone for interactions by treating children with kindness and respect, modeling respectful communication, and encouraging peer interactions. Teachers can facilitate friendships and help children solve social problems by encouraging cooperation and appreciation of each other's contributions. (For more suggestions on supporting peer interactions, refer to the discussion in Chapter 4 about social development in "Social Awareness," pages 77–80, and collaboration with peers in "Relationship Skills," pages 81–83.)

Encourage Independent Problem Solving

Encouraging children to identify and solve problems on their own facilitates a range of cognitive, social, emotional, and physical skills. Teachers who intervene too quickly rob children of the chance to develop independence, whereas waiting too long can lead to anxiety or discouragement.

Effective teachers use several techniques to find the right balance. They encourage children to describe their challenges, which fosters cognitive and language development. They patiently let children generate and try solutions. When needed to prevent frustration or harm (such as can occur when children are arguing over a toy), teachers step in with a well-timed suggestion or direct assistance, always seeking to support the child's self-image as an independent problem solver. (For other suggestions on supporting children's problem solving, see "Responding to Learning Experiences," pages 57–62.)

Building Partnerships with Families

Recognizing that families are primary in their children's lives and their first teachers, intentional teachers strive to create trusting partnerships with families and work with them to support children's learning both at home and at school (Mapp et al. 2022). Open communication with families provides teachers with insights into children's interests and learning preferences, which helps them better understand and support each child's unique needs (Dimock et al. 2017).

Teachers approach families with openness, fairness, and cultural sensitivity. Learning from families about their cultural practices and values, as well as working together to solve challenges, helps to create a more inclusive environment. When families feel welcomed and valued by the school community, they are more likely to be actively involved and engaged in their child's education (Cobb & Krownapple 2019). Seeing their culture and values reflected in the classroom builds trust (NAESP 2016), which positively impacts children's well-being and academic success.

Building and sustaining strong, two-way relationships with families is a shared responsibility between the program and the teacher. Programs and teachers support families by seeking their input on how they would like to participate in the program, providing activities and events they are interested in and at times when they can participate, inviting them to join advisory boards, linking families with community services, helping the transition to new settings, and sharing information in their home languages. Teachers also connect with families both informally and formally through pickup and drop-off chats, family-teacher conferences, and emails. In essence, family-school partnerships are not just about involving families in school activities; it is about building strong, collaborative relationships that benefit each child, each family, and the entire learning community (Weiss, Lopez, & Caspe 2018).

This section focuses on two additional teacher strategies that relate most directly to intentionality: helping families understand how the classroom curriculum uses child-guided and adult-guided learning and partnering with families to connect home and school learning.

Exchange Information About the Curriculum and How It Promotes Children's Development

Effective teachers share curriculum information with families in various ways, including through meetings, newsletters, email, messaging systems, blogs, and resource sharing of books, articles, and video recordings. They explain the curriculum and what children learn—for example, by posting signs in each area that list the kinds of learning taking place there. Teachers seek to forge a reciprocal relationship with each family by listening to and learning from the family as well as sharing information with them. Teachers solicit families' ideas and goals for their children's learning and respond to their concerns. After setting goals together, families and teachers can document and review how children are progressing toward those goals.

Depending on their own school experiences, families may look for teachers to use highly directive teaching strategies as evidence that their child is being taught the information and skills needed in kindergarten and elementary school. When families look for obvious signs of such instruction (such as worksheets) and don't find them, teachers can assure them that they hear their concerns and explain how they use a balance of child- and adult-guided experiences to help children learn. All families share with teachers a desire for their children to succeed in school and in life, so use this common ground to communicate with, support, and respect each other. Displaying and explaining children's work (such as writing samples, charts, experiments, and constructions) will further help families recognize evidence that the learning they care about is occurring.

Partner With Families to Connect Learning at Home to Learning at School

Many families already support learning at home and appreciate simple ideas to build on this. Teachers can offer ideas for weaving learning into everyday home routines, like talking with children while grocery shopping, exploring math concepts by setting the table at mealtimes, sorting laundry, looking for printed words while taking a walk, and reading together at bedtime. Helping families identify these naturally occurring learning situations will promote opportunities to connect school learning to home learning and help families feel confident in supporting their child's academic learning.

Teachers can further connect school and home by asking families to share stories, traditions, or events from home life; learning from families ways to connect their home culture with classroom learning; and providing continuity by using familiar routines, materials, or approaches from home.

Creating spaces for families to connect with each other also fosters a supportive community. Sharing experiences and strategies enriches everyone involved, making school a more collaborative and welcoming place for all.

Assessing Children's Development and Learning

Assessment, when "responsive to the current developmental accomplishments, language(s), and experiences of young children" (NAEYC 2020, 20), gives teachers valuable insights into children's growth and development. Observing, documenting, and assessing children's learning helps teachers plan appropriate learning experiences and also improve their teaching. Both informal methods and structured tools help teachers see how children are progressing toward their learning goals and determine what they are ready to learn next (NAEYC 2022). It's also a chance for teachers to gain insight into areas where they can grow or where more professional development would be helpful.

Intentional teachers assess learning by observing children and documenting their progress on a regular, consistent basis using anecdotal notes or records and audio or video recordings; maintaining portfolios of children's work; measuring progress using developmentally appropriate and validated assessment tools; and sharing assessment results with families. Since multilingual learners know and can do some things in English and some in their home languages, truly accurate assessment for them must include observations and measures in all their languages.

This section focuses on two specific aspects of assessment: how teachers can intentionally apply assessment results to improve their understanding of children's development and plan further learning experiences, and using assessment as a tool for professional growth. (Further guidelines and strategies for carrying out appropriate assessment activities can be found in Chapter 8 of *Developmentally Appropriate Practice in Early Childhood Programs Serving Children from Birth Through Age 8,* fourth edition [Scott-Little, with Reschke 2022].)

Use Assessment Results to Plan for Individual Children and the Group as a Whole

Along with collecting objective assessment data based on what they observe rather than personal impressions, it's important for teachers to be able to interpret and apply the information thoughtfully.

Formative assessment is the ongoing process of monitoring a child's learning over time. By observing and documenting children's play, work, and interactions, teachers gain the information they need to help determine a child's strengths and areas for growth. The information can be gathered and used throughout the year to plan learning experiences to support each and every child's progress in every developmental domain. (Batts 2022, 13)

Using this insight, teachers can choose the best mix of child-guided and adult-guided experiences to support each child's growth.

Use Assessment Results to Identify Areas for Professional Development

Results of children's assessments can also highlight areas where teachers might benefit from professional development. By building their own expertise and skills in specific areas, like instructional strategies or deeper content knowledge, they can more effectively support children's learning. For example, if a valid assessment of literacy shows several children making progress in letter recognition but not in comprehension, perhaps coaching or attending a workshop on strategies for building comprehension, like encouraging recall and prediction during book reading, may help.

● ● ●

Intentional teachers ensure that young children gain the knowledge and skills they need to succeed in school and in life. To fulfill this mission, they thoughtfully address every aspect of early learning—intellectual, linguistic, social and emotional, physical, and creative—through joyful, engaging experiences. They apply the effective practices summarized in this chapter using both child-guided and adult-guided experiences. Moreover, intentional teachers see themselves as lifelong learners. They continuously observe the children in their care and make goals, plans, and adjustments based on their observations; stay up to date on child development theory and research; and collaborate with coworkers and families to support each child's growth.

Intentional teaching also involves self-reflection. When teachers envision today's children as tomorrow's adults, they can better understand the meaningful role they play in helping young learners grow into caring, curious, and capable individuals. This book provides insights and practical strategies to support this mission.

The general principles and strategies of intentional teaching discussed in this chapter can be applied across all areas of early learning, from social and emotional skills to math and literacy. You can refer to these overall strategies as you read the following chapters, which offer specific ideas for promoting growth and learning in the developmental domains and subject-matter areas. As you explore these chapters, keep in mind that effective early childhood education is built on partnerships between children and teachers as well as between schools and families. Considering and using these evidence-based practices will help administrators and teachers create early childhood programs in which adults and children are partners in the learning process.

For Further Consideration

1. How can commercial curriculum materials help teachers provide essential content yet enable them to remain intentional in their teaching? What risks and shortcomings come with such curricula, and what can teachers and programs do to address these?

2. What specific strategies can teachers use to ensure that their practices truly reflect and respect children's identities and perspectives?

3. How can teachers build a two-way partnership with families that goes beyond traditional communication to actively involve them in curriculum planning and their child's learning?

4. What types of professional learning experiences, both preservice and in-service, might best support teachers in deepening their understanding and application of developmentally appropriate practices?

5. Consider specific examples where implicit biases might influence classroom practices or expectations. How can teachers actively work to recognize these biases and foster a learning space that respects and values each child and family?

Learning Objectives

1. To define approaches to learning and describe how they affect readiness for and responses to learning experiences

2. To explain how developmental differences in children's foundational cognitive skills, including executive function skills, contribute to their approaches to learning

3. To identify the roles of the learning setting, teacher interactions, and teaching strategies in supporting children's approaches to learning

4. To describe teaching strategies that build on children's unique strengths and individual approaches to learning to promote persistence, motivation, and successful engagement in learning

CHAPTER 3

Approaches to Learning

Marie L. Masterson and Michèle M. Mazzocco

When Lourdes, age 4, is reluctant to touch the finger paint, her teacher, Ms. Alma, offers Lourdes disposable gloves. After a few minutes, Lourdes removes one glove and dips her forefinger in the paint. She rubs her fingers together then wipes them with a towel. Ms. Alma offers different painting tools like a sponge, pine cone, and cotton balls so that Lourdes has many options to create patterns in the paint that are comfortable for her.

• • •

During outdoor play, 4-year-old Marica watches an ant carry a bread crumb twice its size across a patch of dirt. "He's awful little," she comments. "How can it move something bigger than him?" She crouches and studies the ant carefully. Wanting to support Marica's interest and extend her inquiry and observations, her teacher, Ms. Bisa, introduces Marica to some books about ants. Together, they find answers to Marica's questions. They learn about parts of ants' bodies and how they can grasp and move heavy objects. Ms. Bisa keeps a record of Marica's interest and new learning by placing anecdotal notes in Marica's portfolio.

• • •

Mr. Robert introduces several 4- and 5-year-olds to a game called Jumping Feet, which calls for executive function skills that support self-regulation. The children play the game like hopscotch, except that the path Mr. Robert has drawn has outlines of either one or two feet instead of numbers. When the children see two feet on the path, they jump with two feet. When they see one foot, they jump with one foot. After the children play Jumping Feet this way for a while, Mr. Robert changes the rules. "Instead of using two feet to jump when you see two feet, use one foot. When you see one foot, use two feet." Darcy begins her turn but has trouble switching from the old rule to the new rule. She jumps with two feet onto the outline of two feet. She frowns and glances at Mr. Robert, which suggests that Darcy knows something is not quite right but that she is trying. Mr. Robert acknowledges that it is tricky to switch to the new rule and encourages her to keep trying. (Adapted from Wiltshire & Scott 2024)

Approaches to learning reflect a broad set of skills, attitudes, and behaviors that children use to engage in learning, such as persistence, motivation, and flexible thinking (Bustamante, White, & Greenfield 2018; Head Start Early Childhood Learning & Knowledge Center 2024). As shown in the vignettes above, children's approaches to learning reflect their efforts and desires to attend and engage, their ability to solve problems, and their curiosity and interests (Burts et al. 2016). They demonstrate their joy and enthusiasm (and sometimes hesitation) at engaging with the world around them. Approaches to learning include children's ability to manage their own behaviors, emotions, and attention while working toward learning goals (Anthony & Ogg 2019). The way preschoolers approach learning affects their experiences across content areas during early childhood and beyond. For example, researchers have shown that positive attitudes toward learning may help children compensate for factors that interfere with academic achievement, such as fewer early learning opportunities (Mariano et al. 2019). This is why it is important to intentionally design learning experiences that support children's positive approaches to learning even when children face difficulties, as shown in the Jumping Feet vignette above.

Many strategies can increase children's motivation and engagement (Golubovic-Ilic & Cirkovic-Miladinovic 2020). To influence children's positive attitudes toward learning, you can nurture natural curiosity, encourage autonomy, and provide individual support. You can ask questions and explore answers to topics that interest children, which promote critical thinking and problem solving. To encourage the development of a growth mindset, you can support autonomy and help children see themselves as active agents in achieving goals (Boyland, Barblett, & Knaus 2018). These strategies instill lifelong habits for successful learning.

Strategies for supporting children's approaches to learning appear in "Fitting the Learning Experience to the Learning Objective" later in this chapter, where they are considered separately as child-guided and adult-guided experiences.

Multimodal Learning

Many educators have been exposed to the idea that approaches to learning depend on learning styles that are preferred by individual children. However, learning style theories that suggest each child learns best in a specific way through a particular mode, such as visual, auditory, or kinesthetic, have not been supported by research (Kirschner 2017; Waterhouse 2023; Willingham 2018).

Children learn best when they are exposed to content through *many* forms of communication—including physical movement, spoken and written words, music, objects, and visuals—with the teacher carefully considering which modes match the learning content and goals (McCormick et al. 2023; Rumenapp, Morales, & Lykouretzos 2018). Multimodal instruction encourages children to engage and respond through many forms of involvement. When multiple modes are effectively integrated, children become active learners, gaining understanding and representing their learning in a variety of ways (Clinton-Lisell & Litzinger 2024; Nguyen et al. 2022).

Multimodal instruction is important for all children, including children with developmental delays or disabilities and multilingual learners. For example, by supporting verbal communication with gestures and real-life examples, teachers can promote deeper understanding of content for children who are emergent English learners. By offering reinforcing visuals to a child with an auditory processing disorder, the teacher can help the child make sense of verbal communication. Multimodal experiences provide greater access to information and opportunity for responding.

Young Children's Development in Approaches to Learning

Temperamental traits have been considered important to children's approaches to learning. For example, sensitivity, sociability, or impulsivity may be seen as fixed—that is, traits that cannot be influenced (Kopala-Sibley et al. 2018). Some aspects of temperament, such as a child's level of inhibition and emotional reactivity, can influence how they approach learning. However, while temperamental traits are stable from the age of 3 to 12 years, they also can be influenced by children's early relationships with others, their cultural and social contexts, and their early learning experiences. For example, healthy, secure relationships support children's development of trust and encourage freedom to explore and try new experiences. Cultural and family expectations and beliefs also influence the qualities and kinds of learning approaches that children are encouraged or expected to pursue. For example, children might learn to value or avoid messy activities. Their at-home experience may be mostly structured or mostly unstructured, and it may support children's autonomous or adult-guided activities (Cheung et al. 2022).

Persistence is another trait that is influenced by development yet can be positively shaped by active adult behaviors (Oeri & Roebers 2021). Children who are likely to give up can develop persistence when teachers help them manage and overcome challenges. Teachers encourage children's effort and focus on a growth mindset, which lets children know that effort and hard work pay off. Because children's social dispositions, including their openness to engaging in a group, influence the way they engage with new information, teachers can also model and encourage strategies for successful engagement.

Cognitive Development and Executive Function Skills

Cognitive development and approaches to learning are related concepts that refer to different aspects of how children acquire knowledge, process information, and engage in learning activities. Cognitive development refers to the growth and maturation of processes and skills related to thinking, memory, attention, problem solving, language, and the acquisition of knowledge. It is reflected in how children think, reason, learn, and understand the world around them. In contrast, approaches to learning reflect the strategies, behaviors, and attitudes children use to approach and engage in learning tasks.

Cognitive development is foundational to approaches to learning. Executive function skills, a subset of higher-order cognitive development, play a crucial role in how individuals engage in and adapt to learning experiences. Executive function skills support the ability to hold and manipulate information in one's mind, resist acting on impulses, and think in flexible ways (Suor et al. 2019). These abilities enable children (and adults) to plan, monitor, and control their own behavior in social and academic settings. For example, when children are frustrated with a challenging task, being able to monitor their emotions and use appropriate strategies to manage the task or take a break will help them engage more effectively.

The connection between executive function skills and approaches to learning is strengthened when children learn to problem-solve, adapt to new learning situations, and sustain effort and persistence over time. Supporting the development of executive function skills contributes to children's holistic development and successful learning outcomes.

Teachers can identify executive function skills and use strategies to support individual children. For example, teachers can model and support behaviors that help children plan and engage in a task, such as thinking through needed steps and making adjustments to plans (Moreno, Shwayder, & Friedman 2017). All children at times need help to manage tasks, regulate their emotions, or pause to consider the best option before doing or saying something. Given the foundational role executive function skills play in approaches to learning, references to these skills appear throughout the remainder of this chapter.

Teaching and Learning Using Approaches to Learning

A positive approach to learning is fostered through intentional support strategies. Prepare the environment to encourage children to learn in their own ways, and provide opportunities for them to make choices that support initiative and self-confidence. As children explore the environment and materials, encourage them to ask questions and use their imaginations. Create cognitive challenges that are meaningful to children and involve children in decision making and planning. Offer support and learning opportunities in children's home languages.

Some children may be hesitant and need additional time to process and reflect. Encourage them to try new things and build an awareness that making mistakes and encountering difficulty are part of learning. Appropriate early experiences encourage children to take reasonable risks because they focus on the enjoyment of learning rather than on the fear of failure. Persisting and trying out new strategies will help children experience success and gain confidence (Leonard et al. 2021).

Cognitive Challenges

Young children are motivated to pursue what is just beyond their current understanding or mastery (NAEYC 2020). By providing rich learning experiences for each child that are cognitively challenging but achievable—offering adaptations and supports as needed—teachers foster critical thinking, creativity, problem solving, and a positive approach to learning (Darling-Hammond & Cook-Harvey 2018; NAEYC 2020). Robust instruction that leverages children's strengths also promotes self-agency and equity by "prioritizing opportunities for all children to apply, synthesize, and extend what they have learned" (Schmidtke 2021, 3). Note how Mr. Leo supports Mateo when he encounters a problem:

> After reading *The Three Little Pigs*, Mr. Leo offers a challenge to the children: to build a house that is strong enough to withstand the big bad wolf (represented by a fan). Nora and Mateo work next to each other at the low table using tape and glue, tubes, containers, cardboard, and fabric scraps for their structures. "Mine's gonna be for camping. It's gotta be leakproof," says Mateo. He leans across to reach the tape dispenser, and his elbow knocks the tube away from the bottom carton that is supporting his structure. He grunts in disappointment.
>
> Nora offers some cardboard squares. "You gotta tape these on," she says.
>
> Mr. Leo, who has been observing the two children, says, "You have materials and fasteners. What would make your tent stronger?"
>
> "I need better tape," Mateo says, and he looks through the bin holding different types of tape. He selects the long roll of colored craft tape. "Can you cut it for me?" he asks Mr. Leo.
>
> "How about if I hold and you cut?" Mr. Leo responds. They collaborate silently, coordinating their efforts, until Mateo's tent sides are restored.
>
> "Got it!" he says with satisfaction.

Rather than solve problems for the children, Mr. Leo offers ideas to help them think critically about their designs, promoting persistence and flexible thinking—key components of successful approaches to learning.

Child Decision Making and Planning

Providing opportunities for decision making and planning also supports children's approaches to learning. For example, you might observe children racing toy cars down a ramp and challenge them to think about how the shape or weight of the cars affects their speed, then ask how they could test out their theories. By supporting the children's critical decision making and problem solving, you encourage deeper thinking.

When children make choices about their own learning, they become more engaged, persistent, and attentive (Dabrowski & Marshall 2019). They also experience more joy and motivation (Schmidtke 2022a). During children's self-selected activities, teachers play a key role in guiding and extending children's thinking through meaningful prompts, questions, and suggestions. Knowing individual children and how much support they need for any given task allows you to tailor strategies to meet each child where they are and help them strengthen their skills and make learning gains.

To create a setting that supports each child's positive predisposition to learn and creates multiple avenues for learning, consider how to incorporate the following priorities:

> Sensory experiences: Provide an environment in which children have many opportunities to touch and manipulate objects, explore visual and auditory stimuli, and experiment with movement and balance. Let children repeat and build on previous experiences. Share information with them in several ways. For example, give individual children auditory and visual cues to support their understanding.

> Pacing or timing: All children need a balance of stimulation, including active play outdoors, quieter activities, and more sustained periods of time to explore materials and ideas deeply and to practice skills. Observe and adjust activities to match children's stimulation needs. Children may need opportunities to focus on one thing at a time or assistance to transition gradually between activities or ideas. Learning occurs while children appear to be active and also while children watch, listen, and think, so allow time for them to process information and avoid interrupting these periods of learning. When you step in too quickly, children are deprived of a chance to discover things for themselves and may come to rely on adults instead of developing their own skills.

> Social context: Children need both time to work on their own and time to engage in experiences that require interaction with others. They need time for independent pursuits to quietly and methodically investigate things or practice skills, such as during puzzle or block play. Yet these and many other activities are also well-suited for learning in a group context. Social give-and-take helps children consider new ideas and master new skills, including cognitive and social skills. Peer collaboration offers opportunities for children to develop trust, learn to divide roles, and take on differing responsibilities within a group (Clements 2022).

Connecting Teaching to Children's Lives

By Kimberlee Telford

"Ms. Kerry!" Sawyer, age 4, yells as she races into the preschool classroom. "I saw you at the garden yesterday!"

"Yes, and I saw you too!" Ms. Kerry replies. "It was so much fun to meet your little brother. The carrots you are growing are getting very big."

"When they are big enough to pick, my auntie is going to teach me how to put them in a jar and make them taste like pickles!" Sawyer responds.

"You saw my tomatoes!" Felipe, age 3, says.

"Yes, I did see your tomatoes," Ms. Kerry responds. "You showed me you have three tomato plants." Ms. Kerry counts on her fingers: "One for you, one for your abuela, and one for your mom. What are you going to do with your tomatoes?"

"Abuela chops them up for salsa. It's sooo good," Felipe replies.

After seeing some of the children at the community garden, Ms. Kerry reads a book about gardening with the whole class. The children decide they would like to experiment with their own classroom "garden" in the sensory bin. The following day, Ms. Kerry helps the children pour clean soil into their sensory bin, and the children very enthusiastically select items from a basket to garden with, such as glitter, bouncy balls, glow sticks, pipe cleaners, and craft sticks. Sawyer and Felipe are the first to investigate.

Felipe: These balls are actually seeds 'cause they have a round shape and can fit in the dirt.

Sawyer: Okay, but you have to use the glowers to push them in the dirt. It's pretty hard.

Felipe: This is a bouncy seed. You can bounce it like this.

Felipe throws the bouncy ball into the soil, but the ball does not bounce. "This is not a good bouncy place. Cars and blocks is better," says Felipe as he changes his plan and takes the ball over to the block center.

Ms. Kerry sees that Sawyer is struggling to "plant" the ball in the soil using the thin bending glow stick and is beginning to show signs of frustration.

Ms. Kerry: Hi, Sawyer. May I play with you?

Sawyer: Yeah, but it's really hard to plant these seeds.

Ms. Kerry: Yes, I see that you keep trying different ways to plant your seed using a glow stick. I noticed that you tried pushing down on the top of the seed; you pushed on the side of the seed to roll it; and you tried digging under the seed. You have tried lots of good ideas.

Sawyer: I tried everything. It's impossible.

Ms. Kerry: I wonder why this is so challenging? I saw you and your brother digging in your garden yesterday, and it looked much easier.

Sawyer: Yeah, because we had sticks from a tree. These glowers are too floppy and wobbly. (*Waves around the glow stick.*)

Ms. Kerry: That's a good observation! Is there something here we could use that is like the sticks you and your brother used?

Sawyer: Maybe . . . craft sticks. They're straighter and won't flop around so much. (*Tries moving a ball with a craft stick.*) It's tricky, but you can still do it like this.

When Felipe returns to the sensory bin to plant three "bouncy seeds," Sawyer offers him some of the craft sticks to make the planting easier.

Having a positive approach to learning requires that children feel safe and trust their teachers. Children are open to learning when they know that it is okay to take risks, make mistakes, and try something else. By building on experiences and knowledge familiar to children and supporting children as they deal with challenges in their own ways (for example, Felipe leaves for another activity, then returns; Sawyer persists with a tool in an effort to achieve his goal), Ms. Kerry provides an environment that fosters problem solving and idea generation.

In addition, Ms. Kerry demonstrates intentionality as a culturally responsive teacher. By engaging with her students and their families in the classroom and in the community, she recognizes that many of the families, such as Sawyer's, know a lot about gardening and food. By embedding what she learns about the children and families in the classroom, she connects the children's funds of knowledge to new learning.

Fitting the Learning Experience to the Learning Objective

Children's approaches to learning can be examined in two ways: their readiness or willingness to engage in learning experiences and the way they process or respond to those experiences. The first describes children's initial willingness to explore and engage with materials, ideas, people, and events. Many children eagerly and immediately engage with materials, whereas others prefer time to warm up to new experiences. Children may need to see, manipulate, explore, and hear concepts in multiple ways to make sense of new ideas. The extent to which children are open to experiences reflects what they understand about their own thinking and learning (their metacognition) and their view of learning as a creative, dynamic process influenced by their own self-agency (Puente-Diaz et al. 2022). It may also simply reflect what they are used to doing.

Children also differ in how they think about, relate to, and navigate the physical and interpersonal environment both during and after a learning experience—referred to here as responding to learning experiences. For example, some children demonstrate persistence, often making repeated attempts to solve a problem or reach their goal (such as Sawyer in the earlier vignette); other children seek assistance or move on to something else when they encounter a problem (such as Felipe). A child may follow up on a discovery by repeating it to see if it happens again or by varying an action to see if it changes the outcomes. Children often want to talk about their experience or show someone else what they learned. Over time, emerging cognitive and language skills allow young children to think back in more detail on what they have learned and consider how they can expand on an experience that was interesting and challenging at just the right level. Modeling reflection, sharing, and conversation will help children build these skills.

Children often experience joy in learning when they feel they have the autonomy to explore through child-guided experiences and the support to succeed through adult-guided experiences. This synergy leads to sustained engagement and enjoyment in discovery.

Readiness for Learning Experiences

Children's openness to and readiness to engage in learning experiences is related to their temperament, growth mindset, initiative, persistence, and risk taking. These traits are activated through the strategies children learn to use, the attitudes they develop about learning, and the habits that lead them to understand and apply new information. Being open to learning also helps children engage more fully with content encountered in the classroom. Their approach is related to the cultural values that adults model, such as the degree to which autonomy is supported, as well as the values and interests children bring to their own learning experiences.

Scaffolding

Scaffolding, a term introduced by psychologist Jerome Bruner (1986) and based on the work of Lev Vygotsky (1978), has two parts. The first is to support children at their current level of understanding; the second is to gently extend their learning. Finding the right balance requires sensitivity to each child's approach to learning and developmental level. Supporting a child without extending learning means the child stays at a safe (successful) level without taking on a new challenge and progressing. On the other hand, too much pressure to advance may confuse the child or discourage learning by creating frustration or failure.

Children's inherent curiosity and drive to learn lead them to explore their environment and engage with materials that spark their interest. Although children often initiate explorations spontaneously, their ability to approach learning with more intentional planning is influenced by adult modeling and support. As you seek to know each child well and provide a safe environment for trying things out, you can guide children's exploration and engagement through prompting, scaffolding, and follow-up.

Of the key knowledge and skills in the area of readiness for learning, child-guided experiences are particularly important for the following:

> Taking the initiative

> Engaging with materials

Adult-guided experiences are especially significant for the following:

> Planning

> Engaging with ideas

CHILD-GUIDED experiences are especially important for learnings such as:

| Readiness for Learning Experiences | Taking the initiative |

Young learners are inherently enthusiastic about and engaged with the world. In an environment where they feel secure and are supported to explore and make mistakes, they are eager to exercise mastery and control over their actions, interact with others, and discover the effects of their actions on the environment. They become comfortable with trying new things, taking risks, and generating their own ideas. Children vary in the extent to which they are comfortable taking the initiative, and some need more or less encouragement or time for initiative to develop.

Teaching strategies. Children are often inherently interested in tasks. When adults are involved, children are more likely to approach tasks if they are confident that their initiatives will be met with enthusiasm and support from adults rather than concerns or interference. In addition to the satisfaction children receive from pursuing or mastering something on their own, an adult's support can encourage children to display growing levels of originality, flexibility, and imagination. To help young children express and expand their inherent sense of initiative during child-guided experiences, try the following teaching strategies:

> Focus on children's efforts, not the outcomes of their actions. Emphasize the satisfaction of the learning itself. Take time to observe and understand the goals children have in mind. Provide materials and support to help them carry out their goals.

> Avoid praising children with vague comments like "Great job!" Such statements focus on an outcome and imply judgment; instead, praise children's efforts or offer encouragement by getting down on their physical level and mirroring their actions, commenting on what they are doing, and asking thoughtful questions that can help them move toward their goal.

> Ask open-ended questions so children know you are interested in their thinking, not looking for a correct answer. An open-ended question has many possible answers and elicits thinking through explaining why something is happening or how it is connected to children's understanding.

> Encourage—but never force—children to explore new materials, try out their knowledge and skills, or share an idea or opinion. Let children know that you see and value their courage as well as their curiosity.

> When children don't engage immediately, recognize that learning is occurring even when they are quiet and observing others. Give children time to think and process information. Find gentle ways to encourage engagement, such as moving items closer to the child or modeling a behavior before stepping aside to let the child take over.

> Balance freedom and structure in the environment to let children exercise their curiosity without feeling anxious or confused. An overly structured classroom deprives children of opportunities to make choices and offers fewer opportunities to practice executive function skills involved in planning and problem solving; it also inhibits children who are afraid of messing up the order suggested by adults. On the other hand, a disorganized or chaotic setting with too many materials may be overwhelming.

Readiness for Learning Experiences > **Engaging with materials**

Engagement, an important component of learning and school readiness, requires self-regulation. As children get older and gain more experience, they are better able to maintain engagement. Engagement is best described as children pursuing their own goals and using the materials and other resources at hand to achieve them. Extended engagement often happens as children pursue meaningful, self-selected goals and materials to achieve those goals.

Teaching strategies. For many children, engagement is self-reinforcing. The more they get involved with materials, the more ideas spring to mind, and the more successful they are in pursuing those ideas. Encourage and extend children's exploration and engagement by preparing the learning environment and providing uninterrupted blocks of time for children to devote to activities using strategies such as these:

> Provide a variety of materials and activities so each child finds something to engage their personal interest. New or reintroduced materials also attract and sustain children's attention. Find the right balance between familiarity and novelty. Too much repetition invites boredom, whereas too much novelty induces overload. Offer repeated opportunities for children to

practice and consolidate new skills and concepts to support mastery and enable children to apply their learning in new situations (NAEYC 2020). This approach is especially important for children with developmental delays or disabilities.

> Observe children to discover what works for each individual and for the group. For example, younger children might intently explore one color of paint—experimenting with the concept of redness, for example. Older children may be ready to compare or blend two or more colors or explore the effects of different painting tools.

> Give children ample time to carry out their intentions. Scheduling generous time for self-directed play encourages collaboration with peers and more complex exploration of materials and play themes.

> Be flexible about when individual children move to the next activity and let them transition gradually. For example, children may want to finish a painting before cleaning up and joining a group activity.

> Be sensitive to when children lose interest in an activity. Either modify the activity (for example, introduce backup materials or have restless children move around instead of sing) or bring the activity to an end. If children feel forced to continue, that activity may take on unpleasant associations, and they may resist becoming engaged in it thereafter.

> Minimize interruptions and transitions. Adults may inadvertently hamper children's concentration by assuming young children have short attention spans and need a change of pace or stimulation. When practical, let children stay with their chosen activity as long as their interest is engaged; let them decide when they are ready to move on to something else. Avoid setting up special projects during choice time that pull individual children away from their self-selected activity. Protecting extended playtime is especially important for children with developmental delays or disabilities who receive services with specialists who come to the classroom.

ADULT-GUIDED experiences are especially important for learnings such as:

Readiness for Learning Experiences ⟩ **Planning**

Child planning is a deliberate, goal-oriented cognitive skill supported by impulse control and working memory, and thus it nicely illustrates how executive function skills are interrelated (Ernst, Sobel, & Neil 2022). Planning is a special kind of problem solving that involves thinking about how to achieve a goal, such as deciding on what steps to follow to build a fort or get an object unstuck. The ability to plan is positively associated with children's cognitive development, social and emotional development, school-related behavior, and academic success (Ackerman & Friedman-Krauss 2017). The Head Start Performance Standards and many state standards include planning as a measure of program quality and child learning (Administration for Children and Families 2018).

Planning becomes more complex and detailed as children's working memory span increases, making it possible for children to hold onto mental images, ideas, or a sequence of actions. A young preschooler's plan for engaging with materials is often simple ("I want to play with the trucks"). An older preschooler considers a broader range of materials, actions, or people and describes the sequence necessary to carry out the plan ("Yolanda and I are going to make tacos with playdough and paper. First, we'll roll out the dough, then we'll tear the paper for lettuce"). This child anticipates problems and presents possible solutions.

Teaching strategies. Teachers often confuse planning with making choices among options offered by an adult. For example, a teacher might ask whether a child plans to go to the dramatic play area or the art center during playtime but not encourage the child to verbalize what they envision doing there. To offer young children opportunities to make plans, try the following ideas:

⟩ Provide opportunities for children to plan intentional choices during the day. For example, as children hang up their coats, ask them to think about how they might choose which book they want to look at during arrival time. If they are eating breakfast with a peer with whom they often play, ask if there is anything they want to tell their friend about what they might play with after breakfast. At the beginning of playtime, ask children what materials they plan to use, what they might do with them, and what else they might need to be able to accomplish their plans. Outdoors, you might respond to a child's play choice with a prompt for planning; for example, if a child reports that they will continue building a fort they built the day before, ask, "What else do you need to make the fort? What tools do you need to use?"

> Provide scaffolding for children who need it for making choices and planning. Use visual aids, tactile cues, or gestures as needed to encourage a child to make a simple plan with you. Allow the child ample time to respond.

> Ask questions in children's home languages, such as "Where will you play?," "What will you play with?," or "What do you want to do next?" Even if you do not share a child's home language, you can learn key questions in the home language to guide deeper-level thinking.

> Treat children's plans with respect, showing interest in their choices and decisions. Repeat and extend their ideas, imitate their actions, accept their suggestions, and let them be the leaders.

> Share information with families about the cognitive and social benefits of children's decision making and planning. Ask parents how they support their child to make plans at home. Most of the time, adults make plans for children (for example, the day's schedule). It is, therefore, beneficial for children to set their own agenda when possible.

Readiness for Learning Experiences > **Engaging with ideas**

Preschool children often wonder why events happen and what makes things work. They ask questions and need support to find answers. Adults encourage them to pay attention to the reason(s) behind what they observe through scaffolding.

Teaching strategies. Scaffolding children to engage with ideas means involving them in authentic, give-and-take conversation. Adults and children are equal partners in the conversation, with both voicing their own sense of wonder about what is happening and why. To encourage children to engage with ideas, try the following strategies:

> Describe, and encourage children to describe, what they are doing. Comment on the materials they use, their actions, and the effects of their actions. Personal conversation shows that you are aware of and interested in what the child is doing, which communicates that the child's learning is important. It also invites the child to converse in back-and-forth exchanges. While describing their actions, they also consider possible choices and outcomes. In other words, they begin to think as well as do.

> Give children choices about how to use materials or carry out ideas, even during teacher-planned times of the day. For example, introduce materials with a brief story or demonstration, but then let children explore the materials according to their own interests and curiosity ("Here are the pebbles, leaves, and twigs we collected yesterday. I wonder what you can make with them"). Encourage initiative in making choices and support children's creative thinking and curiosity.

> Ask open-ended questions that spark children's thinking. Questioning young children is the foundation for critical thinking. Asking open-ended questions conveys genuine interest in what the child is doing and leaves it open to the child whether and how to respond. Children's answers show what they know and understand, and their own questions reveal their interests and wonderings and can guide your teaching and planning.

> Invite children to explain their thinking. Conversations that inspire children to engage with ideas focus on thought processes rather than facts. In the process of making a comment or answering the question, a child consolidates (connects ideas and makes sense of learning) what they know and recognizes how they know it. Statements that engage children with ideas include these:

"I wonder why . . ."

"How can you tell?"

"Tell me how you got [the object] to . . ."

"What do you think made that happen?"

"What might happen if . . . ?"

> Take advantage of opportunities to explain your own thinking while reasoning or reflecting. Discuss your own discoveries ("The chirping got louder when I got close to this tree—I wonder if there's a nest here!") and encourage children to help you explain why something happened ("Why do you suppose the mama bird sounds so upset?"). Model your intentional focus on remembering, reasoning, problem solving, and learning from a mistake ("I thought it was a bird because it sounded like chirping! But it is a cicada! It chirps, too; if I listen carefully, how can I tell it is not a bird chirping?").

Responding to Learning Experiences

Just as children approach learning experiences in different ways, they also engage in and reflect on them differently. Children's responses to learning experiences are related to their unique characteristics, current knowledge, executive function skills, and social and cultural contexts.

As preschoolers develop cognitive processing skills, they are increasingly able to analyze a problem and seek to solve it on their own. They also grow in the ability to pursue and achieve goals they set for themselves, readily using available resources to carry out their play ideas. However, young children benefit from adults' suggestions for how they might extend or follow up on an idea, action, or discovery. Children also depend on adult scaffolding and encouragement to reflect on their experiences.

Of the key knowledge and skills in the area of processing experiences, child-guided experiences are particularly important for the following:

> Solving problems

> Using resources

Adult-guided experiences seem to be especially significant for the following:

> Reflecting

> Following up

CHILD-GUIDED experiences are especially important for learnings such as:

Responding to Learning Experiences > **Solving problems**

Children often encounter problems as they carry out their play ideas. (*Note:* This section refers to problems children have with materials. For problems that arise between children, see "Engaging in Conflict Resolution" on pages 86–88 in Chapter 4.) Individual differences in how children approach problem solving often can be observed. For example, children who are anxious about getting things right often avoid situations that may result in failure; children with an orientation toward learning or mastery are often more willing to take on new challenges and focus on increasing their knowledge or abilities. These differences are a reflection of individual personalities, family culture and contexts, adult modeling, and children's experiences with engaging in creative problem solving with others (Maker et al. 2023).

In addition to individual differences, there are developmental changes in the way children approach and persist in solving problems. Younger preschoolers may do so with more enthusiasm and self-confidence but less persistence, and they tend to rely more on trial and error. Older preschoolers are often more persistent and flexible, and they are somewhat more systematic in their attempts to solve problems. These processes reflect the development of executive function and self-regulation skills (Center on the Developing Child 2019). With scaffolding and regular opportunities for practice, children will gain increasing independence in managing the spaces and materials of the classroom.

Teaching strategies. To prepare preschoolers to problem-solve, use the following strategies:

> Encourage children to describe problems that arise during play. They may not see a problem the same way as an adult, but by talking through problems, they become better observers and analyzers. They are then more likely to propose and try solutions. For children who are not yet verbal, state the problem for them ("It looks like the button isn't working"). Describing the situation helps the child recognize what is wrong and encourages attempts to fix the problem independently.

> Anticipate challenges that may be frustrating and talk through alternative strategies with children. For example, "Check to see if your block base is wide enough to support the blocks you are adding on top."

> Call children's attention to what is or is not working. Talking about solutions that did or did not solve a problem helps children establish a cause-and-effect connection, which they can apply to similar problems in the future. Helping children identify and talk about problems helps children reason about possible solutions, which supports them in developing more systematic ways to attempt problem solving in general.

> Give children time to come up with solutions. Although your solution might be more efficient or effective than the child's, simply telling the child what to do erases the opportunity for them to learn and develop confidence in their independent problem-solving abilities.

> Assist children who are frustrated. Sometimes children do need help, especially when their inability to solve a problem keeps them from moving forward with their plans. Provide just enough assistance for children to continue solving problems on their own.

> Celebrate children's joy when they successfully solve a problem. For example, reflect with children on joyful moments of discovery, reinforcing an appreciation for learning and problem solving.

Responding to Learning Experiences   **Using resources**

Children become increasingly adept at identifying and using resources, including manipulating objects, watching and imitating others, and specifying what kind of help they need. As Lilian Katz (1993) points out, the dispositions, or "habits of mind," children bring to these endeavors are the desire to find things out, make sense of experience, strive for accuracy, and be empirical (prove something works). Temperamental differences affect children's willingness to try new resources, but as children grow older, they develop skills to carry out more complex experimentation to satisfy their curiosity (Kagan 2005). The importance of providing age-appropriate and hands-on resources to young children cannot be overstated. For example, open-ended toys are important for children's play and learning, as they promote higher-level thinking, imagination, problem solving, and cognitive development (Cankaya et al. 2023; Howe, Leach, & DeHart 2022).

Teaching strategies. To help preschoolers generate and grapple with ideas, provide the raw materials, or resources, to help spark them. The following strategies can support children to explore ideas and build deeper understanding:

> Provide open-ended materials that appeal to all the senses. Children are more likely to learn meaningful lessons when they experience materials in many ways. Close-ended materials, with one correct way of being used, restrict the possibilities for discovery, and children are more likely to quickly lose interest in them. By contrast, open-ended materials, which have multiple uses, lead to sustained engagement and greater use of imagination. When adapting or modifying materials for children with physical disabilities, ensure the children can engage with the material or activity in multiple ways.

> Some children feel more comfortable watching before interacting. They may need to sit next to you and see you explore materials in different ways. When they see you using a soda straw to poke holes in clay or using the wheels of a toy truck to paint interesting patterns, they may feel more confident to explore on their own. Keep in mind that multilingual learners in particular may observe for a period of time before they feel comfortable trying new approaches.

> Talk with children about how they use resources—for example, the objects and people they interact with, how they use materials to solve problems, what they observe (using all their senses), and the conclusions they draw. These kinds of dialogues focused on problem solving are foundational to developing early critical thinking skills (O'Reilly, Devitt, & Hayes 2022). Encouraging children to verbalize their actions and observations helps children build a vocabulary that in turn supports problem solving (Romeo et al. 2018).

> Encourage children to use resources to answer their own questions. For example, if a child asks you how to do something, encourage them to experiment with materials and observe the results themselves. For example, say "I wonder what you could use to find out" or "How do you think it might work?" to encourage them to experiment with materials and observe the results. Supporting children to find the answers to their own questions often leads to meaningful and lasting insights.

ADULT-GUIDED experiences are especially important for learnings such as:

Responding to Learning Experiences ▷ **Reflecting**

Reflection involves more than "memory or a rote recitation of completed activities. Reflection is *remembering with analysis*" (Epstein 2003, 29). Unlike rote memorization, reflection helps children discover and apply underlying concepts. For example, grasping the alphabetic principle that every letter has a unique appearance and sound allows a child to apply this idea to each new letter. Generalizing information that can be used in other content areas is an efficient way to learn. During the preschool years, gains in children's cognitive and language development support gains in their ability to reflect on their own experiences and apply what they learn to related contexts. As children construct mental representations (images or ideas) of objects, events, and interactions, they can more clearly think about their past and anticipate their future. Words help children encode experiences in their memory, describe their experiences or memory to others, and gradually develop the ability to consider "what if" thoughts about events that have not yet happened.

Teaching strategies. To engage children in meaningful reflection, encourage them to use reflection, being mindful not to detract from their immersion in an activity. Teachers' use of "thinking" language is foundational to early critical thinking skills (O'Reilly, Devitt, & Hayes 2022). Here are some ideas for using thinking language to help children reflect on what they learn from their experiences:

> Use comments and open-ended questions such as the following to encourage reflection on current and previous experiences: "What does this remind you of?," "How else could the story end?," "What if . . . ?," "How else could you have . . . ?," "Why do you think he did that?," and "I wonder where else you could use this."

> Create opportunities for children to describe their actions to peers. For example, refer them to one another for help ("Jonetta got her tissue paper to stick. Maybe she can tell you how she did it"). Collaborative problem solving encourages children to think about what they did so they can explain it to someone else. Ask children to tell as well as demonstrate their ideas.

> Use photographs and other mementos to help children remember and reflect on experiences, such as by using them to create documentation panels. Images are particularly useful for multilingual learners, who can begin to attach simple labels (names of objects or actions) to their experiences. A sequence of photographs helps children recall the order of events and highlights if-then connections. For example, viewing pictures of children building a bridge across a stream helps them recall the series of steps that led to the final structure. They may have discovered that they needed extra support in the middle of the stream to hold up the bridge. Likewise, an object representing an event, such as something brought back from a field trip, can elicit reflections about the objects and incidents most memorable to each child.

As preschoolers pursue an interest or a discovery, they might not spontaneously choose to continue doing so in greater depth. Once finished with an activity, they may lose interest, look to see what others are doing, or simply move on to something else. When a child remains absorbed by a set of materials or an activity for a prolonged period, however, it suggests that they may be ready to go deeper—to follow up a personal interest. In early childhood, the capacity to explore more deeply increases with age. Encouraging creativity and ingenuity helps children expand learning in their areas of interest.

Teaching strategies. You can encourage children to follow up their interests and discoveries by structuring the program schedule with extended and flexible time, providing ready access to a variety of materials each day, and showing genuine interest in and curiosity about each child's pursuits. Try the following strategies:

> Provide opportunities for children to elaborate on the play themes that interest them. Rather than discourage repetitive play, think of creative ways to build on it. For example, if the same group of children plays superheroes every day, offer a variety of materials they can use to make props. Pose questions such as "Suppose he lost his power to become invisible; how else could he sneak inside?" Encourage them to move like superheroes at large group time or invent a song a superhero might sing about their special powers.

> Follow up with children's interests and curiosity. Your genuine involvement in what they are doing communicates that their activities and learning are important. Demonstrate your interest by engaging in authentic conversations, asking questions, playing with children as partners, discussing their activities with families, and suggesting ways families can extend a child's interest at home.

A positive approach to learning is an important component of school readiness. Supporting children in this area begins with understanding each child's individuality, including their unique personalities, their developmental levels, and their family, cultural, and linguistic experiences. Intentional teachers create an environment that acknowledges children's emerging sense of themselves as doers and thinkers. The program setting provides choices, supports initiative and persistence, offers appropriate cognitive challenges, and involves children in decision making and planning. Children have many opportunities to experience satisfaction through successful engagement with a variety of materials, people, activities, and events. Each child, and the children together, thrive and anticipate that learning will be interesting and rewarding.

For Further Consideration

1. How can teachers recognize and respect their own approaches to learning while allowing children to approach learning in ways that are consistent with their own personalities, developmental levels, and cultural contexts?

2. How can intentional teachers support, guide, and extend children's play while respecting children's initiative and not taking over their play themes?

3. Think of one learning center in the classroom (such as the dramatic play area, art area, or music and movement area). What types of materials can you provide to accommodate differences in preschoolers' interests, desire to play alone or with others, and developmental levels?

4. In scaffolding children's learning, how can you find the right balance between supporting children at their current level of understanding and providing gentle extensions that encourage children to use additional resources, engage with ideas as well as materials, try alternative ways to solve problems, or follow up on their experiences and discoveries?

CHAPTER 4

Social and Emotional Learning

Keri Giordano

Manuel, age 4, watches his mother leave after she drops him off and says to his teacher, Miss Irene, "Estoy triste."

Miss Irene replies, "Estás triste. You are sad because your mother left."

Manuel nods and says, "Sí."

Miss Irene asks, "Would you like a hug, un abrazo?" She opens her arms, and he cuddles inside them. "A hug," Miss Irene repeats.

"Hug," says Manuel, trying out the word, and he smiles.

• • •

At the beginning of small group time, Travon, a younger 4-year-old, observes his teacher, Mr. Devon, wrapping a wide rubber grip around a red pencil before placing the pencil on the tray of Keira's wheelchair. Later, when Keira says she wants to use a blue pencil, Travon says, "I'll get you one!" He fetches a blue pencil from the pile on the table, wraps it with a rubber grip, and puts it in the middle of Keira's tray.

• • •

Nia and Caleb crouch together, each holding a small plastic watering can. Ms. Marva has just lifted a tray of plants from a shelf and placed it

Learning Objectives

1. To define social and emotional competence and describe five areas of social and emotional competency

2. To identify how children's social and emotional development thrives in the context of supportive and responsive adult relationships and age-appropriate peer relationships

3. To recognize the impact of culture on social and emotional development and to begin to apply a lens of cultural humility when considering children's social and emotional development

4. To apply a variety of teaching strategies across the five domains of social and emotional development

on the floor where the children can help her pick off the dead leaves and water the containers. Nia nudges Caleb with her elbow, pleading as he grabs one of the plants. "But I want to do that one."

Ms. Marva helps Nia and Caleb make a plan. "What could we do so you both can water?" she asks. Caleb answers, "I can water these ones," and points to a few of the plants closest to him. Ms. Marva responds: "So you can water those plants." Nia says, "Okay. I can water the stripey ones." Ms. Marva agrees: "And you can water the plants with the striped leaves. That's a good plan."

Social and emotional learning has always been an essential—even the primary—domain of early childhood education. When children feel valued and have meaningful and satisfying learning experiences and interactions with others, their feelings of competence and interest in pursuing learning are enhanced. Strong social and emotional skills have significant long- and short-term positive outcomes—including academic success, improved interactions with others, and more positive behaviors and attitudes—as well as decreased problem behaviors, stress, and substance misuse (Cipriano et al. 2023; Durlak, Mahoney, & Boyle 2022). Indeed, social and emotional development holds equal importance with academic development to children's learning.

Social and emotional development has been defined as

> the process through which all young people and adults acquire and apply the knowledge, skills, and attitudes to develop healthy identities, manage emotions and achieve personal and collective goals, feel and show empathy for others, establish and maintain supportive relationships, and make responsible and caring decisions. (CASEL, n.d.-c)

Today more than ever, young children need adults to help them develop these skills. Children are living in a world that has experienced a global pandemic and is grappling with the growing effects of climate change. They face increasing academic pressures, experience ongoing systemic injustices, and are exposed to a never-ending stream of intense and violent local, national, and international events. The good news is that educators can help children thrive by supporting them to develop skills to manage themselves and positively engage with others and the world around them.

Young Children's Development in Social and Emotional Learning

The social and emotional developmental domains are often considered together, as the skill set in one area closely impacts functioning in the other. The development of social and emotional competence includes emotional skills (related to recognizing, expressing, and regulating one's own emotions and identifying the emotions of others) and social skills (the principles and strategies children need for interacting successfully with others, such as making and keeping friends, solving problems, and engaging in socially and culturally accepted behaviors).

Resources on Social and Emotional Learning

The National Center for Pyramid Model Innovations (NCPMI) provides training, resources, and technical assistance with the goal of supporting the social, emotional, and behavioral needs of infants and young children (NCPMI, n.d.). The Collaborative for Academic, Social, and Emotional Learning (CASEL) also provides a variety of resources, trainings, and advocacy tools aimed at providing high-quality social and emotional learning in all settings (CASEL, n.d.-a). ZERO TO THREE shares comprehensive resources for child development of very young children, including social and emotional development (Zero to Three, n.d.). See also the NAEYC resource page on social and emotional development (NAEYC, n.d.).

According to CASEL (n.d.-a), social and emotional competence is made up of five interdependent core competencies:

> Self-awareness is an area of emotional development that involves identifying one's own emotions, feelings, values, and thoughts.

> Self-management falls in the area of emotional development and involves regulating one's thoughts, feelings, and emotions in ways appropriate to a situation.

> Social awareness is an aspect of social development and involves knowledge of social and cultural norms and customs. Social awareness includes an ability to take the perspectives of others and to demonstrate empathy and concern.

> Relationship skills are a key component of social development and involve a range of appropriate strategies for interacting with others, including effective communication, teamwork, conflict resolution, and problem solving.

> Responsible decision making involves both emotional and social development and includes the ability to make thoughtful choices that are safe, support one's own well-being, and are considerate of the needs and desires of others. Skills include being open to multiple perspectives, defining a problem, using information to determine positive solutions, and considering the impact a choice might have on others.

Children are not born with these competencies; adults support children's development in these domains over time in the context of responsive and supportive relationships and through intentional, planned learning experiences. Supporting children's social and emotional development through both child-guided play and adult-guided interactions can lead to a joyful discovery of self and others. Strategies for incorporating the five core competencies into your practice appear in "Fitting the Learning Experience to the Learning Objective" later in this chapter, where they are considered separately as child-guided and adult-guided experiences.

The Role of Teacher-Child Relationships

Infants rely on adults to meet their needs, and the way that adults meet these needs determines young children's future interactions (Lally & Mangione 2017). Early sensitive and responsive reactions from adults set the stage for a child's long-term healthy social and emotional development. A warm, supportive relationship between a child and teacher, for example, creates a positive environment in which the child can practice social and emotional skills and gain competence in these areas.

Positive relationships are related to numerous outcomes in the areas of behavior, social skills, and academics. When teachers have high levels of closeness and low levels of conflict with children, children are less likely to display externalizing behaviors such as aggression, disruption, and so on (García-Rodríguez, Redín, & Abaitua 2023). Children with more positive relationships with their teachers do better academically and like school more. They are also more likely to have positive relationships with their peers and are better able to regulate their emotions (García-Rodríguez, Redín, & Abaitua 2023). Gartrell explains, "Only when children know and trust us in day-to-day interactions will they listen to us when conflicts happen" (2020, 15). Perhaps Urie Bronfenbrenner summed it up best when he said, "Every child needs at least one adult who is irrationally crazy about him or her" (Brendtro 2006, 163).

Cultural Considerations in Social and Emotional Development

Social norms vary by culture and family; expected behavior in early learning programs and children's homes or other settings may be different and thus confusing for children. This can include behaviors such as making eye contact, waiting for an adult to acknowledge them before speaking, or demonstrating independence in self-care activities. Further, developmental milestones may not account for the ways some children's cultures and experiences impact how they develop and use their social and emotional skills. Teachers should keep these things in mind when they observe and assess how children express themselves, interact with others, and use other social and emotional skills so that they do not misinterpret children's behavior and abilities or judge how families promote children's independence and set behavioral expectations. Practicing cultural humility and expressing curiosity and openness about families' values and cultural practices can help teachers broaden their understanding, act with intention toward children and families, and develop appropriate expectations for children. Cultural humility involves an openness to reflecting and adapting your perceptions through the development of relationships with others, where you hear, respect, and appreciate their voices and values.

In much the same way that cultural and family norms can impact social and emotional development, so can ability status. Throughout this chapter, ages are used to indicate when most children develop particular skills. These are used as points of reference and will not apply to all children. Learning about individual children and their families is critical to understanding children's strengths and supporting their social and emotional development.

Teaching and Learning in Social and Emotional Development

Intentional planning on the part of the teacher, through both structured, planned activities and support in spontaneous situations, is key in facilitating children's social and emotional growth. Based on work that integrates the best of both child-guided and adult-guided learning experiences in these domains, following are some general strategies to consider as you work with your class as a whole, as well as with small groups and individual children, to facilitate children's social and emotional development:

> Communicate your respect for children. Give children your positive, respectful attention throughout the day, focusing primarily on them and what they are doing rather than spending class time arranging materials, cleaning up, or interacting with other adults. Speak calmly, avoiding shouting, shaming, or using harsh words and actions. Address comments directly to children rather than talk about them as though they weren't there. As you convey respect for and guide children in the ways of being a valued member of the community, they learn to respect themselves and engage in positive relationships with others.

> Model positive behaviors and self-monitoring. One way children learn is by watching others, observing the reactions to those behaviors, and imitating them. For example, children learn positive behaviors when they see you being empathic, solving problems, taking risks, admitting mistakes and talking through how to address them, and so on. This learning is enhanced if you occasionally make explicit what you yourself are doing—for example, pointing out that you are listening to each child.

> Coach children to use successful strategies. Like modeling, coaching can be done with either individual children or groups. Coaching entails dividing a positive behavior into its component parts, providing children with explicit instruction on how to perform and sequence the parts, creating opportunities for them to practice the behavior, and offering feedback on their efforts. For example, you can coach children in key aspects of play, such as gaining a peer's attention, sharing and requesting toys, organizing play, and giving compliments (NCPMI 2019). Coaching may be especially helpful with children who do not seem to be accepted by their peers and whose reaction to this only increases peers' rejection of them.

Explicit Social and Emotional Instruction

More schools and early learning programs have begun using explicit social and emotional curriculum resources. As the child-guided teaching strategies in this chapter show, young children benefit from authentic opportunities to learn about themselves and how to engage with others through play experiences, child-initiated learning, and informal interactions with peers and adults. Quality preschool classrooms continue to prioritize these open-ended experiences. But as research continues to build showing that children benefit from explicit instruction focused on social and emotional skills (Bierman & Sanders 2020), many programs have implemented a formal social and emotional curriculum in their program. Social and emotional learning is typically integrated into existing classroom routines and activities (Jones et al. 2021). Although a review of the many social and emotional programs in existence is beyond the scope of this chapter, several organizations (for example, CASEL, n.d.-b; Jones et al. 2021) offer guides with more information about the various options available.

> **Provide repeated opportunities for practice.** As in any domain of learning, repetition and practice are vital to mastering appropriate social behavior. Meuwissen explains, "Viewing children's social skills as an experience-dependent process emphasizes that learning such skills will take practice and repetition, not simply aging, to develop competence" (2022).

Whether you are using a formal social and emotional learning curriculum or have a less formal approach, your strategies should be individualized as well as group oriented. Be flexible and adaptive to support all children, including children with developmental delays or disabilities. Some children will need additional scaffolding and modifications as you help them on their way to becoming socially and emotionally competent. Above all, remember that a lack of such skills does not mean children's attitudes or behaviors are bad or naughty. Young children simply do not know any better—yet. These skills must be taught and modeled, and retaught for some children, just as skills in literacy or math or any other content area.

Fitting the Learning Experience to the Learning Objective

The remainder of this chapter identifies the social and emotional skills that children typically develop around preschool age. These skills are examined in the context of CASEL's (n.d.-a) five core competencies, outlined previously, and organized into skills and knowledge that children seem most likely to learn through child-guided experiences (including through peer interactions) and those that may require adult-guided instruction. As with every curriculum area in this book, the division between the two types of learning experiences is not rigid. Both child-guided and adult-guided experiences require adult support, and both occur in an atmosphere the teacher has created.

Social and emotional skills often overlap. As a general rule, dealing successfully with one's emotional state is a prerequisite to socializing effectively with others. Conflict resolution, for example, involves both emotional self-regulation and social problem-solving skills. Yet, differentiating between emotional and social learning can help early childhood educators think about the skills needed to promote learning in each area.

For both emotional and social learning, a central role of teachers in child-guided experiences is to create a warm and caring program environment, as discussed in Chapter 2. Preschoolers form primary emotional attachments to their parents and caregivers. Therefore, family members, in conjunction with teachers, play a crucial role in making a child's transition to the school setting successful. Adults need to understand the challenges young children face when they find themselves among strangers, in a place with unfamiliar social and behavioral expectations and perhaps unfamiliar languages. Even if the personal and social values and expectations of a child's home and school are congruent, children face an adjustment to the group nature of the classroom. Teachers who establish a supportive climate help young children to discover themselves and begin to form positive relationships with others. Children's social and emotional confidence will be enhanced if they can navigate this environment on their own—with adults providing support only as needed.

In addition to creating a supportive environment, teachers in adult-guided experiences guide young children to acquire social and emotional skills and knowledge. They address their own biases so that they do not affect their interactions with children. Teachers promote children's positive attitudes about themselves and others, which allows them to develop the self-control and motivation to solve problems with others and become respectful, contributing members of the community. Although these goals may sound lofty when applied to preschoolers, the early years lay the groundwork for children's later beliefs and behaviors as friends, family members, coworkers, and citizens.

Self-Awareness

As noted previously, self-awareness involves recognizing one's own emotions and having a growth mindset. Of the key knowledge and skills in this area, child-guided experiences may be particularly important for the following:

> Developing a positive self-identity

Adult-guided experiences may be especially significant for the following:

> Developing feelings of competence

> Recognizing and labeling emotions

CHILD-GUIDED experiences are especially important for learnings such as:

Self-Awareness Developing a positive self-identity

Self-identity refers to the way one defines and feels about oneself as a person. The healthy development of a child's self-identity hinges on establishing trusting, secure relationships with the important caregivers in their life, including family members, teachers, and others. As identity formation continues during the toddler and preschool years, the child comes to recognize multiple aspects of their identity, such as their name, gender, family structure and role in the family, physical appearance, abilities, race, ethnicity, and languages. It may include other elements, such as religious group and neighborhood, as well as the greater community and the media—and who is visible and represented versus who is not. As self-awareness develops, children come to understand who they are within the context of their relationships and communities.

Teaching strategies. Teachers help children develop a positive sense of who they are by supporting their transition from home to the early childhood setting, working in respectful partnerships with families, establishing a classroom environment in which every child sees themself reflected and feels valued, and providing labels for the many facets of children's identities. Children's positive self-images are fostered when teachers use strategies such as these:

> Provide books, toys, music, artwork, and so on that reflect the cultures of the children, families, and community so that children see themselves represented. Also include materials and activities that allow children to learn about people, places, and events that they might not otherwise encounter (NAEYC 2020).

> Support children through their separations from family members as they gradually gain confidence that they can handle things on their own. Acknowledge and accept their feelings. Work with family members to help in the transition process—for example, to institute a goodbye ritual and make it clear to children when their loved one will be back. Allow children to enter classroom activities at their own pace or to reenter them later if they get upset and withdraw.

> Provide many options for families to engage in the program so they can choose what interests them and works best for them. Seek to learn what is important to families and bring that into the classroom in various ways. (See also "Building Partnerships with Families" on page 38 in Chapter 2.) Children gain a sense of security when they can see that their families and teachers are working together as partners.

> Support children in expressing their feelings. Make them aware that others in similar situations share such emotions; for example, "Clare, I understand why you are upset that your dog chewed a hole in your shoe! Tushar also felt angry when his puppy tore up his book."

> Address differences positively. Children are curious about differences in gender, skin color, religious observances, family composition, and so on, so don't shy away from naming and discussing them. Young children need straightforward, accurate information from adults as they try to understand what they observe. Supply respectful, factual language; for example, "Tomoko has trouble walking, so she uses a wheelchair," "Hassan is Muslim, Gemma is Catholic, and Marva is Jewish," or "Journee lives with her mommy and daddy, and Milo lives with his two daddies." Approach these topics with a sense of cultural humility; listen to and value children's voices and lived experiences (see also "Valuing Diversity" on pages 246–248 in Chapter 9).

ADULT-GUIDED experiences are especially important for learnings such as:

Self-Awareness | **Developing feelings of competence**

Competence is being able to do something well. Feeling competent means having the self-confidence to undertake tasks with the expectation of success. It is important to judge young children's success by what the child sets out to accomplish, not according to adult standards. Children gain confidence and competence when they experience success. How children feel about themselves and their abilities when they enter school has a great influence on their motivation and willingness to undertake challenging learning tasks. It is especially important for teachers to recognize and support the strengths of children of color, multilingual learners, and children with developmental delays or disabilities, who may face biases and lowered expectations. When you convey your expectation that a child can accomplish something, and provide specific feedback that highlights their efforts and successes, you affirm their abilities and help them build a sense of themselves as capable doers. For instance, acknowledging a multilingual learner's skill in navigating two languages or celebrating a child's creative problem-solving strategy can enhance their self-perception as competent learners. This targeted support helps children feel valued and capable, reinforcing their motivation to engage fully in their learning.

Teaching strategies. Helping young children develop a positive and realistic sense of confidence in their abilities is arguably the single most important task of early childhood educators. Many of the following strategies were introduced in Chapter 2 as effective practices in general; they are especially pertinent in this discussion of self-confidence:

› Encourage self-help skills in ways that are consistent with children's abilities and developmental levels. Give them time to do things on their own (such as putting on their outdoor clothing or cleaning up spills), even if the tasks are not done perfectly. Introduce the next level of challenge once children have mastered the current one and are ready to move on. Let children practice a task as often as they want to achieve mastery.

› Acknowledge and encourage children's efforts and accomplishments. Although praise ("What a nice picture you've painted" or "I love what you wrote to your grandpa!") can make them depend on the judgment of others to feel good about themselves, acknowledgment or encouragement ("You really put a lot of detail into your drawing") helps them evaluate their own competencies positively. Avoid offering false praise in an effort to buoy self-esteem; instead, scaffold children's efforts as they work toward mastery of a skill or concept.

› Provide opportunities for all children to be leaders. Do not force or require children to lead, but give everyone the opportunity to do so.

› Be aware of implicit and explicit biases you may hold that could prevent you from fully supporting a child's sense of competence. Avoid falling into the pattern of a fixed mindset yourself, viewing children's abilities as limited, and join children in problem-solving new ways to accomplish tasks.

› Set up opportunities where children can use their strengths to solve a problem or accomplish a task.

Self-Awareness › **Recognizing and labeling emotions**

Emotional awareness is the understanding that one has feelings as distinct from thoughts, identifying and naming those feelings, and recognizing that others have feelings that may be the same or different from one's own. Having this vocabulary and these skills, including how to express strong feelings in nonhurtful ways, serves children well throughout their lives (Gartrell 2020).

Teaching strategies. One's emotions arise naturally, but knowing what they are, what they mean, and how they are labeled by one's culture are things children learn from others. Being able to successfully label emotions is key for children to learn self-regulation (Tominey et al. 2017). Here are some strategies to try:

> Accept children's full range of emotions. Do not judge emotions as good or bad. Of course, do stop cruel or unsafe behavior that may result from emotions such as hurt, anger, fear, and frustration. Acknowledge with your words, facial expressions, and gestures what the child appears to be feeling ("You're frustrated that the marker keeps smudging when you try to write. How can I help?" "I know you really want to go outside, but it isn't time yet. First let's clean up, and then we can go out. Do you want to start with the plastic animals or the cars?").

> Label children's emotions and your own with simple words, such as *angry, happy,* or *sad.* For multilingual learners, pair the word in their home languages with the word in English, and use a picture if possible. For children with developmental delays or disabilities, consider tools such as social stories or visual cues to help them become aware of their emotions and communicate their needs effectively.

> Plan small group activities that focus on feelings. Preschoolers do not often talk about emotions in the abstract, but they can do so readily by reading books, acting out situations with puppets or person dolls, or creating and discussing artwork about people and events that evoke emotions.

> Share with families that showing a range of emotions in acceptable ways and helping children label their feelings are an important part of early learning. Although families and cultures have their own beliefs about the acceptability of emotional expression, families and teachers can agree that they want their children to succeed. Learning families' perspectives and sharing with them the ways emotional competence adds to school readiness opens the door to exploring a range of comfortable avenues for encouraging appropriate emotional expression at home.

> Clearly state rules, routines, and expectations so that children are aware of what is coming and what they need to do, reducing the need for continual self-regulation.

> For recurring behavior resulting from a child's strong feelings, consider carefully what is behind the behavior and how the environment might be contributing to it. Find ways to support behavior that will help the child meet their needs in a more acceptable way.

Self-Management

Self-management skills enable children to regulate their own emotions, manage impulses, achieve goals, and develop organizational skills. Successfully managing one's emotions and actions, especially after overcoming a challenge, can bring a deep sense of satisfaction and confidence. Of the key knowledge and skills in the area of self-management, child-guided experiences may be particularly important for the following:

> Engaging in and persisting at tasks

Adult-guided experiences may be especially significant for the following:

> Managing emotions
> Demonstrating agency

CHILD-GUIDED experiences are especially important for learnings such as:

| Self-Management | Engaging in and persisting at tasks |

When children persist at tasks, they learn that persistence pays off. This results in a sense of achievement and an increased willingness to keep trying new things.

Teaching strategies. From birth, children are motivated to explore their world and the people in it (National Scientific Council on the Developing Child 2018). However, the experiences adults provide for children, and the way they interact with them, can either encourage or discourage children's own motivation. Observe children and promote their motivation and persistence with strategies such as these:

> Support children's explorations through play and positive interactions with each other. Play is intrinsically rewarding for children, and it is active, meaningful, socially interactive, and joyful—all ingredients in motivation and persistence that lead to learning (National Scientific Council on the Developing Child 2018; Zosh et al. 2022). Encourage children in solving problems as they arise in their play. Provide challenges for each child that are at just the right level, allowing them to persist and succeed. Provide specific hints or suggestions as well as feedback. When a child struggles, you might reduce the level of complexity of the task.

> Offer new activities, challenges, and ways of doing things to help sustain children's motivation and eagerness for learning. If you usually do an activity indoors, for example, take it outside!

> Provide lots of choices for children so that they can pursue tasks that are personally meaningful to them. Embrace the perspective that every child has unique sources of motivation rather than thinking that a child is just not motivated. Every behavior is motivated by something. Developing authentic relationships with each child gives you opportunities to learn what they enjoy and find motivating; use this information to help them sustain engagement and motivation.

> When children make choices that may not align with expectations, reflect with them on why they made that choice. Help them consider alternative actions that could meet their needs in constructive ways. This approach empowers children to recognize their own agency and develop positive strategies to get their needs met.

ADULT-GUIDED experiences are especially important for learnings such as:

| Self-Management | Managing emotions |

Managing emotions for young children involves deciding how to express their feelings or impulses and choosing to do this in appropriate ways (Gartrell 2023).

Teaching strategies. To be successful in social contexts, children need to learn socially acceptable ways of expressing their emotions. You can help support this in the following ways:

> Model healthy ways to manage emotions, such as taking deep breaths or using positive self-talk, to demonstrate how to cope with feelings effectively.

> Designate a quiet area where children can choose to go to calm themselves when they are upset. Note that this is *not* to be used as a time-out situation, which does not teach children how to better manage their emotions and actions and often leads to feelings of shame. This area might contain cushions, fidget toys, stuffed animals, books, sensory bottles, noise-canceling headphones, photos of family members, and/or posters illustrating calming breathing techniques that you have introduced and practiced with the children. Observe who uses this area and what they seem to find the most helpful, and let this guide you as you consider what items you might add or switch out.

> Teach simple mindfulness exercises, such as deep breathing or focusing on senses. Mindfulness practices, which involve focusing on the present moment and an awareness of body sensations and the space around oneself, have been found to help support the development of self-awareness and self-regulation (Savina 2020).

> Privately acknowledge moments when a child is using positive coping strategies and expressing their emotions appropriately. Remember to acknowledge small steps that indicate a child is working toward self-management, even if the effort isn't perfect. For example, for a child who yells instead of hits another child, this is progress. Acknowledge the effort and focus on guiding the child toward further management of their emotions (Gartrell 2023).

> Teach children simple problem-solving skills to help them resolve conflicts and manage difficult situations. (More on the conflict resolution process is discussed in "Engaging in Conflict Resolution" on pages 86–88.)

Demonstrating agency involves setting goals, making plans, and taking actions to achieve those goals. This is important as it allows children to begin to realize that they have some control over their choices and related outcomes.

Teaching strategies. To develop a sense of agency, children need meaningful experiences in which they can make choices and have those decisions respected and encouraged. Try strategies like the following:

› Provide children with choices throughout the day, such as what to play with, what to eat for snack, or where to sit during large group time. Allow for extended periods of time for children to choose what to do, alone or with other children, and initiate and direct their own activities (Masterson 2022).

› Help children set achievable goals based on their interests and abilities. Break down larger goals into smaller, manageable steps so they can experience success.

› Encourage children to think of solutions to problems they encounter rather than immediately provide an answer for them. Ask open-ended questions to guide them in finding solutions.

› Acknowledge children's efforts and perseverance, even if they don't succeed at first. Encourage them to keep trying and celebrate their progress with them.

Social Awareness

Social awareness incorporates the abilities to take another's perspective, empathize, understand social norms, and feel a part of the learning community. Understanding and empathizing with others' feelings helps to create joyful connections and a sense of belonging to the learning community.

Of the key knowledge and skills in the area of social awareness, child-guided experiences may be particularly important for the following:

› Feeling empathy

Adult-guided experiences may be especially significant for the following:

› Developing a sense of community

CHILD-GUIDED experiences are especially important for learnings such as:

Social Awareness	Feeling empathy

Empathy involves comprehending another person's feelings and being able to imagine oneself in that person's place. Being empathic includes traits such as care for others, compassion, and altruism. Empathy has both a cognitive and an affective dimension. To be fully capable of experiencing and demonstrating empathy, a child must be developmentally capable of seeing a situation from someone else's perspective (Cigala, Mori, & Fangareggi 2014; Piaget [1932] 1965). This is an ability that is just emerging in the preschool years. Yet, there is evidence that even infants and toddlers have some ability to pick up on another's emotions (Bulgarelli & Jones 2023; Decety & Holvoet 2021; Uzefovsky, Paz, & Davidov 2019).

Teaching strategies. The main strategies intentional teachers use to support the development of empathy are modeling, acknowledgment, and encouragement. Here are some examples:

> Demonstrate concern and empathy in your interactions with children and others. Describe your reactions and actions; for example, "I'm giving Taryn the fuzzy monkey to cuddle. She's sad because her grandma is going away today." Other children notice these displays and will begin to follow your example.

> Help children recognize and understand the feelings of others through role playing or discussing scenarios where empathy is important. Engaging children in activities where they can take on different roles and perspectives can help them understand how others might feel in different situations.

> Help children recognize emotions in others by pointing out facial expressions, body language, and tone of voice. When discussing behavior, help children understand how their actions affect others and how they would feel in the same situation: "Look at Cammi's face. She's looking down at the floor, and her lip is trembling. I think she feels sad that you took the last puppet."

> Help children develop skills to resolve conflicts and problems peacefully, which requires understanding the perspectives of others (see "Engaging in Conflict Resolution" on pages 86–88).

ADULT-GUIDED experiences are especially important for learnings such as:

| Social Awareness | Developing a sense of community |

The early childhood classroom is often children's first experience with a community outside of the home. This community should provide a physical, emotional, and cognitive environment that values the contributions of each member and supports the collective growth of the group (NAEYC 2020). Early childhood communities are grounded in sensitive and responsive adult-child, child-child, and adult-adult relationships.

Teaching strategies. Intentional teachers create a sense of community in the classroom by employing strategies such as these:

> Show interest in each child's knowledge, skills, and experiences, and use opportunities to talk about these. Encourage children to reflect on the unique contributions of their peers.

> Expect children to be respectful and kind to each other, and model how this is done. Refer to the children and adults in the classroom with phrases such as "our class," "all of us," "our group," and "all together." Using the word "friends" can be problematic and displays a false cheeriness; it's okay if a child feels they are not "friends" with a peer. Support children's right to make choices in who they want as a friend. Respect for and kindness to others, however, is always important.

> Call attention to occasions when children are working or sharing an experience together as a group. The occasions can be routine ("We got our things put away at cleanup so we can find them tomorrow at choice time") or special ("Look at all the pine cones we gathered outside. I wonder what we could do with them?").

> Organize activities that foster children's participation with others. Supporting children in social engagement not only helps to strengthen their social skills but also is "the key to teaching social-emotional skills and preventing challenging behavior" (Hemmeter, Ostrosky, & Fox 2021).

> Model an understanding that all children have different ways they play. For example, if a child with a developmental delay or disability wants a pretend hamburger for a longer period, explain to a peer that the child wants to hold on to it because that is their favorite toy and they find comfort in it. Encourage or suggest ways for peers to play with a child who has a developmental delay or disability, if needed. During classroom routines, make sure a child with a developmental delay or disability does not always go first or last.

> Create comfortable and convenient opportunities for families to be active in the community. For example, many programs invite families to read books to the children, but this activity may exclude families who are hesitant about their reading skills, have poor vision, or prefer not to be the center of attention. Provide a variety of opportunities that families can choose from or ask them how they would like to engage in the program.

> Some children share your interests, temperament, and/or culture, so making a connection with them is easy. When this does not occur, make an extra effort to build a relationship by making contact with the child each day, even if just for a minute. Strategies that can help build positive relationships with all children include greeting children by name, acknowledging and celebrating accomplishments, delivering positive messages to families in front of the child, and finding out about and incorporating the child's interests into your conversations and classroom (Joseph & Strain 2019). As you do this, monitor yourself to see whether your previous perceptions of a child, especially those whose culture or home expectations differ from yours, are changing for the better. This helps you to have a clearer perspective, especially if a child's behavior or personality is challenging for you.

Connecting Teaching to Children's Lives

By Kimberlee Telford

Keith, age 4, and Nevaeh, age 4, are tugging on and arguing over a green scarf in the music and movement center. Keith loses his grip on the scarf and falls backward as Nevaeh runs off with the scarf to a different center. Mr. Cliff walks toward Keith, who is visibly upset, and sits next to him.

Mr. Cliff: Hi, Keith. Are you all right?

Keith: (*Pounds his fists on the floor.*)

Mr. Cliff: I see you banging your hands on the floor. It looks to me like you are feeling frustrated.

Keith: (*Speaks in a growling voice*) No, I am inikk.

Mr. Cliff: Oh, inikk. That means angry, right?

Keith: (*Nods.*)

Mr. Cliff: Why are you feeling inikk?

Keith: I wanted that scarf for my dancing! Nevaeh ripped it away from me. Now I don't have anything.

Mr. Cliff: I understand that you would like to dance with a scarf. How do you think we can solve this problem?

Keith: I don't know.

Mr. Cliff: Perhaps we could go and talk to Nevaeh about the scarf, or we could look for a different scarf you could use for dancing.

Keith: (*Pauses.*) Let's look for a different scarf.

Mr. Cliff and Keith look through the scarf basket together, and Keith selects a blue scarf.

Keith: Blue is my mom's favorite color. Mr. Cliff, can you get my music from home?

Mr. Cliff retrieves the music Keith's mother shared with him and plays it in an open space. Keith starts bouncing and dances with his arms in the air. Isabella, age 4, hears the music and comes over.

Isabella: This is kind of like my mom's mountain music, but different. (*Turns in large circles as she begins dancing.*)

Mr. Cliff: (*Notices Nevaeh watching the children dance.*) Nevaeh, do you and your dad like to dance at home?

Nevaeh: (*Nods.*) Oh yeah, we dance and sing a lot! But we don't have this music. It's kind of weird.

Mr. Cliff: Oh, this music is different from what your family listens to at home. Would you like to try dancing to this music today? Maybe your dad could send me some music your family plays, and you can share that with your classmates tomorrow.

Nevaeh: (*Nods.*)

Mr. Cliff: Isabella, would you like to show Nevaeh how you dance to this music?

As Nevaeh hesitantly enters the dancing space, Isabella approaches her and offers Nevaeh her hand. The girls dance together holding hands. As more children gather in the open area, they use the scarves, ribbons, and percussion instruments that are available. Some children choose to dance in a twisting line, using scarves to connect each of the dancers. Other children choose to sit together in a group playing the instruments. This allows Mr. Cliff to engage in further conversation with the children regarding the music, dancing, and instruments they have in their homes and communities.

Mr. Cliff demonstrates intentionality as a culturally responsive teacher as he reinforces Keith's home language, that of the Siksika (Blackfoot) Nation, by echoing his words. The teacher also uses familiar elements like music to help Keith address his feelings and then reengage in the learning space. By incorporating the family's values, traditions, culture, and language, Mr. Cliff both enhances learning and builds trust.

Relationship Skills

Building friendships and collaborating with others can lead to joyful shared experiences between children that strengthen their social bonds. Of the key knowledge and skills in the area of relationship skills, child-guided experiences may be particularly important for

> Building relationships

Adult-guided experiences may be especially significant for

> Engaging in cooperative play

CHILD-GUIDED experiences are especially important for learnings such as:

| Relationship Skills | Building relationships |

Relationships facilitate other types of learning and are rewarding in their own right. Relationship skill development depends on other social and emotional skills, such as self-regulation and self-awareness, and continues to evolve as children grow in those areas.

Infants as young as 6 months have a beginning understanding of friendship (Liberman, Kinzler, & Woodward 2021), and these skills continue to grow into the preschool years, when children are able to take turns, support their peers, and problem-solve as a group (Barros Blanco et al. 2022).

Teaching strategies. Adults play a vital role in encouraging and supporting young children as they navigate the complex terrain of relationships. Accepting overtures from others as well as reaching out can be risky for preschoolers. They need to know they are socially and emotionally safe and that their autonomy will be respected as they interact with others. This can be especially true for multilingual learners and children with developmental delays or disabilities that affect social interaction. To help children establish relationships with others, try these ideas:

> Be genuine and authentic in your interactions with children. Children sense when adults are disinterested, impatient, or mechanical during conversations. If you talk to children with warmth and respect, they will learn to converse in kind with others. Children from some cultures and language backgrounds may have ways of showing emotions or responding to adult questions that are different from yours. Spend time with children and show interest in what they are doing without putting pressure on them to respond.

> When possible, maintain a stable group of children and adults so relationships can grow over time. Create clusters in which one adult and a small group of children (no more than 10, if possible) stay together for several weeks or months to share meals or snacks and small group activities. Stable groups allow children to get to know the personalities and interests of their peers and the adult. They can also help preschoolers feel safe and secure, which further encourages them to reach out to others.

> Support children's friendships. Encourage and support budding relationships by first simply acknowledging them ("Emelia, I saw you and Sam playing store in the house area"). Then, keep these children together if you re-form small groups.

> Provide opportunities for children to interact with less familiar people, too. For example, ask two children to help with a task ("Daniel and Abby, can you help me carry the scarves outside?"). Providing opportunities to interact allows children to discover peers they might then choose to form relationships with. However, avoid asking multilingual learners to serve as interpreters for children who are not as fluent in English—this sets a new purpose for their relationship and is often not appropriate for their language development.

ADULT-GUIDED experiences are especially important for learnings such as:

Relationship Skills | **Engaging in cooperative play**

Cooperation is acting together toward a common goal. In early childhood, it includes sharing toys, space, friends, conversations, resources, skills, and ideas. By 3 to 4 years old, children are generally able to work together to collaboratively solve a problem (Barros Blanco et al. 2022).

Teaching strategies. Young children learn to play with others by watching and imitating, as well as by trial and error. As social beings, children are intrinsically motivated to interact. Yet, teachers perform a vital function in helping children elaborate their roles in interactive play. Here are some strategies to try:

> Promote interaction through your use of space and materials in the classroom. Do not arbitrarily limit the number of children who can play at one time in an area because it models exclusionary behavior. Whenever possible, provide enough of the same type of materials so that children can freely interact with the materials and each other. If space or supplies are limited (for example, the classroom has only one beanbag chair or only two tablets), problem-solve with the children to decide how to accommodate everyone who wants to use them. (See "Engaging in Conflict Resolution" on pages 86–88 for individual and group problem-solving ideas.)

> Model cooperative play, showing how to take turns, share, and communicate effectively. Get down on the children's level, imitate their use of materials, and follow their ideas and play leads. Help children learn to express their thoughts and feelings clearly and listen actively to others.

> Acknowledge and encourage children's efforts at engaging in cooperative play and demonstrating positive social skills.

> Set up situations for children to work together to accomplish a goal, such as this teacher did:

Ms. Patricia shows David and Marco, both 5, a card game in which they will practice cooperation and further develop their number sense. She explains the need for a "caller" who distributes the cards and directs the other players when to flip over their top card. When Anna walks over and watches, the teacher asks her to join the game. After another round, Ms. Patricia excuses herself, and the players vote for Anna to become the caller.

Before long, Marco throws his cards on the floor, frustrated that Anna is telling him what to do. Ms. Patricia reminds the group about their vote, and they continue playing. When another child later joins in and the same problem arises, this time Marco explains that one person needs to be the caller (MacDonald 2018, 33).

> After play activities, discuss with children what they enjoyed about working together and any challenges they faced. This will help them learn from the experience.

> If a child or group of children need support to work together in a group activity, suggest specific roles or tasks. Respect their decision to act on your decision or to try something else.

Responsible Decision Making

Although it takes many years to learn all the skills needed to make good choices about one's behavior and interacting with others and the environment, with adult support and modeling and plenty of practice, young children can gain and apply these skills. Making thoughtful choices and seeing positive outcomes can inspire a sense of pride and joy, reinforcing the value of responsible behavior. Teachers play a crucial role in helping young children make responsible decisions through modeling, asking open-ended questions, and prompting thinking about how a choice might impact themselves or those around them. In particular, children need guidance to learn to use problem-solving strategies when they have social conflicts. NCPMI (2023) provides useful tools for teachers to show children how to use the problem-solving process.

Of the key knowledge and skills in the area of responsible decision making, child-guided experiences may be important for the following:

> Evaluating the consequences of one's actions

Adult-guided experiences may be particularly important for the following:

> Engaging in conflict resolution

> Developing a framework for moral behavior

CHILD-GUIDED experiences are especially important for learnings such as:

| Responsible Decision Making | Evaluating the consequences of one's actions |

Preschool-age children are typically goal oriented, focused on their own needs, and tend to act intuitively ("I want that truck, so I'll grab it"). Although they can often see the consequences of their actions on others, they may need adult guidance to think through the possible consequences and learn how to choose a response that is less hurtful to others in the future (Gartrell 2023).

Teaching strategies. Setting and reinforcing group guidelines or rules can facilitate children's understanding of consequences. To further support children in evaluating their choices and their effects, try the following strategies:

> In some situations, let children discover the consequences of their actions, provided no one is being hurt or endangered. They will adjust their own behavior accordingly, especially if they are rejected by their peers. Here's an example recorded by a preschool teacher:

> Zack brings his new fire truck to school and announces that no one is allowed to touch it. When he brings the truck over to where Omar and Maggie are playing with toy cars and ramps, they tell him he cannot join their game. This continues for two days. On the third day, Zack puts his truck on the ramp and says to Maggie, "You can push it if you want." She does and then gives it to Omar. Maggie asks Zack, "Do you want to play racing cars with us?" Zack says yes and joins their play, letting his friends take turns with his truck.

This teacher didn't jump in to give social directions, offer opinions or interpretations, or solve problems for the children. If the teacher had insisted Maggie and Omar let Zack play with them, Zack might not have figured out how to alter his behavior to achieve his social goal of inclusion. Teachers also can point out the beneficial consequences of cooperative behavior to encourage children to continue or increase it. However, the focus should be on how the behavior makes the child feel rather than on how it pleases the adult. For example, you could say, "You're having fun racing your cars together" rather than "It makes me happy to see you sharing."

> Introduce children to NCPMI's Solutions Kit (2020) (see "One Approach to Conflict Resolution"). When a problem arises, discuss the various solutions and what consequences each might have. Or use this technique in role-playing situations, such as with puppets, which can remove the emotions from the situation. This helps children to focus on the skill.

ADULT-GUIDED experiences are especially important for learnings such as:

| Responsible Decision Making | Engaging in conflict resolution |

Conflict resolution—also known as problem solving and other names—refers to using appropriate, nonaggressive strategies to discuss and develop solutions to differences between people. Resolving conflicts when needs and emotions are running high is a challenge; in such situations, even adults sometimes cannot or choose not to use their own skills to evaluate the consequences of their actions and identify solutions to problems.

Teaching strategies. Intentional teachers explicitly model, coach, and teach children the behaviors necessary to interact harmoniously with others and resolve conflicts. Key to this process is understanding that children are not misbehaving but rather making mistakes (sometimes referred to as *mistaken behavior*) as they learn how to behave appropriately (Gartrell 2023). So, for example, teachers avoid value-laden or negative terms, such as "Stop being mean" or "When you act up like that, you can't sit with the other children." Instead, adults seek to build secure relationships with each child and use guidance, which are responses to conflicts that calm and teach rather than punish children.

When conflicts arise, as they inevitably will, use the occasions to teach children conflict resolution skills and help them learn how to handle future disagreements. To become skilled at conflict resolution takes repetition, but preschoolers can begin to implement problem-solving strategies on their own with sufficient modeling and support from their teachers. Some become skilled enough that they can eventually engage in the process on their own without adult help or even act as the facilitator in other children's conflict resolution. Consider the following general strategies for helping children learn to successfully resolve their conflicts. (For a specific six-step process to facilitating the process, see "One Approach to Conflict Resolution" on page 87.)

> Establish a safe classroom. Let children know that the adults present will not allow them to be physically or verbally hurt. Stop children's hurtful or dangerous behaviors and words immediately, including aggression, rejection, and taunting. Set and discuss a few clear limits ("No hitting") and expectations ("Everyone gets a turn") with the children, and post these where children can easily see them. Add a picture or symbol as well to clarify the expectation. Be consistent in implementing rules and following through on expectations.

> Convey calmness through your voice, body language, and facial expressions during a conflict. Show concern but not alarm. Be aware of your own emotional triggers beforehand to help prevent overreacting during a conflict situation. Acknowledge and respect all the children's feelings. Act and speak sincerely; for example, make eye contact with all the children involved, and reflect warmth and concern in your voice. In nonthreatening ways, touch or hold children to reassure them and help them regain self-control.

One Approach to Conflict Resolution

Recommended approaches to conflict resolution vary, but they all contain the same basic elements. Here is one six-step procedure (NCPMI 2023), followed by an example:

1. Set the tone. Approach the children calmly. Be supportive and validate each child's emotions. Acknowledge their attempts to self-regulate.

2. Ask each child to identify, from their perspective, the problem. Listen actively and reflect back what you hear each child saying.

3. Support the children in brainstorming potential solutions to try. Ask each child to offer a solution. NCPMI (2020) has a great tool for facilitating this process, the "Solutions Kit: Classroom Addition," that includes picture cue cards.

4. Support the children in evaluating each of the solutions.

5. Implement the solution the children all agree to.

6. Follow up to see whether the solution is working. If conflicts reemerge, repeat the problem-solving steps.

Miss Zara, who teaches 4-year-olds, notices a commotion in the block area. Markus is crying, and Karina is lying on the floor, covering all the red blocks with her body. Miss Zara bends down and calmly says, "It looks like we are having a problem. Markus, I see that you are very sad, and, Karina, it looks like you are covering the blocks. Markus, let's practice taking some deep breaths so we can talk about this. Karina, please stand up. I will keep the blocks safe while we figure this out. Tell me what's going on." The children explain that Karina has all the red blocks and that Markus needs them in order to make his house.

Miss Zara: So, the problem is that Karina is using the blocks to make her birthday cake, and Markus is sad because there are no red blocks to make his house. What can we do to solve this problem?

Markus: She could give me all the red blocks.

Miss Zara: That's one solution. I wonder how Karina would feel about that?"

Karina: (*Shakes her head vigorously.*)

Miss Zara: It looks like she might be pretty upset if she has to take all the cherries off her ice cream. I wonder what else we can try?

Karina: We can trade; I can use two pink blocks for my ice cream and give you two red blocks.

Markus: Good. Here!

The children trade blocks and continue to play. Miss Zara observes for a few minutes and then says, "It looks like trading solved the problem! Now everyone has the blocks they need for their project."

> Observe children's behavior while mediating a conflict, and collect information to arrive at an insightful interpretation. Be aware of your own biases; for example, if Keely has recently been involved in a few disputes with other children, do you assume that you will find her in the middle of the new one that just started in the block area? When a conflict arises, do you assume the child at fault is the one whose culture is different from yours, the one who can't sit still, the one whose family never shows up when you ask to talk with them?

> You can use the same general approach to conflict resolution outlined in the sidebar when children exhibit challenging behaviors, such as throwing toys or refusing to follow routines. In such cases, the problem solving takes place between the adult and the child. Acknowledge that the child helped to solve the problem.

| Responsible Decision Making | Developing a framework for moral behavior |

Moral development, the forming of personal beliefs about right and wrong, is a long process that extends well into adolescence and even early adulthood. Preschoolers, especially older ones, are beginning to wrestle with questions of moral behavior, particularly with regard to the treatment of others, including empathy and fairness (justice). Young children are interested in, and capable of, reflecting on their own and others' choices, especially when encouraged to do so by adults and supported to think about how things are fair or not fair to some people and how unfairness hurts. Teachers seek to build on

children's innate, budding capacities for empathy and fairness as well as their cognitive skills for thinking critically about what is happening around them. [The teacher's goal is to build] a sense of safety—the sense that everyone can and will be treated fairly. (Derman-Sparks & Edwards, with Goins 2020, 16)

Teaching strategies. Individuals' moral sense develops to a great extent through their following (or sometimes explicitly rejecting) the examples set by significant others in their lives, particularly in their home settings. Still, teachers help lay the groundwork from which children build their own value systems by modeling and encouraging appropriate behavior in the classroom. To support children as they begin to construct a moral framework, you can employ several strategies, including these:

> Be consistent and fair-minded, striving to be equitable in your actions as well as to facilitate children's growing abilities to recognize, describe, and address unfairness (injustice) (Derman-Sparks & Edwards, with Winters 2020).

> Establish clear and age-appropriate expectations about behavior. Communicate them to children clearly and apply them consistently (NAEYC 2020). Emphasize collaborative problem solving rather than blame or punishment by guiding children to identify solutions together.

> Take time to reflect on how you respond to each child, checking for unintentional biases that may lead you to focus on certain behavior. Be mindful to respond equitably, providing all children with similar opportunities for positive reinforcement and redirection. Remember that young children are observant and will learn from your example; when they see you treating everyone in a just way and hear your explanations, they are more likely to model this respect and empathy with their peers.

> Verbalize in simple terms the reasons for your actions and decisions that involve moral matters, such as fairness. For example, "I'm making sure every child who wants a muffin has one before giving out seconds. It isn't fair if someone gets two before every child has had one." When children have questions or strong emotions about more complex issues, ask them questions to find out what they think about the issue. Listen carefully and give honest answers. If you don't know the answer, be honest and let the children know that you need time to find more information. Then be sure to follow up.

> Work respectfully with children's families to understand their values and beliefs, with the goal of achieving as much congruence between home and school values as possible. When you find that a family's values and beliefs diverge from your program's principles, listen carefully to their reasoning. Refrain from judging the beliefs the family holds that conflict with yours. Explain your own position clearly and simply, and build on the relationship you have built with the family to problem-solve conflicts over how situations are handled in the two settings. For example, in some cultures families may see it as a sign of disrespect if a teacher covers a child's new outfit with a spattered smock, but they may also be upset if paint gets on the child's clothes. In this case, acknowledge the family's discomfort, and do your best to explain the important concepts children learn by exploring messy materials. You might ask for a spare set of the child's old clothes or if the family would prefer a different or more effective cover-up.

● ● ●

Social and emotional learning is an essential developmental domain for young children. They need to understand, regulate, and express their feelings appropriately in order to experience satisfying interpersonal relationships. Educators help young children construct and master emotional and social skills by valuing every child's strengths, nurturing a relationship with each child outside of conflict situations, bolstering children's sense of competence and initiative, and creating a classroom environment in which their problem-solving abilities can thrive. Teachers also provide explicit guidance in the complex rules of social intercourse by helping children grasp and adhere to classroom and societal norms and offering suggestions when children's own resources prove insufficient to achieve their goals.

Between their intrinsic motivation to be social and teachers' desire to support their social development, young children can and will develop the skills they need to be ready for interpersonal and civic relationships inside and outside of school.

For Further Consideration

1. If you are an experienced teacher, what are your emotional triggers when you are working with children? If you are a novice teacher, what do you expect will be your emotional triggers? How can you recognize them in order to remain calm and in control when helping children deal with their feelings and the situation that upset them?

2. How can you use relationship-building strategies with children who exhibit aggressive or antisocial behaviors? How can you support children in generalizing strategies from your relationship with them to the relationships they have with their peers?

3. How can teachers plan both child-guided and adult-guided social and emotional learning experiences that meet the needs of children with varying levels of skill development, ability, and cultures?

4. How might you integrate strategies for enhancing social and emotional learning into other areas of the curriculum?

5. How can you collaborate with families whose views on social and emotional learning and development differ from yours?

Learning Objectives

1. To explain the intersection between physical development, health, and other developmental domains; the long-term benefits of developing healthy physical activity and nutrition habits; and the consequences of not developing these habits during early childhood

2. To articulate strategies for preparing and planning learning environments to create accessible physical activities that promote motor skill development for all children, including adaptations and accommodations to differentiate and individualize instruction

3. To develop structured and unstructured physical activities that integrate opportunities for children to learn fundamental motor skills and movement concepts

4. To describe developmentally appropriate ways to enhance children's self-help skills in food preparation, hygiene, and safety, thereby promoting healthy lifestyles

CHAPTER 5

Physical Development and Health

Lori E. Meyer

In keeping with the standards her program uses for physical development, Ms. Rachel has been challenging her preschoolers to develop their motor skills by moving in different ways. One day during outside time, Cody tells Ms. Rachel that he is a "crooked horse" and starts galloping in a zigzag pattern. "I see," says Ms. Rachel. "You galloped in a crooked path to the tree. I'm going to move like you did." Ms. Rachel imitates Cody's movements and says, "Sometimes I call this 'going zigzag.'" Several other children, drawn by the activity, begin to gallop in a zigzag path, too. After a few minutes of doing this, Ms. Rachel says to them, "I wonder what other kinds of paths we could gallop in." One child suggests "circles," and the children gallop in a series of curves. When Malcolm joins the group in his wheelchair, he suggests "forward and back." Malcolm maneuvers his wheelchair back and forth as the other children gallop forward and backward beside him.

Developing and using basic physical abilities are essential to children's health and well-being across their lifespan. Gross and fine motor skills serve multiple functions across everyday activities and routines at home and school. Physical coordination is essential to accomplishing many, if not most, everyday tasks. For children with physical delays or disabilities, using and increasing their motor skills may be particularly gratifying, especially when it leads to greater independence and control within their daily routines and environments. The ability to initiate self-directed movement and to influence, participate, and engage in one's physical environment not only is a powerful motivator for young children but also supports growth in other areas, such as cognition, communication, spatial awareness, and problem solving (Catalino & Meyer 2016).

In addition, movement is, or should be, inherently pleasurable. Children (and adults) experience joy in moving their bodies, whether they are feeling the freedom of using their muscles in a variety of ways or expressing creativity through music and dance (Isbell & Yoshizawa 2016). Movement offers many opportunities for creative expression. Children move to music in dance-like ways and experiment with direction and speed as they maneuver their bodies and objects through space. Such experiences allow children to move uniquely, express their inner thoughts and feelings, and build confidence in themselves as movers.

Furthermore, significant health benefits are associated with engaging in physical activity. Movement experiences promote healthy weight and cardiovascular fitness, enhance other body systems (such as increasing lung capacity and strengthening children's respiratory systems), and decrease depressive symptoms (Yogman et al. 2018).

Decreased physical activity, however, along with poor diet, has contributed to an unprecedented rise in the prevalence of childhood obesity in the United States and is occurring at earlier ages than in the past, which is associated with a number of health issues in adulthood (Cunningham et al. 2022). Nearly 13 percent of 2- to 5-year-olds are identified as having childhood obesity (Stierman et al. 2021). Further, obesity disproportionately affects some groups of children more than others. Between 1998 and 2010, there was an increased risk of developing obesity among children from the least socioeconomic advantaged households (Cunningham et al. 2022).

To avoid adverse effects on children's health and well-being and promote lifelong habits of daily physical activity, the Society of Health and Physical Educators (SHAPE) America has set national guidelines for children from birth through age 5. These guidelines encourage adults in children's homes and learning settings to support children's movement, exploration, and motor skills through developmentally appropriate physical activity (SHAPE America 2020). SHAPE America recommends that each day young children experience both structured, adult-led physical activity (30 minutes for toddlers, 60 minutes for preschoolers) and unstructured, child-led physical activity *at least* one hour a day for both toddlers and preschoolers (a combined total including home and other settings). For children ages 5 through 12, SHAPE America (n.d.) recommends at least 60 minutes of age-appropriate physical activity daily.

Adults may assume that children will develop physically on their own provided they receive adequate nutrition, have safe opportunities to move around in the environment, and do not have a disability or medical condition that impacts their physical development. Indeed, there is a typical progression in what children are capable of in terms of their gross motor and fine motor development. However, the development of physical skills in the early childhood years is not purely maturational, and young children do not learn fundamental motor skills simply through play (Goodway et al. 2020; SHAPE America 2020). Children need instruction, modeling, encouragement, and lots of opportunities to practice if they are to grow in their fundamental motor skills. In addition, early childhood represents a unique time when children's physical activity levels impact their ability to perform basic gross motor skills (Coe 2020). This relationship later inverts, with physical activity levels relying on an individual's motor proficiency. To ensure that children gain the basic gross motor skills they need, teachers plan movement experiences and structure physical activities that introduce a range of movement options.

Many early childhood educators already incorporate movement into their settings and daily routines, such as large group time and transitions, within games, during songs, and through dance. Intentional teachers plan various indoor and outdoor activities to support children's physical development and build on their existing strengths. By intentionally observing children's play and motor skills and consulting your program's standards, you can identify areas where you can offer additional support or challenge, such as providing more opportunities for specific types of movement or differentiating activities to meet children's needs. Given the increase in physical inactivity and obesity among young children, intentional teaching is important for children's physical development and health.

Teachers also have an important role to play in supporting children's personal care skills and healthy behavior, including nutrition. Intentional teachers can enhance children's self-help skills and encourage a lifelong commitment to healthy eating by actively involving children in preparing snacks, measuring ingredients, exploring different foods and textures, discussing food characteristics, and providing child-sized utensils for making and cleaning up after food preparation experiences.

Young Children's Development in Physical Development and Health

Implementing intentional teaching strategies for physical development and health requires an understanding of how young children develop physically. Learning new movement skills is a process with both biological and environmental influences (Goodway et al. 2020). A contemporary model of children's motor development is Clark and Metcalfe's "Mountain of Motor Development," in which they propose that ". . . progression up the mountain was specific to an individual's experiences, and the constraints they experienced along the route" (Goodway et al. 2020, 67). The mountain's phases of motor development include

> The "Reflexive" period (birth–2 weeks): Skills observed include movements linked to stimuli (e.g., reflexive sucking as oral motor movement).

> The "Preadapted" period (2 weeks–1 year): Skills often correlate with independent feeding (e.g., object manipulation, eye-hand coordination, grasp and release) and early locomotion skills (e.g., crawling, cruising, walking).

> The "Fundamental Motor Skills" period (1–7 years): Considered the mountain's "base camp" where locomotion (e.g., running, skipping, hopping) and manipulative coordination skills (e.g., dribbling, kicking, catching) are more advanced and serve as the foundation for future skill success.

> The "Context-Specific Motor Skills" period (7–11 years): Skills are continually refined and are combined for more complex movements needed within sports and games.

> The "Skillful" period (11 years–adult): At the top of the mountain, individuals have developed and mastered a very specific set of skills within a particular activity or sport (e.g., volleyball spiking, swim stroke technique). (Favazza & Siperstein 2016, 227)

An individual child's "mountain of motor development" might be better conceptualized as a "mountain range" containing multiple peaks of various heights (Goodway et al. 2020). Thinking in this way, it should be evident that individual children will not reach the highest motor development phase across all sports, games, and activities. Each child's physical development journey is unique. Children who do not get opportunities to learn and practice a particular motor skill, such as throwing or dribbling a ball, may grow up unable to perform that skill. Or perhaps they do not develop these skills because they do not have sufficient time, adult support, or motivation to practice. Research suggests that young children are not motivated to practice a new skill unless they experience success close to 80 percent of the time—that is, the task cannot be too hard or too easy, because in either situation the child will lose interest (Graham, Elliott, & Palmer 2016).

Resources on Physical Development and Early Childhood Programs

Several documents provide summary statements about early physical development as well as guidance on how to apply the information in program settings. In 2019, the American Academy of Pediatrics, American Public Health Association, and National Resource Center for Health and Safety in Child Care in Early Education released the third edition of standards titled *Preventing Childhood Obesity in Early Care and Education Programs*, designed to describe best practices based on evidence on nutrition, physical activity, and screen time. These standards are part of the comprehensive standard set titled *Caring for Our Children: National Health and Safety Performance Standards; Guidelines for Early Care and Education Programs* (CFOC). A special feature of the CFOC standards is their online database, which allows for periodic updates based on new science and recommendations for practice (National Resource Center for Health and Safety in Child Care and Early Education 2024). In addition, in 2020 SHAPE America issued its third edition of early childhood standards in a publication titled *Active Start: A Statement of Physical Activity Guidelines for Children Birth to Age 5.*

The development of any motor skill is sequential, and there are key fundamental motor skills that set the stage for physical activity enjoyment and participation later in life. Goodway et al. explain:

> These skills [fundamental motor skills, or FMS] do not naturally "emerge" during early childhood; rather, they result from many factors influencing the child's motor skill development. Therefore, movement experiences early in one's life play a substantial role in acquisition of FMS and are seminal within one's journey toward being physically literate. (2020, 68)

Like other content areas, the physical development and movement curriculum should be designed so that later learning builds on earlier experiences and skills (Goodway et al. 2020).

An effective physical development and movement curriculum provides appropriate opportunities for young children to develop in two separate but related gross motor areas: fundamental motor skills and movement concepts. Children learn about movement concepts as they practice fundamental motor skills, so teachers do well to incorporate both in preschoolers' physical activities (Graham, Elliott, & Palmer 2016). These two areas are cornerstones to becoming physically literate and represent two of the four current national physical education standards (SHAPE America 2024):

Standard 1: Develops a variety of motor skills

Standard 2: Applies knowledge related to movement and fitness concepts

Gross Motor Development

Fundamental Motor Skills

Fundamental motor skills refer to the movement skills that young children need to develop and refine to become physically literate. They can be thought of as the ABCs of physical activity (Goodway et al. 2020). Although researchers have grouped fundamental motor skills in various ways, these skills fall primarily into three categories (Logan et al. 2018):

> **Locomotor:** The body is transported horizontally or vertically from one point in space to another. Children's locomotor skills, the first of the three types of movement to develop, are walking, running, hopping, skipping, galloping, sliding, leaping, climbing, crawling, chasing, and fleeing.

> **Balance/stability:** The body remains in place but moves around its horizontal or vertical axis, or it balances against the force of gravity. These skills develop next: turning, twisting, bending, stopping, rolling, balancing, transferring weight, jumping/landing, stretching/extending, curling, swinging, swaying, and dodging.

> **Object control/manipulative:** The body moves to apply force to or receive force from objects with hands, feet, or other body parts. These skills develop last: throwing, catching/collecting, kicking, punting, rolling, dribbling, volleying, striking with a racket, and striking with a long-handled instrument such as a bat). Manipulative skills are essential in many games and sports, such as kickball and baseball. The fine motor skills needed for tasks such as writing and drawing are also manipulative skills, although they are less vigorous than the gross motor skills.

Movement Concepts

Movement concepts are the knowledge component of the curriculum. Whereas fundamental motor skills relate to *what* the body can do, movement concepts relate to *where, how, and in relationship to what* the body moves. Put another way, movement skills can be thought of as *body verbs* and movement concepts as *body adverbs*. Learning these movement concepts helps to modify or enrich children's range of motor skills and the effectiveness of their use of the skills (Graham, Elliott, & Palmer 2016). These categories of movement concepts or awareness will be discussed in more detail further on in the chapter: where the body moves in space; how the body moves in space (such as speed and control); what connections the body makes with other people, objects, and the environment; and self-awareness (body parts, body shapes).

Fine Motor Development

Young children use a variety of fine motor movements to manipulate materials and tools. Common actions that require these types of movements include molding, squeezing, poking, smoothing, positioning, writing, stacking, pouring, and cutting. Between the ages of 3 and 5, children gain strength, eye-hand coordination, and endurance. They grow more skilled at manipulating age-appropriate materials such as scissors, pencils, markers, crayons, blocks, puzzles, string, beads, pegs, hammers, screwdrivers, paintbrushes, clothes fasteners, eating utensils, snap-on and screw-on lids, switches, buttons, levers, and gears on toys and technology. The more proficient and confident preschoolers become in their fine motor skills, the more eager they are to try working with new tools and materials.

Some children with developmental delays or disabilities need fine motor activities adapted or modified to their specific strengths or needs. Tools are available that are easier for children to grasp to allow for success, such as adapted scissors. Providing opportunities for accessible fine motor practice, such as buttoning and unbuttoning clothes and opening and closing zippers, can support long-term life skills. Other items that may work well include puzzle pieces with pegs, larger beads for beading, and larger/built-up crayons and markers.

There are, however, physical limits to all preschoolers' fine motor abilities. For example, children's early writing tends to be large because they cannot make fully circular wrist motions; the cartilage in their wrists does not harden into bone until about age 6 (Berk 2023). Therefore, writing, drawing, and cutting with precision are still difficult for them. Handedness is generally established by age 4, yet children still experiment with using the nondominant hand beyond this age. It is important to keep children's developmental progressions in mind so you can effectively scaffold children's learning at each stage and avoid holding unrealistic expectations for what children can and cannot do.

Development of Personal Care Routines and Healthy Behavior

Young children enjoy taking care of themselves and often practice self-help skills intently and repeatedly. They learn to serve food and eat on their own, get dressed, use the toilet, wash their hands, brush their teeth, use and dispose of tissues, and so on. Children with physical or other developmental delays or disabilities also enjoy—and may insist on—doing as much for themselves as possible. The development of fine motor skills enables children to assume more of these self-care responsibilities. As they learn to care for themselves, children may also show interest in taking care of others, including pets as well as people. They may not always perform these tasks to adult standards (such as missing a spot of paint on their hand), but their pride is evident, and their efforts should be accepted and acknowledged by adults without overemphasis on correctness.

Performing daily self-care routines, along with learning about the natural world as part of science explorations (see Chapter 8), makes children aware that they have to take care of their bodies just as they take care of toys and equipment. Preschoolers start to grasp that some foods are more healthful than others, and being involved in growing, choosing, and preparing foods can increase their interest in eating them. Physical activity and good nutrition are essential not only to healthy development but also to academic achievement (Asigbee, Whitney, & Peterson 2018).

Teaching and Learning in Physical Development and Health

As mentioned previously, children benefit from both unstructured times when they are free to explore their interests independently and without undue influence from adults as well as from structured times when adults participate, model, teach, and encourage children's efforts and developing skills. In other words, physical education, like any other content area, requires adults to take an active and deliberate instructional role. Intentional teachers fulfill these recommendations by creating an appropriate learning environment, regardless of who guides the learning, and using effective interaction strategies with young children. Each interaction strategy can be used with both child-guided (unstructured) and adult-guided (structured) experiences but may vary depending on the skill. For example, modeling and using explicit cues may be useful to support child-guided experiences, but they are more often necessary in adult-guided experiences.

Likewise, challenges make learning enjoyable in both instances, but they become more salient in adult-guided instruction to suggest movement possibilities and raise awareness of health issues that children are unlikely to think of on their own.

Young children with developmental delays or disabilities are placed at an increased risk for adverse health concerns related to lower rates of physical activity than their peers (Catalino & Meyer 2016). Collaborations between a child's medical provider, therapists, special educator, or child care health consultant can support additional planning needed to promote the child's full inclusion in physical activity and movement programs (Massare & Myers 2024). Such collaborations and planning are important, even for commonplace activities such as yoga. Yoga is recommended by the American Academy of Pediatrics as beneficial for all children and especially children with developmental delays or disabilities and others who would benefit from skills to enhance their mental health and well-being (National Center for Complementary and Integrative Health [NCCIH] 2020). Other considerations specific to planning yoga activities, beyond those already discussed for physical activity and movement activities in general, include attending to incorporating variations and adaptations of favorite poses to foster continued engagement and practice and being flexible in response to children's pace and accuracy (Zuccaro 2023).

Physical Education Learning Environment

Intentional teachers consider several aspects of an environment suited to foster children's engagement in physical activity: scheduling, activity intensity, group size, indoor and outdoor spaces, equipment, and the participation of every child (SHAPE America 2020). Although several of these have already been touched on in this chapter, a few points are worth emphasizing and expanding here.

First, movement education should be a scheduled activity, like small group time, snack time, or any other part of the daily routine, and should include both structured and unstructured opportunities, as noted previously. As Massare and Myers explain, "Including at least two structured activities daily can encourage higher intensity levels that increase younger children's engagement in activity play" (2024, 85). Although specific requirements vary from state to state, most state licensing regulations for early childhood programs include provisions related to physical activity, outdoor play, and opportunities for large motor play. The key is to be consistent and create a predictable schedule for movement, especially for children who rely on knowing what comes next in their day. You can also integrate opportunities for movement across curricular areas and within ongoing classroom routines and activities. Incorporating movement activities into learning experiences and transitions supports children's social and emotional development, physical development, and cognition (August et al. 2023)

Second, plan with the knowledge that young children engage in short bursts of activity throughout their day, and their activity intensity varies. Choose movement activities that match children's energy levels and needs, such as a jumping song as part of a whole group time that also includes listening activities. Further, given that preschoolers' attention spans are short, in general, you might plan several movement variations to use during an activity and several different games within one physical activity time (for example, leading children in four 5-minute physical activity games; Meyer et al. 2020). Incorporating children's ideas and interests into movement activities can also increase their attention span and engagement.

It may be helpful to explain to children that when they engage in more vigorous physical activity, they might notice body cues like their heart beating faster, their breath becoming heavier, their face feeling warmer, and their body sweating. This information helps children understand that these sensations are signs of their bodies working hard and getting stronger—especially helpful for children who are more inactive, because they may feel concerned about having these physiological responses. Children might also enjoy learning more about how their bodies work— for example, why their bodies sweat ("When we play hard, our bodies get hot. To cool us down, our bodies make a special liquid called sweat. When the sweat leaves our bodies, we feel cooler. This is called evaporation" or "Sweat is like a tiny rainstorm on our skin. It helps us to cool down, just like a rainstorm cools the air").

Third, regarding group size, teachers should simultaneously consider learning goals, space, children's development and abilities, safety, and equipment needed for the movement experience planned. It may be important to have smaller groups when the children need more individualized instruction during a structured activity—for example, if multilingual learners or children with developmental delays or disabilities are participating. In such situations, a greater portion of teaching strategies may involve individual feedback, such as touching the children, gesturing, guiding their movements, and keeping them engaged. Some children with developmental delays or disabilities may need visual support to understand new skills and movements, tasks broken down into smaller steps, repeated opportunities for practice, and planned adaptations of the movement experience.

Fourth, access to indoor and outdoor spaces for physical activity and movement is particularly important in the development of gross motor skills. For some activities, the amount of space required is more than the dimensions of a typical classroom, and movement activities may take place elsewhere if available, such as a gym, multipurpose room, large hallway, or outdoors (although children are more likely to be engaged in movement activities when outside [Massare & Myers 2024]). Children who use a wheelchair or walker need additional space to safely move around. When planning your classroom space, move through the environment, considering the adaptive equipment children may use to ensure that everyone can move throughout the entire space. Wherever movement learning takes place, the environment should be free of obstacles.

Fifth, equipment is a key component (see "Basic Equipment and Materials for Early Childhood Movement Programs" on page 102). In acquiring movement resources, consider scale, accessibility, and quantity. Equipment should be child sized and appropriate for children with developmental delays or disabilities. Storing equipment (such as hoops, balls, mats) near the movement space helps ensure that it will be used frequently and spontaneously. Depending on the type of activity, it may be important to have a sufficient number of materials so that every child can participate without waiting. That means if the activity is throwing and there are 12 children in the class, have 12 items to throw (such as balls and beanbags). Every child does not need to have the same item as long as there is something appropriate for each child. Another option is to create multiple activity stations for children to visit so that fewer items of each kind are needed. Remember too that outdoor equipment does not need to be limited to permanent structures. Loose parts can be used to promote vigorous physical activity and gross motor development. Loose parts could include natural materials (such as stones, tree stumps, logs, leaves, water, and dirt) and manufactured materials (such as crates and bins, plastic pipes, rope, and hoops).

Finally, the principle of active involvement and the participation of all children is crucial. In some cases, it is a distinguishing difference between a movement program and sports. Rather than winning, the goal of each childhood physical activity or movement program is to have children refine their skills and have fun while doing so (Logan, Cuff, & AAP Council on Sports Medicine and Fitness, 2019).

With this in mind, think about elimination games such as Duck, Duck, Goose or Musical Chairs. Players spend most of their time in these games sitting or standing, and some are excluded altogether—making them poor choices for physical activities. These games can be adapted, however, so that there are no winners and losers (for example, after each round of Musical Chairs, have all the children continue to play, or replace chairs with Hula-Hoops and encourage children to fit, sometimes including more than one child, inside a hoop when the music stops). Likewise, races can promote feelings of inadequacy and discouragement for all except the winner and are, therefore, not appropriate for young children. Instead thoughtfully consider scheduling, activity level, group size, space, ability, and equipment to ensure every child is an active participant and has experiences that are just the right level of challenging yet achievable.

Physical Education Interaction Strategies

Participating in movement activities with children will encourage them to try new ways of using their bodies and play equipment and increase their enjoyment in the activities. The following general interaction strategies promote movement learning of all types in young children.

Facilitate access and exploration by providing materials, space, and time for young children to explore movement. Make modifications and individualize instruction and materials based on children's strengths, interests, and needs to support all children's access to and exploration of movement skills.

Model a skill to demonstrate to children how to use their bodies or equipment to accomplish a physical objective. This demonstration technique is especially beneficial for children who do not easily process verbal instruction, have limited vocabulary, or are multilingual and are learning the language spoken by the teacher. The goal is to help children get the basic idea of the movement skill and practice it independently. Use caution when modeling and providing verbal instruction to prevent or correct errors. Tricia Catalino explains,

> As children practice, they will use feedback from the external environment (i.e., hitting or missing the target) and from their bodies (i.e., how hard did I have to kick to hit the target or what part of my foot hit the ball when I missed the target) to refine and improve this skill. (Personal communication, April 7, 2024)

Add descriptive language. Describing movement makes children more aware of what they are doing, so they pay attention to their bodies. It also increases their vocabulary. Once they hear movement words from teachers, children begin to use labels such as *over* and *under, straight* and *bent* not only as part of movement activities but also to convey concepts in mathematics and other content areas.

While children are practicing and refining a new skill, provide small bits of key information (cues) about that skill to help them learn it more quickly and correctly. Cues can be verbal, visual (demonstration), or hands-on guidance (Grisham-Brown & Hemmeter 2017). A *verbal cue* might be telling a child, "Hold your hands in front of your body to catch the ball." *Visual cues* can replace or supplement verbal cues; for example, pointing to your eyes as a reminder to the child to look at the target when throwing a beanbag. For *hands-on cues,* with the child's permission gently move the child's body into a more efficient position, such as centering the child's body over a balance beam. Be sensitive to which type works best for each child, skill, and situation and individualize your cues. (See "Movement Skills and Verbal Cues" on page 111 for examples of movement skills and associated verbal cues.)

Create skill challenges to increase children's interest and enjoyment, encourage them to stay with a task longer, and help them apply skills to other situations. For example, you might say, "I wonder how many different ways you can bounce the ball," "How many times can you skip to the bookshelf and back before the music stops?," or "Who has a different way to . . . ?"

Invite children to lead a movement activity, making verbal suggestions or demonstrating an action to be copied by the class. Being leaders develops children's confidence and independence and makes them more aware of verbal labels and motions because they must communicate them to others. Most children want to be leaders, but allow them to volunteer. You may find that children who typically don't speak up in a group feel comfortable leading. Children who are pre- or nonverbal or who are multilingual learners can also lead physical activities.

Basic Equipment and Materials for Early Childhood Movement Programs

Some of the following items are only available commercially; others can be made or collected at minimal cost, especially with contributions from children's families and local businesses (such as empty recycled cereal boxes). Materials should be appropriately sized for young children, varied, and plentiful. Access to adaptive equipment will ensure participation of children with developmental delays or disabilities and an inclusive learning environment. Modifications to existing equipment can be made so that children with developmental delays or disabilities can use it better (such as adding Velcro strapping to paddles and bats to make them easier to hold). Other equipment may need to be collected or made (such as a kicking aid for children who use a wheelchair). Note that not all the equipment listed below is needed to provide sufficient movement experiences and a well-rounded program.

Bag: Large mesh bag for carrying materials; bucket, box, wheelbarrow, storage cart

Balancing equipment: Beams, boards, planks, or platforms on or raised slightly off the ground; includes railroad ties, bricks, blocks, or rocks arranged in various configurations

Balloons of different sizes and weights: Sometimes recommended for indoor use only to avoid potential environmental hazards; heavy-duty recommended, 12 inches in diameter, children should be closely supervised to avoid choking hazards

Balls of many types: Different diameters; lightweight foam, rubber, and plastic balls; old tennis balls; yarn, fleece, and cloth balls; smooth and textured balls; wiffle balls; beach, tennis, basketball, football, softball, and soccer balls; audible balls with a bell or beeping sound for children with visual impairments

Baskets, bowls, and boxes: Various heights and widths, to throw things into

Basketball hoop or other types of anchored net: Including soccer net, child sized

Bats: Plastic and foam rather than wood; other striking materials include hockey stick, recycled two-liter bottle (dowel rod could be connected to bottle to create a handle)

Beanbags: Square and cubed; about five inches per side; filled with dried beans, rice, sand, birdseed, or plastic pellets

Bowling set (pins and ball): Recycled two-liter bottles could serve as pins, other "sets" include T-ball, badminton, hook-and-loop catching mitt/ball

Bubbles: Encourage jumping and other gross motor movements

Climbing equipment: Jungle gym, ladder, tree stumps, boulders, snow piles, stackable steps

Cones: Plastic or vinyl for marking boundaries, creating obstacles, and movement paths; taller cone could serve as a T-ball stand

Disks: Frisbees, foam, paper plates, plastic paint can lids

Gardening tools: Tools for digging, raking, and so on; these help to develop upper body strength

Hoops: Plastic; 24-inch diameter; smaller diameters are better for young children

Jump ropes: Five to six feet on average, considering a child's height and coordination; longer ropes (seven, eight, or nine feet long) may be appropriate for three children playing together (such as two children hold the rope and a third child jumps); a jump rope cut in half with knots or small counterweights at the ends for children who use a wheelchair

Launch boards: Stomp-and-catch games where a child steps on one end and a beanbag at the other end flies up for the child to catch; includes stomp rockets

Mats: Four feet by six feet; don't teach tumbling or rolling without them!

Music: Recorded or child-created (see rhythm sticks below)

Nets: For tennis/pickleball; a lower net (around two feet tall) can be made of construction netting and PVC pipes for poles

Paddles: Soft, foam; includes hand paddles

Parachute: 12 feet in diameter

Pool noodles: Can be used as bumpers for bowling or markers for pathways/boundaries

Pull and push toys: Wagons, toy lawnmowers, shopping carts, doll strollers, vacuum cleaners, wheelbarrows, a laundry basket or box with weights added

Rackets: Plastic

Rhythm sticks: Wood or plastic; include other rhythm instruments such as egg shakers, hand drums, wrist bells

Ribbons, ribbon wands, ribbon sticks: To perform expressive rhythmic movements; ribbons three feet long; use longer ribbons with older children

Ring toss set: Plastic or foam

Rocking toys: Wooden or plastic horse, boats

Scarves: For throwing, catching, juggling, and rhythm activities; lightweight scarves fall slowly, so they are ideal for catching

Sliding equipment: Commercial slide, fireman's pole, waterslide

Spots: Vinyl for use indoors or outdoors; used for place or path markers; directional arrow spots also available; recycled mouse pads, carpet squares, floor tape, or string may also be used indoors

Swings: Commercial swings, tire swings, rope swings

Targets: Plywood or other sturdy material (such as cardboard), or sheets with targets painted on them; cereal boxes; two-liter bottles or hoops can also serve as targets for throwing practice

Tunnels: Purchased or made with recycled boxes

Wheeled vehicles: Tricycles, toy cars and buses, scooters; always wear helmets

---

Adapted from SHAPE America 2020 and Carissa Wengrovius, personal communication, April 11, 2024.

Promoting Personal Care Routines and Healthy Behavior

Eating and physical activity patterns are established at a very young age. For that reason, early childhood programs play a vital role in helping children establish healthy habits. Establishing healthy habits can even start in the classroom, as children's questions may inspire food-related activities and curriculum ideas. Because their stomachs are small, young children do best with several smaller meals and snacks spread throughout the day. Water intake is also important. Variety is another aspect of healthy nutrition, and it allows children to experience different tastes, textures, and smells. Likewise, good exercise habits are built on children enjoying a variety of large motor activities as a normal part of the daily routine. When teachers are active alongside them—not watching from the sidelines—children get the message that an active lifestyle is vital for adults, too. Finally, eating and exercise have important social dimensions. Eating in a pleasant and relaxed setting develops positive attitudes about food. These attitudes are fostered when meals and snacks in the classroom are conducted family style, with adults and children passing around the food, serving themselves, and conversing while they eat.

Connecting Teaching to Children's Lives

By Darcy Heath

It is lunchtime in Mr. Miguel's classroom of 4-year-olds. Each day the class eats their lunch family style at a table. Mr. Miguel likes to use this time to learn more about the children, including their interests, families, and things that are important to them.

"Mr. Miguel, look! We are having noodles for lunch today!" yells an excited Ayla as she sits down at the lunch table.

"I love noodles, too," adds Amir as he joins the table.

"Me too, me too!" chime in Greyson and Jayla.

"It sounds like a lot of us like noodles. What kind of noodles do you like to eat at your house?" asks Mr. Miguel as he passes the bowl of noodles and the tongs to Jayla to serve herself. Jayla struggles to squeeze the tongs to pick up the noodles to put on her plate. Mr. Miguel smiles at Jayla and quietly encourages her to try again. The second time, Jayla picks up the noodles with her tongs and puts them on her plate. Mr. Miguel gives her a thumbs-up and continues to listen to the conversation among the children as he passes the bowl to Meilee.

Ayla: My favorite noodles are pancit that my lola makes for me. They are really good.

Meilee: My yaya makes me Dan Dan noodles, and I eat them with chopsticks.

Mateo: What are chopsticks?

Mr. Miguel: Chopsticks are like a fork in that people use them to eat food. After lunch we can look up some pictures of chopsticks and see how they work.

Meilee: My chopsticks have a special clip that holds them together. It makes it easier for me to pick up the noodles with them.

Mr. Miguel: That sounds like fun. Maybe we can find a picture of chopsticks with a clip. What about you, Amir? What kinds of noodles do you like?

Amir: My Dad makes spaghetti. He lets me put as much cheese on it as I want. I love cheese and noodles!

Greyson: Me too! Macaroni and cheese!

Mateo: I can't eat noodles or cheese because I'm allergic to them. But my mom makes me rice, and I like that.

Mr. Miguel: Isn't it great that everyone eats different things at their homes? Everyone's family has different foods that they enjoy. That is one of the differences that make us each unique and special. Some people, like Mateo, can only eat certain things because of allergies. Why don't we finish up our lunch and I'll find some pictures of chopsticks and some of the different types of noodles that you all like. After you wash your hands and brush your teeth, we can see how our favorite noodle dishes are the same and different.

During this lunchtime, Mr. Miguel builds warm, authentic relationships with the children by noticing and celebrating each of the children and their customs. He celebrates their successes and values their individual and family differences. He listens and pays attention to their stories, interests, and challenges. Valuing their cultural differences, he shares information about the children's cultures with the group.

Mr. Miguel also provides opportunities for children to develop their fine motor skills by allowing them to serve themselves lunch and offering tools that require fine motor skills, such as tongs. He demonstrates the use of the tongs for children who are unfamiliar with them, and then gives quiet encouragement and support while the children practice these skills. The children experience sharing a physical space with each other at the table and developing spatial awareness. Mr. Miguel integrates healthy eating habits and the difference between diet and allergies into the conversation.

Fitting the Learning Experience to the Learning Objective

The rest of this chapter examines movement skills (gross motor and fine motor), movement concepts, and the development of personal care routines and healthy behavior. Each section is in turn divided into those skills or concepts that are acquired primarily through child-guided or adult-guided experiences. Keep in mind that, as with all areas of development, this division is not rigid.

Movement Skills

Movement learning, more than other content areas, can be difficult to attribute to either child- or adult-guided experiences. Locomotor skills, for example, often mature on their own, and children spontaneously engage in and improve at them with ample opportunities to explore and discover. Yet, movements that are more difficult or complex and involve greater eye-hand coordination or coordination of muscles and senses require a certain amount of direction and refinement. In addition, there are some locomotor skills that require intervention before children can come to a more mature form and eventually combine and apply them in games and sports. More challenging skills often require adult support and supervision to ensure safe and efficient execution.

CHILD-GUIDED experiences are especially important for learnings such as:

| Movement Skills | Locomotor skills: Crawling, walking, running, climbing |

These four locomotor skills are primarily learned by children through exploration and discovery. Preschoolers become increasingly coordinated in their running and can maintain better balance while climbing.

Teaching strategies. Although young children enjoy moving, teachers play a critical role in creating a physical environment that supports movement exploration. Their attitudes are also important in helping children overcome their fears and in sharing their joy of discovery. To provide support, teachers can implement a variety of strategies, including these:

> Promote children's free exploration and practice of locomotor skills. Accept and respect children's originality and creativity. To encourage children to move in new ways, make interesting or novel suggestions, such as "Imagine you are a squirrel scampering along the ground . . ."

> Select a favorite storybook (or make up a story) at large group time and integrate opportunities for movement while you read or tell the story.

> Use basic locomotor skills to enhance other areas of learning. For example, if children are exploring short and long strings during small group time, encourage them to take short and long steps during or while transitioning to outside time.

| Movement Skills | **Stability skills: Turning, twisting, bending, straightening, curling, stretching/extending, swinging, swaying, pushing, pulling, rising, falling, dodging, stopping** |

These stability skills seem to be primarily acquired through exploration and discovery. Children typically use these skills while standing in place. Although these stability skills can be practiced by children individually, they are often done in groups, such as swaying together to music.

Teaching strategies. Build on young children's spontaneous movements by suggesting games and challenges that will further develop their basic stability skills. Many of these activities can be done during large group time, with each child on a carpet square or small mat or on a soft surface outdoors. Dramatic play also offers opportunities for children to act out the stability movements natural to animals or illustrative of characters in stories. Try strategies such as these:

> Demonstrate and practice stability skills with children, such as curling and stretching/extending fingers and toes. Explore the words *curl* and *stretch* with familiar situations. For example, ask children to pretend to be sleeping kittens in a curled-up position before waking up.

> Have a child lead the group in an activity exploring a stability skill such as swinging, letting the child choose which body part to swing and how. Encourage the leader to describe the movement before performing it. Supply the words for body parts and motions.

| Movement Skills | Manipulative skills: Throwing and kicking |

These are the manipulative skills children typically discover on their own. Throwing is the easier skill, and children may naturally use an underhand, overhand, or sidearm motion. Kicking develops later because children's lower body control typically lags behind upper body control.

Teaching strategies. Children naturally throw and kick things because they are curious about the effects of such motions. They may also imitate the actions of older siblings or sports figures. Although their abilities are rudimentary at first, children enjoy seeing their accuracy improve with practice. Teachers can encourage this practice with strategies such as these:

> Encourage children to practice and explore manipulative skills. For example, they can toss a beanbag overhand and underhand or kick a ball with their toe (in a sturdy shoe) or the side of their foot. Encourage them to use their nondominant as well as dominant leg or arm.

> After children master basic motions, provide targets for them to throw or kick objects at. Begin with large, close, and/or low targets, moving to targets that are smaller, farther, or higher; also progress from stationary to moving actions.

> Use children's interest in throwing and kicking to explore positional and distance words. For example, challenge them to throw a beanbag up or down, stand near or far away from the target, or kick a ball above or below a target. Invite them to suggest other variations and encourage their use of position and distance words.

Movement Skills	Fine motor skills and eye-hand coordination: Grasping, pinching, tearing

Fine motor skills require eye-hand coordination. Preschoolers practice grasping, pinching, and tearing with a variety of materials, such as small objects (animal and people figures, food), clay and playdough, collage materials, and different types of paper. At first, children enjoy mastering fine motor skills for their own sake. Later they apply them to fulfill their intentions as they build structures, create art, engage in dramatic play, and carry out self-help tasks.

Teaching strategies. The following strategies will support young children as they practice, master, and apply a variety of fine motor abilities:

> Provide quiet, protected spaces for fine motor activities. Young children benefit from spaces without competing visual or auditory distractions when focusing on tasks requiring eye-hand coordination. Uncluttered tables at the children's height, allowing their feet to be firmly placed on the floor, also support their balance and stability.

> Provide flat surfaces for working with small toys, writing tools, art materials, and so on. Preschoolers can also work comfortably on the floor, at easels or slant boards, on paper tacked to the wall, on outdoor pavement, at sand and water tables, in flower and vegetable gardens and digging areas, and many other such spaces where they can use their small muscles and hone their eye-hand coordination with a variety of interesting materials and tools. Some children with developmental delays or disabilities may find it less taxing to stand at an easel for painting and drawing, where they can use larger shoulder movements, than sitting at a table and using their smaller hand muscles (Brillante 2014).

> Provide a variety of fine motor materials, tools, and equipment, such as art materials, writing tools, dress-up clothes, household utensils, blocks and other construction toys and tools, puzzles, stacking and nesting toys, beads, and items that can be taken apart and put back together. Give children opportunities to exercise their small muscles throughout the day; for example, using serving and eating utensils at snack time or putting on safety goggles and hammering nails or golf tees into wood, cardboard boxes, or playdough at choice time.

> Provide similar objects in a range of graduated sizes and shapes so that children can feel a sense of accomplishment as their fine motor skills develop. Examples include DUPLO and LEGO blocks, jigsaw puzzles with pieces that vary in number and size, fat and skinny crayons and markers, and doll clothes with different types of fasteners. Encourage children to begin with the easiest materials and then gradually attempt to work with more challenging ones. Materials in larger sizes, brighter colors, with rubber grips, and so on are also useful for children with motor or sensory needs.

> Modify materials so that children with physical delays or disabilities can use them more easily. For example, add small knobs to puzzle pieces, pencil grips to crayons and markers, and large paper clips to book pages to make them easier to turn (Brillante 2014).

ADULT-GUIDED experiences are especially important for learnings such as:

Movement Skills	Locomotor skills: Hopping, jumping, galloping, sliding, slithering, marching, plodding, leaping, chasing, fleeing, skipping

Once children have mastered basic locomotor skills through child-guided experiences, there is an almost endless range of variations to explore. However, children may not create or chance upon more complex movements on their own (see "Movement Skills and Verbal Cues" on page 111). Some locomotor skills, like chasing and fleeing, use cognitive and movement strategies in addition to physical strategies to anticipate or avoid the other person.

Teaching strategies. Adult interventions such as the following can help open up the world of movement for children:

> Provide targets or goals to locomote to; for example, say, "Let's gallop to the fence" or "Hop to the coat rack to get ready for outside time." Ask children to suggest targets.

> Provide ways for each child to participate in movement activities that match their developmental goals. For children with limited mobility or low vision, problem-solve with them to find alternative ways to meet movement challenges. For example, ask how many times they can roll a wheelchair back and forth between two points before the music stops, or how they can use tactile feedback to navigate moving through a narrow space.

> Invite families to share their favorite movement games from their childhood (such as hopscotch, jump rope songs, and "What time is it, Mr. Fox?").

| Movement Skills | Stability skills: Transferring weight, balancing, jumping/landing, rolling |

Adult-guided experiences that focus on stability skills extend the skills learned primarily through child-guided experiences. These activities build on a young child's growing muscle control and coordination.

Teaching strategies. Stability—bodily control—underpins many movement tasks. For that reason, your role in helping children master these foundational skills is particularly important for lifelong physical activity. For example, try the following strategies:

> Stretch two pieces of tape or string along the floor that start close together and get farther apart. Have children jump over them, beginning at the narrow end and progressing as far as they can toward the wide end. Children can suggest other ways to cross over, such as leaping or jumping sideways.

> Suggest balancing challenges for the floor or a low beam, such as varying the position of a raised leg. Ask children to suggest other positions. For a child with a visual impairment, use tactile modeling: support a peer in a particular position while the child feels the peer's leg and arm positions to learn how they are arranged.

> Design a balance trail with an interesting arrangement of items that children can stand or walk on. As they become more competent, gradually add more difficult items. For example, begin with wide planks on the floor and taped pathways; later add twisted ropes and low elevated beams.

| Movement Skills | Manipulative skills: Catching, dribbling, volleying, punting, striking with a racket, striking with a long-handled instrument |

Catching (sometimes called fielding) is difficult for young children because it involves visual tracking plus motor coordination. Children may be startled by the approaching object and close their eyes or freeze. Children can dribble, if primitively, with their feet (such as by kicking a pebble along the path) before they have the control to dribble a ball with their hands.

Teaching strategies. The development of these fundamental manipulative skills is critical for children's later participation in sports or games. Because some involve interacting with others (throwing, catching, volleying), their mastery also opens a world of social relationships. Try these strategies to support children's manipulative skills:

> Begin by offering items to catch, volley, and strike that are soft and slow moving, such as scarves, beanbags, and oversized balls. Children who have difficulty standing can practice these skills from a sitting position.

Movement Skills and Verbal Cues

Movement Skill	Verbal Cue Examples
Balancing	"Spread your legs," "extend your arms," "bend in stages for balance," "keep your head and body still"
Stopping	"Allow enough time," "try to slow down gradually," "lean back slightly"
Throwing	"Look at the target," "hold your arm far back," "step forward with the foot opposite your throwing arm"
Skipping	"Lift the knees," "step, hop, and land on one foot and then the other"
Galloping	"Put the same foot forward every time," "begin with a big step forward"
Catching	"Watch the ball," "move to where it is," "bring the ball toward your body and hug it to you"

› Recognize children's strengths and pair them with classmates who could use additional support. For example, a child who uses a wheelchair may have incredible arm strength for throwing and catching. Be alert to who is perceived as the one giving or receiving help within partnerships and strive for all children to have experiences in both roles.

› Build children's skills in sequence. For example, at first children should use their hands to strike stationary objects (such as a balloon placed on a table or batting tee), and then they can progress to striking objects suspended from a string or rope. Next would come dropping the object in front of the child and finally throwing a moving object to the child.

Movement Skills | **Fine motor skills and eye-hand coordination: Cutting, folding, writing**

Some fine motor movements, such as cutting, folding, and writing, require both greater eye-hand coordination and the precise use of small muscles. Although children are highly motivated to master these abilities on their own, many need guidance and encouragement from adults (or peers who have already mastered the skills), particularly if children are perplexed or frustrated in their independent efforts. Provide assistive devices, such as magnifying lenses or large or easy-to-grip writing tools, for children with developmental delays or disabilities. Younger preschool children may also find such aids useful as they develop these skills.

Teaching strategies. Mastering complex fine motor skills depends on children having access to a variety of interesting and gently challenging materials and experiences. Consider the following ideas as you supply the classroom and create opportunities for children to use their small muscles:

> Appeal to children's interests when supplying materials that promote fine motor skills, and place the materials in all areas of the room—for example, scissors (art area), thin rods (block area), magazines (book area), small figures (toy area), eggbeaters (house area), measuring spoons (sand and water table), and chalk (outdoor playground).

> Include a variety of fine motor materials and activities during small and large group times so that children can use their hands and eyes to make and build, transform, investigate cause and effect, and represent things (write, draw, sculpt).

> Integrate children's cultures by inviting families to share card games that they enjoy playing. Teach the rules to children in small group settings, and then add the playing cards to a fine motor or manipulative area in the classroom.

Movement Concepts

Children develop an early awareness of their body and space, which is further enhanced through exploration and adult guidance, especially when adults supply appropriate labels. Understanding concepts like body parts, shapes, and spatial relationships often requires direct instruction or conversation, particularly in multilingual learning environments.

CHILD-GUIDED experiences are especially important for learnings such as:

| Movement Concepts | Understanding how the body moves (self space) and how to move it around others and objects (shared space) |

Children learn primarily through self-discovery about the space they themselves occupy versus the space they share with other people and objects. Preschoolers continue to explore the boundaries between themselves and others, especially when trying out movements they do not yet fully control.

Teaching strategies. Viewing the world from their own perspective, young children naturally test the boundaries of their bodies. Teachers can facilitate this exploration by providing both limited and wide-open spaces for children to navigate. Minimize sharp edges and provide soft surfaces (such as carpeting) so that bumps do not result in injuries.

This area of physical development has both individual and social aspects. Here are some strategies to support this learning:

> Introduce self- and shared-space activities gradually. Begin with large group activities where children stay in their own space and perform movements such as swaying or bending. If needed, provide visual markers, such as carpet squares or tape on the floor, to help children stay in their own area.

> Provide children with opportunities to discover their personal body boundaries; for example, have them move through narrow and wide spaces, or low and high ones. Use existing spaces and create others with furniture, cartons, sheet-draped tables and chairs, beanbag chairs, Hula-Hoops, and the like. For example, challenge children to perform increasingly difficult motor movements while inside a hoop (raising the arms, lifting one leg).

> Ask each child to choose a partner and perform the motions while inside the same hoop together. This activity also presents a good opportunity for children to engage in social problem solving, such as agreeing on rules about how to avoid actions that might hurt the other person.

| Movement Concepts | Understanding speeds |

For preschoolers, speed concepts include slow, moderate or medium, and fast as well as accelerating and decelerating (going faster and slower).

Teaching strategies. Children love to play with speed—the more extreme, the better. They challenge themselves and one another to go faster or be the fastest. However, children also enjoy experimenting with slow movements, especially if they are exaggerated (for example, "verrrry sloooow!"). Teachers have many options for supporting this natural fascination with rates of movement, including these:

> Call children's attention to moving things and comment on their rate of speed. Describe the speed of various activities; for example, say, "Those are slow-cooking cookies. I'm getting hungry" or "The water from Charlie's faucet is coming out faster than the water from Nicola's. Charlie's bucket will fill up sooner." Comment on the speed of objects in the environment and of creatures and events in nature, such as the rate at which animals travel or leaves fall.

> Ask children to name things that move at a slow, fast, or medium speed and demonstrate the corresponding movement. Then copy the children's movements and ask, "Am I moving too fast or too slow?" Follow their suggestions for making a movement faster or slower.

> Invite families to share their favorite songs and various styles of music from their cultural backgrounds. Encourage children to move their bodies to the music while discussing the music's tempo during or after dancing.

| Movement Concepts | Understanding the body, its parts, and the shapes it can take |

At its most basic, body awareness is the relationship a person has with their own body. Children come to understand that their body comprises various parts and that those parts take various shapes, as does their whole body in relation to the world around them (such as whether they move on top of or underneath something). The shapes (or characteristics) that preschool children can create with their bodies and comprehend with minimal adult intervention include round, straight, tall, long, short, small, and big. They can also experiment with and experience the concept of like and unlike (see also Chapters 8 and 9).

Teaching strategies. Young children's fascination with their own bodies offers many natural openings for teachers to support their learning of relational movement concepts, including the following strategies:

> Refer to children's body parts by name in natural conversation; for example, "Lyla, can you show Ian how you kicked the ball by turning your foot to the side?" Read books, tell stories, and sing songs and chants that feature body parts. Use various rhythm instruments, and ask children to represent the sounds with their bodies. For example, they might show a jingly bell sound by wiggling and a gong sound by standing up straight. Describe the sounds, acknowledge children's labels, and provide additional vocabulary words.

> Pose movement challenges and problems to enhance body awareness. This problem-solving approach is more effective than showing or telling. For example, "Can you make your body round like a ball?" and "Can you touch your ear to your shoulder?"

ADULT-GUIDED experiences are especially important for learnings such as:

| Movement Concepts | Understanding where one is in space and how to move through space |

Levels refers to the position of the body or a body part in space—that is, high, middle or medium, and low. Direction concepts include up/down, forward/backward, beside, and sideways. (They also include right/left, but most preschoolers are not yet ready to learn these concepts.) Pathways are straight, curved or circular, and zigzag movements.

Teaching strategies. These spatial awareness areas have important implications for physical education and other domains. As teachers help young children move in different ways through space, they are also creating the foundation for many areas of mathematics (geometry), science (physics), and social studies (geography). Teachers can use the following strategies to help develop these areas of spatial awareness:

> Devise activities in which children move their bodies or manipulate objects in different directions or along different pathways. For example, suggest they crawl across the room forward and backward. Ask them to suggest ways to move forward and backward, up and down, sideways, and in straight or zigzag patterns.

> Whenever possible, reinforce physical literacy and vocabulary in academic areas. For example, discuss vocabulary associated with falling snowflakes while moving like snowflakes, such as *twirling, swirling, falling, floating, spinning.* Support multilingual learners by providing vocabulary in the children's home languages.

> Create pathways that are circular, straight, or zigzag using chalk, tape, traffic cones, large blocks, and other materials. Suggest ways to move in, out of, and around these paths. Include ways for children with developmental delays or disabilities to use these pathways.

> Use naturally occurring situations to supply vocabulary words that describe level and direction as children move about the room and play outdoors.

Movement Concepts	Understanding how to move with different rhythms and how much force to use

The component of time in which adult intervention plays a salient role is rhythm—in particular, helping children develop and keep a steady beat, a core skill in making music (Williams 2018). Force is about how hard or soft to do something (such as clapping hands or hitting a xylophone with a mallet). Control is about how well a child can move their body, whether simple or more complex, and whether they are starting the movement or stopping it. Rhythm and control are part of an awareness of one's efforts.

Teaching strategies. Just as space awareness concepts apply to other domains of learning, effort awareness concepts do as well. For example, they contribute to children's understanding of patterning in math (Geist, Geist, & Kuznik 2012). Try strategies such as these to support children's learning in effort awareness:

> Incorporate different strategies to increase children's familiarity with rhythms. Use poems, chants, and songs with steady beats. Instrumental music is best for this because children are not distracted by the lyrics.

> Emphasize beats with your gestures and words, such as by clapping your hands, tapping your foot, nodding, and accenting syllables.

> Provide children with different experiences that involve weight and force. As they work with objects of different weights, comment on their level of effort: "Lucy carried that heavy box all the way across the room!" Ask children to pretend to carry things of different weights: "Let's imagine we're lifting a hammer over our heads. Now pretend it's a feather from a tiny bird."

Roles that children create with their bodies include copying; leading/following; meeting/parting; passing; mirroring; and acting in unison, alternately, solo, with a partner, or as a group. Children also use their bodies to create relationships with other people and objects; this concept is called locations. Locations includes above/below, near to/far from, over/under, in front of/behind, on/off, together/apart, facing/side by side, around/through, between, and into.

Teaching strategies. Awareness of body relationships has both social and cognitive implications for young children's development. Thoughtful teachers can use the following strategies to support the learning of these movement concepts with those impacts in mind:

> Give children opportunities to manipulate equipment (such as Hula-Hoops, pool noodles, scarves, cartons) to help them discover relationships between themselves and objects. For example, for hoops you might challenge children to walk (or march, hop, or jump) around the outside of their hoop or to lift the hoop up around the outside of their body and then down. Emphasize that as movers, people move in a variety of ways and may use mobility tools to assist them (such as wheelchairs, a cane, or leg braces).

> Encourage children to use their bodies to express emotions such as friendly, sad, mad, frightened, brave, shy, silly, and adventurous. Say, "How do you move your body when you are happy?" or "Let's move to the snack table as though we're tired and sleepy." Ask them to suggest feelings to represent with their bodies.

> Provide vocabulary words to describe the body's position relative to people and objects; for example, "Tawana is moving her finger along the shelf to find a book that begins with the letter *T*" or "Let's stand farther apart while we do 'Hokey Pokey' so everyone has room to *shake it all about!*" For multilingual learners, provide the vocabulary words in their home languages and English.

> Create obstacle courses and associated course rules that encourage children to consider that their bodies move at different speeds depending on their skills, strengths, and objects/obstacles present. For example, create multiple pathways within an obstacle course that allow children to choose which path they would like to take (such as more or less challenging). Or encourage children to practice a motor skill in place (such as hopping on one foot) as they wait for a peer in front of them to navigate through a challenging section of the obstacle course.

Personal Care and Healthy Behavior

Young children enthusiastically seek independence and focus on mastering self-help skills, such as eating and dressing themselves. Other behaviors, such as hygiene, safety, and healthy habits, require more explicit adult guidance.

CHILD-GUIDED experiences are especially important for learnings such as:

| Personal Care and Healthy Behavior | Feeding and dressing oneself |

Children have many opportunities at home and in school to practice self-help skills related to feeding and dressing themselves, including using serving and eating utensils and putting on and taking off outerwear. Although preschool children sometimes turn to adults for help with these skills, and children with developmental delays or disabilities may need additional scaffolding or assistance, most children are likely to learn these skills on their own and/or by watching how others carry them out.

Teaching strategies. The role of adults in the development of these skills is primarily to provide time and appropriate materials. Here are some strategies:

> Let children do things for themselves. Young children benefit from multiple opportunities and ample time to learn to perform these actions on their own. Daily schedules—the time allotted to get ready to go outside, for example—should accommodate this need. Teachers often dress or serve food to children because it is faster or neater, and some families perform these actions for their children because they are a valued part of their culture. If a family prefers that you do the same at school, listen carefully to their wishes and work together to find an acceptable solution. Keep in mind that preschoolers should not be expected to carry out these tasks according to adult standards. Acknowledge when children meet the goals they have set for themselves, such as buttoning a sweater, even if some buttons are misaligned. Correcting or improving on what children do may discourage them from further attempts.

> Preschoolers practice many self-help skills during pretend play, such as preparing food and washing dishes while playing house, writing up "prescriptions" for patients at the veterinarian's, or using various fasteners when they create or put clothes on dolls and stuffed animals. In addition to encouraging this direct practice of skills, provide other tools and activities that help children develop the manual dexterity to zip a jacket or hold a pitcher steady. Examples include beads and string, scissors, staplers, hole punches, sponges, tape, wooden spoons, and brooms. Even turning the pages of a book is practice for separating the top paper towel from the stack.

Without the distractions of technology, children readily engage in vigorous physical play. Children with physical disabilities, too, work hard at moving those parts of their bodies that function partially or fully. Although moving their bodies has the advantage of strengthening their muscles, to the children the satisfaction of moving is benefit enough. The movement is itself a pleasurable sensation, and it creates other sensations—a vision of spinning trees, the wind against one's face. In the process of exercising, young children also learn about their bodies and the many ways they can move. They gain mastery over their muscles, learning to control and coordinate the direction, speed, and precision of their movements.

Teaching strategies. As mentioned previously, there is increasing concern today about the lack of physical exercise in young children's daily experiences. Adults can help to correct this imbalance by providing time and interesting materials that take advantage of children's instinctive desire to play. They can also set an example by exercising themselves. Here are some helpful strategies:

> Provide time and materials for young children to engage in vigorous activity throughout the program day, particularly during large group time and outside time. Preschoolers can also move in safe ways during choice time and transitions. Although running through the room may pose safety hazards, children can glide, twirl, and explore other ways of moving in place or from place to place.

> Join in active exercise with the children yourself. Children pick up healthy behavior by imitating adults. When they see you exercising regularly, preschoolers are more apt to adopt these behaviors, too. In addition, convey a positive attitude. If you express displeasure, as though exercising were a distasteful task forced on you, children may internalize the same negative sentiments. However, if you express pleasure in actively using your body, children will trust the joy they experience in exercise, too.

ADULT-GUIDED experiences are especially important for learnings such as:

Although dirt is visible, most germs are invisible and therefore may seem abstract to young children. The need to wash their hands to free them of disease-causing bacteria or to prevent decay by brushing their teeth is not obvious to preschoolers. On the other hand, most do have firsthand experience with getting sick and can comprehend that concrete behaviors might lessen the need for a trip to the doctor's office. The specific techniques needed to clean one's hands and teeth are not intuitive, however, so this is an area where explicit adult guidance and modeling can help children learn healthy practices. If there is no visible dirt on children's hands, a possible alternative to hand washing is the application of an alcohol-based hand sanitizer for children older than 24 months (Alkon & Shope 2023).

Teaching strategies. Children are less likely to resist cleaning their hands and brushing their teeth if they perceive performing these acts as taking on adult responsibilities, rather than as tasks imposed on them by adults. The following strategies can help preschoolers develop positive attitudes toward these self-care behaviors:

> Model and guide emerging physical skills in self-care. Preschoolers will watch you washing your hands and brushing your teeth with interest and attempt to copy you. Describe your actions in simple terms and demonstrate them as often as needed ("I'm spreading the soap all the way to my wrists"). Don't expect young children to be as thorough in these rituals as you, but do encourage and appreciate their attempts.

> Provide daily opportunities for children to practice hand washing and toothbrushing. Realize that if something more interesting beckons, children's efforts at cleaning themselves may be cursory, so don't pull them away from other activities for these routines. Keep the routines low-key and schedule them after one activity has wound down and before another begins.

Personal Care and Healthy Behavior | **Practicing self-hygiene and interpersonal hygiene**

The kinds of hygienic practices necessary to protect the health of others—using and discarding tissues or covering one's mouth when coughing (or coughing into one's elbow)—appear arbitrary to young children. In essence, they are trusting the adult's word that such practices help to guarantee the health of others. As preschoolers develop empathy (see "Feeling Empathy" on page 78 in Chapter 4), however, they are concerned with doing what is right and helpful for those they care about. Therefore, they will become more motivated to follow such practices, provided adults demonstrate and explain how to do so.

Teaching strategies. Adults encourage young children to follow hygienic practices when they routinely use such behaviors themselves and acknowledge children's efforts, even when less than perfect. Try these ideas:

> Call attention to hygienic practices. Briefly describe how and why you blow your nose into a tissue, throw it away, and wash your hands or cover your mouth with your elbow or a tissue when you cough or sneeze. For example, you might say, "The tissue catches my germs so no one else gets them" or "I'm making sure no one gets sick by covering my cough." At first, children might copy the behavior without understanding why it is important, but gradually, as they begin to comprehend cause-and-effect relationships, they will accept that certain behaviors lead to better health and help protect others.

> Acknowledge when children use hygienic practices. Make simple statements describing when children use tissues appropriately or cover their cough, and link it to the associated benefits for themselves and others. Don't praise them, since the purpose of engaging in such practices is *not* to be rewarded by an adult. Instead show you are aware that they are behaving in a helpful manner. If children forget to use a tissue or cover a cough, don't criticize them; offer a gentle reminder.

| Personal Care and Healthy Behavior | Differentiating between healthy and unhealthy foods |

To many young children, food is simply food. Their preferences are based on taste and texture, not nutrition or health. Children therefore depend on adults to distinguish which foods are good for them to eat. Fortunately, preschoolers' interest in classification makes them as curious about sorting food into "healthy" and "not healthy" groups as they are about sorting blocks by color or toy vehicles by type. The US Department of Agriculture (USDA) publishes materials (such as the illustrated MyPlate to teach the five food groups and the MyPlate Champion pledge and certificate) and online resources, games, and applications (such as Team Nutrition MyPlate eBooks and Breakfast Around the World) that can help teachers and families introduce simple concepts about good nutrition (USDA, n.d.).

Teaching strategies. As adults who have attempted to change their own eating habits know, it takes time and vigilance to make healthy eating a routine part of the day. The following ideas will help both teachers and children approach food as a health-promoting option that can be shared and enjoyed in a relaxed, inclusive social atmosphere full of learning opportunities suitable to foster growth:

> Integrate nutritious food into the daily routine. If your program provides food, work with the individuals who are responsible for planning and purchasing it to select a variety of healthy options that meet USDA guidelines for young children, emphasizing vegetables, fruits, whole grains, and low-fat dairy and protein. If the families provide their children food to eat at the program, share ideas for healthy food options.

> Plan small group times in which children can explore healthy foods and describe and discuss their properties, including appearance, sound, smell, feel, and taste. Provide foods children are familiar with from their cultures and offer some new ones to try. Also, cook simple recipes with children and find ways for them to assist with food preparation.

> Serve new or unfamiliar food at the same time as food the children enjoy in order to create a more familiar context and promote exploring new tastes. Do not pressure children into trying food. Let children make their own choices based on the food provided to them. They may need to see the food served multiple times before wanting to try it.

> Label foods as more or less healthy. This makes children more aware of what they are eating and its effect on their bodies ("Candy and oranges are both sweet, but oranges are healthier for our bodies. All of us need the right amounts of food and the right balance to help our

bodies feel good"). Verbal labels also increase vocabulary and classification skills (words such as *vitamins* and categories such "good for you" and "not good for you"). Preschoolers will start to apply the words they hear to identify and sort foods on their own and will begin to reflect on the implications of their choices.

Personal Care and Healthy Behavior	Following safety procedures

Most health and safety rules are imposed by licensing agencies or by adults following guidelines or applying common sense. However, there are some practices that children can appreciate as directly applying to them because they have witnessed, or even experienced, the consequences of not following them. These include such procedures as not walking in front of a moving swing or walking around a spill until it is cleaned up.

The more preschoolers develop a sense of cause and effect, they more they can see the need for certain rules. Also, as they form mental images of the past and future, children can better understand the reasons behind these procedures. They may even offer their own ideas about how to improve or enforce them!

Teaching strategies. Because the logic behind many safety policies is not self-evident, young children depend on adults to explain, demonstrate, and gently enforce them. Often a simple explanation or calm reminder is enough to encourage compliance. The following strategies will help teachers create a safe classroom while not overly restricting children's explorations:

> Model safety procedures yourself. However, periodically ask yourself if a safety rule is necessary or if it exists to reassure or simplify things for adults. Unnecessary policies might unduly restrict children's explorations. For example, rather than having a safety rule forbidding the use of water in the house area, have a conversation with the children to explain your concerns and problem-solve with them ways to minimize or wipe up spills. Children are more likely to follow rules when they discuss and participate in setting guidelines.

> Acknowledge when children follow safe practices. Encourage rather than praise (or criticize) their efforts. Children will become more reflective about their behavior when you describe it and casually mention its benefits ("Antonio, you walked around the edge of the playground instead of in front of the swing so that you wouldn't be hit by it").

> Provide picture cues—preferably using photos of the children in your program—as reminders of safety rules and procedures for children who may need visual reminders. Add phonetically spelled phrases in children's home languages so that teachers, substitute teachers, or visitors can verbalize safety cues in the appropriate language.

> Encourage children to remind one another about safety procedures. Once children have learned to follow safety policies themselves, they are often eager to remind their peers to obey them, too. Don't be overly concerned about children being tattletales. In most instances, being reminded by a peer is more effective than being reminded by an adult.

● ● ●

Facilitating children's development of physical skills and healthy behaviors during the preschool years is essential to forming healthy habits that may last a lifetime. Movement experiences and health awareness can also enhance learning in other domains. Teachers play a vital role in these accomplishments by arranging and equipping the learning environment, scheduling physical education activities in addition to time for children's self-directed play, offering physical challenges, providing concrete cues to help children develop physical knowledge and skills, modeling and remarking on healthy behaviors, and offering daily opportunities to exercise and eat healthy foods.

For Further Consideration

1. Think about the kinds of physical activity you enjoyed as a child. How can you plan ways to include similar activities in your early childhood program daily? What kinds of physical exercise do the children in your program (or programs you have observed) seem to enjoy? How can you create opportunities for them to build on their interest and pleasure in such movements? What support do you need to allow yourself to engage with children in physical activity?

2. What role can and should early childhood education play in preventing obesity, inactivity, and other physical conditions that predispose children to later health and related problems?

3. What advocacy and practical roles can early childhood educators play to promote gross motor activity in neighborhoods where children do not have access to safe outdoor play areas? What role can or should the early childhood community play in bringing fresh, healthy foods to areas where there is a lack, and in encouraging healthier eating options?

Learning Objectives

1. To design a language-rich classroom that invites children to talk with each other, share ideas through speaking or drawing, and build connections

2. To describe characteristics of learning environments that foster a love of and encourage development in language and literacy, including for multilingual learners and children with developmental delays or disabilities

3. To plan ways and identify materials for supporting early literacy, including teaching vocabulary, reading comprehension, letters and sounds, and writing

4. To identify ways to integrate language and literacy learning throughout the curriculum

5. To identify ways to honor all the languages and literacies that children bring to the early learning setting

CHAPTER 6

Language and Literacy

Susan Bennett-Armistead

The preschoolers are going for a walk around the block. As they get ready to leave, their teacher, Miss Genevieve, leads them in a rhyming game about what they might see, using the children's first names.

"Walker, walker, what will you see? Maybe a house. Maybe a tree. I'm a walker. My name is [child's first name, such as Benny]. I think that I will see a [rhyming word, such as *penny*]."

Kai says he will see "the sky," Wren thinks she will see "men," and Zayn comes up with "train."

After each child responds, Miss Genevieve makes a comment such as "Yes, *sky* rhymes with *Kai.*" Miss Genevieve offers "Benevieve," and everyone laughs, acknowledging that the made-up word does rhyme with her name.

When Sophie says she will see a "dog," Miss Genevieve does not correct her but instead says, "I wonder if you'll see something else that rhymes with Sophie." When she replies uncertainly, "Sun?" Miss Genevieve acknowledges that *sun* begins with the same sound as Sophie's name and asks the other children for words that rhyme with *Sophie.* Zayn, whose older sister's soccer team recently won a championship, shouts, "Trophy!"

Elena, whose English language skills are developed enough to understand the opening rhyme (*see* and *tree*) and the basic idea of the chant, nevertheless has trouble thinking of an English word that rhymes with her name. Miss Genevieve says, "En español" to encourage her. Elena's face brightens, and she says, "Reina!" Miss Genevieve tells the class, "*Reina* is the Spanish word for *queen. Elena* and *reina* end with the same word part. They rhyme."

Imagine a typical "person on the street" interview. A reporter holding a microphone walks up to a person and asks, "What is literacy?" The person might think for a minute and say, "Reading." The reporter nods, thanks them, and moves on to the next person. That person also says, "Reading." For an hour, the reporter hears "reading" and occasionally "reading and writing." Indeed most people think literacy is reading and writing. The definition has changed over time, however. It used to be that a person was considered literate if they could just make a mark for their name on a document. To be considered literate today, a person must possess more complex skills. A person who believes that literacy is just reading and writing may also believe that literacy doesn't start until age 5 or 6—and they may miss valuable opportunities to support the language and literacy skills that will lead to literacy success for children.

The National Council of Teachers of English offers a definition of literacy that includes reading, writing, listening, speaking, and creating in order to communicate with and understand one's world (Peterson 2020). Literacy involves both receptive skills, such as reading, listening, and gaining comprehension from viewing pictures, and expressive skills, such as writing, speaking, and creating visual information like drawings or charts. The process of becoming literate begins very early. In fact, babies are born able to respond to their mother's voice apart from other voices. That means that they have been processing the human voice in utero—a receptive skill—for some time. In time, they will respond with babbling of their own, an expressive skill. If literacy starts at or before birth, so too should adults' intentional support of literacy.

Language and literacy are often talked about as if they are the same thing, and they do have a very close and dependent relationship. Language is the foundation for effective communication, enabling children to express their thoughts, needs, emotions, and ideas and comprehend others' expression of these things. It also fosters social interaction and lays the groundwork for successful relationships. Literacy encompasses not only the ability to read and write but also a range of other skills, including comprehension, critical thinking, and creativity. Proficient literacy skills empower children to navigate the complexities of the modern world, opening doors to knowledge, information, and opportunities. Together, language and literacy development play a crucial role in shaping young children's cognitive and social development, creating a strong educational foundation by enhancing academic success, supporting overall well-being, fostering a love for learning, and preparing children for a lifetime of meaningful engagement with the world around them.

Knowledge of language and how it works is divided into five dimensions: phonological knowledge, syntactic knowledge, semantic knowledge, morphological knowledge, and pragmatic knowledge. As you work with children, analyzing how they use and understand language and, eventually, literacy will enable you to better assist them along the developmental continuum of language knowledge.

Phonological knowledge is the knowledge of the sounds that make up one's language. English has about 44 sounds, or phonemes, that make up spoken words. Being able to hear, discriminate, and produce those sounds is a critical part of learning to listen and speak. Later, those skills will be the basis of decoding words when reading.

Syntactic knowledge is the understanding of how word order can affect the meaning of an utterance. Consider this sentence: *The green and purple, loud, big dragon shot fire from its mouth.* It likely doesn't sound right to you. Although the sentence is technically correct, its adjectives are not in the expected order. Contrast it with this version: *The big, loud, purple and green dragon shot fire from its mouth.* It's unlikely that anyone ever explained to you that size comes before color in a lineup of adjectives, but speakers of English learn over time that that is the expected convention. Syntactic knowledge is also how English speakers know the difference between a question and a statement. "Where did Daddy go?" is different from "Go, Daddy!" Providing rich oral language and reading aloud soak children in the rules of a language without the need to talk about those rules.

Semantic knowledge is the understanding that words have meaning and which words mean what. For example, saying the word *cat* conjures a mental image of a furry mammal with whiskers and pointy ears. The word *cat* isn't an actual cat, but when you hear it, you know it represents a real feline. Similarly, the word *cat* does *not* represent a furry mammal that barks. There is a different word for that animal, *dog.* Knowing which word is matched to which thing is semantic knowledge. Building children's vocabularies is an important part of developing their ability to effectively communicate and understand when they are spoken or read to. When they are readers themselves, they will have better comprehension if they understand more words.

Morphological knowledge is the understanding that changing the structural components of a word can also change its meaning. For example, adding an *s* to *boat* turns one boat into multiple boats. Adding the prefix *un-* to *dress* turns it into *undress,* which is the opposite of the original word. This knowledge helps learners hear or read unfamiliar words and break them apart to better understand their meaning, a critical component of comprehension.

Finally, *pragmatic knowledge* is the understanding that language is used in different ways in different circumstances. For example, people talk with their friends differently than they might talk with a judge or a supervisor. With friends they use informal language. They might make eye contact with them more often, stand closer to them when talking, and use gestures in different ways. Their volume and tone may be more varied and less reserved. Consider the baby who is pretending to talk on a phone. They play with tone and gestures that they have heard and seen adults using. "Ba, ba, ba, ba, ba?" and "Ba, ba, ba, ba, ba!" sound completely different simply by

raising the tone at the end of the utterance. Pragmatic knowledge also helps a person to speak French to their French-speaking grandma and German to their German-speaking grandpa. Pragmatics can be applied to written language as well. A book that starts with "Once upon a time . . ." indicates a certain type of story. Children learn this by being exposed to many genres of written material and by talking with and to knowledgeable adults.

Thus, language and learning about it is the twin to literacy. Focusing on developing children's awareness of language and how it works will translate well into conventional reading and writing later, but supporting language skills is also important *right now* for the child learning to communicate their needs, interests, and ideas.

For many years, educators talked about oral language as part of reading readiness; children did not receive reading instruction until first grade. But more recently, early education has adopted the idea of emergent literacy. In this view, literacy is not an all-or-nothing skill acquisition (that is, it does not begin with the introduction of the alphabet) but rather a gradual progression that begins in infancy with hearing language, having "conversations" with others, and being exposed to books. The preschool years can build on early experiences to prepare young children for the next steps. Literacy learning continues through the formal reading and writing instruction of elementary school. Although Snow, Burns, and Griffin (1998) caution against replicating in preschool the formal instruction of later grades, they do note that while providing "optimal support for cognitive, language, and social development . . . ample attention should be paid to skills that are known to predict future reading achievement, especially those for which a causal role has been demonstrated" (5).

Because listening, speaking, reading, and writing are all instrumental in children's development of language and literacy skills, intentional teachers prioritize frequent opportunities for children to engage in each. Strategies for fostering children's competencies in these four areas appear in "Fitting the Learning Experience to the Learning Objective" later in this chapter, where they are considered separately as child-guided and adult-guided experiences.

Young Children's Development in Language and Literacy

Reading research has yielded useful information about how language and literacy develop, from which the following are summarized (Collins & Schickedanz 2024; Ranweiler 2004):

> Language and literacy are connected from infancy onward. Speaking, listening, reading, and writing develop concurrently rather than sequentially.

> Differences between children's home languages and cultures and those of the program can affect children's language and literacy development. It is essential that educators understand language development in monolingual and multilingual learners and seek to "provide experiences that build on a child's funds of knowledge and are culturally and linguistically responsive" (NAEYC 2020, 23).

> Children differ in their rate of learning. Some children pick up literacy skills easily and quickly; others need more explicit help and time.

> Some language and literacy learning is incidental. It arises naturally during play and other everyday experiences. Other learning depends on the explicit instruction that occurs during formal teaching. Thus, children actively construct their own knowledge, but they also need support from adults to further their development.

> Children acquire language and literacy as they interact with others, learning to talk, read, and write because they are social beings. They want to communicate with adults and peers at home, school, and other familiar places.

> Children learn best when instruction is relevant and meaningful to them. When children can apply language and literacy to their everyday interests and activities, that learning will be genuine, deep, and lasting.

> Language and literacy learning happens through activities children initiate, such as engaging in dramatic play, exploring print materials, and using inventive writing. It also happens through instruction such as book reading, letter identification practice, and performing or composing songs and poems using alliteration and rhyming.

To be successful in the world, children need to learn to communicate their thoughts, needs, and ideas. Although young infants do express their basic needs and emotions—quite effectively!—through cries and other early vocalizations, they also begin very early to communicate their more intangible thoughts. At the earliest stages of life, they catalog the sounds of their language and learn to make those sounds more than sounds that are not part of their language. They discover that those sounds mean something and that the same sounds over and over mean the same thing over and over. Eventually children realize that those sounds strung together can mean different things when strung together in different ways. They start to play with the sounds and listen carefully when others make the sounds. They memorize the strings of sounds and start to use them. They slowly develop the understanding of words. *Dog* stands for that big, fluffy thing that leans over the side of the crib, breathes loudly, and sometimes makes a big noise. Children might learn that the sound string /mama/ represents the responsive person who snuggles and feeds them. Those sound strings are stand-ins for the actual thing in the real world. This is the earliest understanding of representation.

Representation also exists in the written word. As noted previously, the word *cat* isn't furry and doesn't say "meow," but when you see it in print, you have some mental representation that matches the word. In this way, language and literacy share a code and a way of representing the world as well as thoughts.

In 2009, researchers looked across more than 300 research studies on early literacy for the National Early Literacy Panel report. This foundational report, which is still relevant today, found that six variables linked to literacy predicted the later success of children as readers and writers:

1. Expressive and receptive oral language development

2. Understanding of the alphabetic code

3. Phonemic awareness and the larger category of phonological awareness

4. Use of invented spelling (understanding and representing the letter-sound connections, even if not correctly spelled)

5. Print knowledge, including awareness of environmental print

6. Other skills such as rapid word naming of letters and numbers, name writing, and visual perception abilities (drawn from a summary of the 2009 NELP report in Morrow, Dougherty, & Tracey 2019)

The early childhood community has had a difficult time deciding what to do with this information. Some have interpreted the value of rapid word naming to mean teachers should be using flashcards to speed young learners along. Others have jumped on the chance to use worksheets to reinforce concepts. But as mentioned previously, children learn best when concepts are relevant to them. All six variables are learned best through play, multiple exposures that are authentic and engaging, and experiences that are meaningful and interesting to children. In particular, children recall word meanings best when adults provide an explanation of the word in context, repeat as needed, and give a deep-enough explanation for the learner to understand the concept and make the word relevant. In short, children learn most effectively when concepts are repeated, relevant, and real.

Consider the vignette with Miss Genevieve at the opening of this chapter. It's an excellent example of playing with words and the sounds of language, all while engaging children in personally meaningful language use. There is no word more important to a child than their own name. Miss Genevieve wisely crafted an activity to play with the sounds of children's names while they were already engaging in a compelling activity (going for a walk). Because the game used each child's name, each child could be successful. When there was a moment that Sophie seemed uncertain, Miss Genevieve supported her and invited others to do the same. Miss Genevieve, whose own name did not lend itself to rhyming with a real word, cheerfully modeled a nonsense word that *did* rhyme, and she could have done the same for a child in the same situation if needed. The activity was playful, was relevant, and offered repeated examples of the concept of rhyming.

Joyful, play-based language experiences like these create a positive foundation for literacy, making learning enjoyable and fostering a love for words and language. To become literate, young children must see reading and writing as not only useful but also pleasurable. Adults play a key role in promoting this positive attitude, particularly through the use of guided play (Hassinger-Das, Hirsh-Pasek, & Golinkoff 2017).

Teaching and Learning in Language and Literacy

As with all curriculum areas, a balance of child-guided and adult-guided experiences is essential in early language and literacy development, and the division between the two is not well-defined. Even though children have language and literacy experiences and acquire some literacy skills on their own, support and intentional instruction from thoughtful adults who understand the necessary elements for literacy learning and can support children in meeting learning goals are critical to sustain the children's motivation and supply essential information.

NAEYC's professional standards and competencies (2019c) apply research findings to create a list of expectations for teachers, including having a deep knowledge of academic disciplines, understanding how children learn in each discipline, and using effective methods of teaching content. These standards note that to help young children gain academic knowledge, including the skills necessary to become readers and writers, educators engage in genuine, reciprocal conversations with children; foster oral language and communication skills; ask questions that probe and stimulate children's thinking, understanding, and theory building; and provide early literacy experiences both in English and in children's home languages.

Even child-guided experiences offer opportunities for teachers to observe and consider ways they might scaffold children's learning while still honoring child choice and discovery. An example of this might be children playing together in a dramatic play area set up to be a fire station. Children are choosing how to use the provided materials, and a nearby adult might augment the play by modeling how to use a map to drive to the scene of the emergency. The teacher can also add vocabulary to the play by pointing out some of the following: "Make sure to wear your helmet! Did you jump into your turnout gear?," "Someone needs to hook up the hose!," or "Did the dispatcher give you the address of the fire?" By using these words while playing with the children, teachers help children see the connection between the language and the materials around them. The importance of the words is underscored by their use in advancing the play.

Language, Literacy, and Intentional Use of Digital Tools

Using digital tools, such as touch-screen tablets, intentionally in early childhood settings allows teachers to support children's language and literacy development while balancing their use with play and other real, hands-on experiences. Effective integration of technology requires planning experiences that are interactive, purposeful, and enhance learning outcomes (Armstrong & Moses 2023). For example, along with providing high-quality print books in different genres, teachers can support children's literacy skills by using ebooks and interactive storytelling apps that let children see themselves and their experiences represented in media, fostering connection and engagement.

Digital tools should complement—not replace—hands-on activities, providing opportunities for children to create, narrate, express themselves, and collaborate with each other. By considering the purpose of a particular technology experience and teaching children ways to use the technology for storytelling, drawing, writing, and documenting what they have created, teachers support self-expression and language development while building an informed awareness of use. Balancing screens with active play helps children learn to engage thoughtfully with technology and offers multimodal communication.

Making practical and developmentally appropriate technology choices may require a shift in teachers' perspectives to determine, as NAEYC's position statement notes, how "technology and interactive media can help to support developmentally appropriate practice" in educators' own settings so "the uses of technology and media by children are active, hands-on, engaging, and empowering . . . [the uses] become normal and transparent—the child or the educator is focused on the activity or exploration itself, not the technology" (2020, 13).

Through careful selection, intentional use, and scaffolding of high-quality, age-appropriate devices and media, teachers can make technology a valuable component of language and literacy learning, fostering critical thinking, creativity, and collaboration.

Language-Rich Communication

This section is adapted, by permission, from Schmidtke 2022b.

To most effectively promote children's language and literacy development, it is critical to view the processes of speaking, listening, reading, and writing as interconnected, dependent, and supportive of one another. This foundational understanding demonstrates the value of promoting children's engagement in language-rich communication across all aspects of children's daily life, including both informal (social conversation) and formal (academic discussion) (Cavanaugh et al. 2017).

The value of children's interactions with teachers and peers that include opportunities for both expressive and receptive language is significant for young children. Children's learning is enhanced through conversational turn-taking, even before they have developed enough words to fully engage in a verbal back-and-forth exchange. Frequent, sustained back-and-forth exchanges (both social and academic) support children's brain development and academic achievement (Flynn 2016; Romeo et al. 2018). Teachers promote language by modeling it, providing varied and frequent opportunities for children to express themselves verbally, offering encouragement for language attempts, uncovering shared and unique experiences in conversations, restating and expanding on what children say, and asking responsive questions that encourage children to think more deeply.

Teachers also support variations in storytelling, such as stories about themselves, stories that are unconnected to the current time or place, or stories that are completely made up with fictional or fantastic characters (Flynn 2016). Storytelling offers rich opportunities for language learning:

> When children engage in storytelling, they actively construct narratives to express their ideas. Through storytelling, children learn to organize their thoughts, articulate ideas, and develop a sense of narrative structure. They begin to understand character development, plot progression, and story elements—essential components of reading and writing stories. (Joseph 2024, 10)

By supporting children's storytelling, teachers also reinforce the important role that storytelling plays in many cultures. Indeed, many cultures use oral storytelling and the sharing of poetry and story songs more than they use books with young children. It is a joyful, culturally significant activity where children and adults work together. Incorporating these practices in the classroom can be an important validation for children and families.

Children benefit from opportunities to deepen understanding of academic content through dialogue, including increasingly complex academic vocabulary. For multilingual learners, these conversations are especially valuable. In literacy-focused conversations, educators can discuss story elements, ask children to predict what happens next, and encourage them to summarize key points. This approach helps children build both language and comprehension skills. In math-focused conversations, teachers might support children's ability to compare, gather information, and understand basic math concepts. Science-focused conversations support children's observation, planning, and scientific inquiry skills. Social-focused conversations support children's abilities to communicate about past experiences, thoughts, feelings, desires, and motivations (Curenton 2016). Through intentional support in these areas, educators can create a rich linguistic environment that fosters the academic growth of all children, including multilingual learners.

Beyond the Word Count: Rethinking Early Language Development

In their examination of the early language environments of young children from different socioeconomic backgrounds, researchers Hart and Risley (1995) found that by the time the children entered preschool at age 4, children from low-income households had heard roughly 13 million words, and those from higher-income households had been exposed to 45 million. The findings from this study became widely known in the early childhood field as the "30-million word gap," and they have had a profound impact on the field of early childhood education, influencing policies and programs aimed at closing the gap.

On the positive side, this study led to increased emphasis on early language and literacy interventions, such as the promotion of book reading and language-rich interactions in early childhood settings. However, the research has also been heavily criticized for promoting a deficit-based view of children from low-income households that highlights the perceived deficiencies of low-income and families of color rather than recognizing their strengths and the values they hold for the way language is used.

Subsequent studies have failed to validate that there is a significant gap in the number of words heard by children from families with low income compared to those from families with high income (Raz & Beatty 2018). These studies point out that it is language directed *to* children (rather than overheard speech as investigated in the original study) that is crucial for language development. Another finding is that children benefit more from interactions where language is tailored to their interests, providing contextual cues that help them link words to their concrete examples and real-world experiences (Golinkoff et al. 2018). This suggests that it is the quality of the talk, rather than the quantity, that is crucial, emphasizing the need for tailored, engaging interactions with children.

It is vital to move away from a deficit-based view of children and families and instead focus on their strengths, including the rich language experiences in their homes. Families have different ways of using language based on their own personal and cultural experiences and practices, and intentional teachers value and seek ways to use these experiences to help all children achieve their highest potential.

Conversations with Multilingual Learners

This section is adapted from Chapman de Sousa 2019.

Having conversations with children who are multilingual learners is an essential skill for early childhood educators. Such engagement has implications for multilingual children's developing identities as valued and knowledgeable members of their communities as well as for their language learning. Conversations provide children with models for using language and responsive communication and offer teachers frequent opportunities to check for comprehension. Conversations also make topics relevant to multilingual learners and potentially motivate them to practice using their new language just beyond their independent level.

In small or large group activities, notice how multilingual learners respond when they sit in different places in relation to you. Some may contribute more to the conversation when they are right next to you. Other children may prefer direct eye contact from you to cue them to contribute, so having them across from you may promote their participation. Factors such as culture, family practices, and personal preferences also influence how children engage in conversation. This is a great time to be a teacher-researcher and notice ways you can adjust your position in relation to children to encourage their engagement.

Even if you do not speak the home languages of children in your program, you can still include their languages in conversations. Get help from family members by inviting them to teach you and the class important words; also ask them for recommendations on literature and songs written and recorded in their languages. In addition, remember that it is always possible to respond to children's communications, regardless of whether or not you speak the same language. You can do so with body language and other ways, such as using pictures and objects. Responding to children's multilingual contributions sends the message that diversity is valued in your classroom. It shows multilingual children that they have important ideas and questions to contribute, and that all forms of communication are of value.

Connecting Teaching to Children's Lives

Ms. Bernice is exploring a transportation unit with her mixed-age preschool class. All of the children are multilingual learners, with Spanish as their home language. In addition to small group lessons and read-alouds related to transportation, Ms. Bernice wants to visibly incorporate families' experiences into the unit. She asks families to audio or video record themselves narrating a short story (in Spanish) about a traveling experience they had with their children and to share a poster or collection of photos related to the story.

The responses, which come in via the class communication app, are swift and enthusiastic. As families send in their stories, Ms. Bernice creates QR codes for their recordings and videos, which she attaches to the collages and posters the families created. She hangs these at eye level in the library area so that children can use the class tablet to scan the QR codes and share the stories with each other. The children enjoy having their families featured in the classroom virtually, and they revisit the artifacts several times a day.

Ms. Bernice watches the videos and listens to the recordings alongside the children, asking them follow-up questions and sharing stories about her own family's travels. Lupe, a 4-year-old who is often reluctant to speak in group settings, holds up the picture collage she made with her mother. She tells Ms. Bernice, "Buelo driving the car, and I was in the car, and I went to the mountain, and I went to the bear, and I went to the unicorns, and Buelo bought me a bicycle, and the end." As Ms. Bernice asks Lupe more about her trip, they continue to chat about her mode of transportation (a car) and how it differs from the buses, planes, and boats featured in other children's stories.

Ms. Bernice exemplifies intentionality as a culturally responsive teacher by centering the voices and experiences of families in her curriculum. By inviting families to share their travel stories in their home language, she not only honors their cultural identities but also fosters a strong home-school connection. The integration of family-created artifacts, QR codes, and multimedia into the classroom environment gives children the opportunity to see themselves and their loved ones reflected in their learning. Ms. Bernice actively engages with the children by listening to their stories, asking meaningful questions, and connecting their personal narratives to broader learning concepts, creating a welcoming and inclusive space where all children feel valued and confident in sharing their ideas.

Besides drawing on research examining the role of oral storytelling for Latino/a families (Reese 2012), these recorded stories allow Ms. Bernice to intentionally embed family experiences within the classroom (Melzi, Schick, & Scarola 2019). Ms. Bernice's use of technology enables her to get to know families asynchronously and to incorporate their cultures, languages, and experiences into an ongoing topic of study that all the children are interested in. She is able to share this topic with families, bring in relevant family stories about it, provide an opportunity for children to see their families reflected in the learning space, and build content knowledge by relating new ideas to children's actual lives. These strategies, which build on families' home literacy assets and practices, are key for working with multilingual learners as well as engaging families in reciprocal ways.

Adapted from Figueras-Daniel & Vasquez 2024

Fitting the Learning Experience to the Learning Objective

The following discussion—grouped according to skills in language (listening and speaking), reading, and writing—can help educators sort out the "what" and "how to" in early literacy instruction and learning. Within each of the three areas, the sample teaching strategies are grouped according to knowledge and skills gained primarily through child-guided or adult-guided experiences, but this is not a rigid division. Careful attention to children's emerging abilities will help you decide which approach works best for each child at any given time.

Listening and Speaking

Intentional teachers prioritize opportunities for children to speak and listen because they understand that reading and writing skills are built on the foundation of oral language. Multilingual learning is included in the child-guided category because multilingual learners gain a great deal from their monolingual English-speaking peers. However, adults are also vitally important, for example, in helping multilingual learners develop English vocabulary and in facilitating communication between monolingual children and multilingual learners when gestures and context do not suffice. Furthermore, adults are critical in encouraging multilingual learners to maintain their home language at the same time they are acquiring proficiency in English (NASEM 2017). One way to do this is to make an effort to learn at least a few words of the child's home language. Labeling the classroom with multiple languages can also help the adults and children learn more than one language together.

Of the key knowledge and skills in the area of listening and speaking, child-guided experiences may be particularly important for the following:

> Practicing conversational skills

> Promoting multilingual learning

> Enhancing sound awareness and production

Adult-guided experiences seem especially significant for the following:

> Promoting phonological awareness

> Expanding vocabulary

> Gaining knowledge of narrative/comprehension

CHILD-GUIDED experiences are especially important for learnings such as:

| Listening and Speaking | Practicing conversational skills |

Conversation is the verbal exchange of information, observations, thoughts, and feelings. Having a conversation means using the give and take of language for social intercourse. Conversational skills comprise listening (especially active, engaged listening), initiating talking with adults and peers, and responding appropriately to the talk of others.

Teaching strategies. The most important thing to remember about conversation is that it requires at least two participants. Patience and silence are virtues when you want to encourage preschoolers to express themselves. Here are some strategies:

> Model active listening as well as talking with children. Remind yourself not to take over conversations. Preschoolers are not always fluent in their speech. Wait patiently while they frame and express their thoughts. Get down on their level, make eye contact, pause to listen, repeat or clarify what they say, summarize their thoughts, and accept and expand on their ideas.

> Model standard language (vocabulary and pronunciation, grammar and syntax). Use more complex sentences as children's verbal skills increase.

> Create natural opportunities for conversations throughout the day, such as during meals and snacks as well as greetings and departures. Use these times to talk with children about their interests.

> Play games that use verbal directions, such as Simon Says, to encourage children's listening. The gestures that accompany the verbal directions are especially helpful for multilingual learners to understand body and action vocabulary words.

> Offer times of the day for turn-and-talk moments, when children sit knee to knee and talk with another child about what they think about something. During book reading, this could be "What do you think will happen next? I think _____."

> Expand children's verbalizations. For example, if a preschooler says, "More juice," you might say, "You'd like me to put more juice in the pitcher." Expanding a one- or two-word statement into a short sentence is especially valuable for multilingual learners as it builds on their language in context and is thus easier to understand.

> Encourage children to talk to one another. Plan group activities that promote collaboration. Support peer conversations by redirecting children's attention to one another, restating the topic of the conversation, and suggesting they share ideas. Support dramatic play among children. The desire to join in such play is a strong motivator for multilingual learners to communicate in a way that their peers can understand.

> Create situations in which children will have to talk to each other to solve a problem. For example, rather than having three paint pots of the same colors on each side of an easel, place two colors on one side and two different colors on the other. If a child would like to use the paint from the other side, they need to ask their peer when they can use it. This is best supported by having an adult nearby to offer scripts for asking to share when they notice a child looking at their peer's paints. For example, an adult can say to Keisha, "It looks like you'd like to try another color. You can say to Sasha, 'Sasha, may I use the yellow?'" The adult then supports the trade by asking Sasha if there is a color on Keisha's side that she would like to use and modeling that ask as well. Planned conflict can provoke language use for problem solving but should be scaffolded like any other new skill in the classroom.

> Use information talk to describe what children are doing when playing, and invite their comments. For example, say, "Kanye, you used lots of blue in your painting. I wonder how you made these swirly marks at the top." For multilingual learners, make simple informational statements in both their home language and English.

> Engage children in decontextualized talk. Converse about objects, people, and events that, while familiar to children, are not immediately present or occurring. Talking about things that children cannot simply show you or point to encourages them to use more language. (Think of information talk as "here and now" and decontextualized talk as "there and then.")

> Create opportunities for children with developmental delays or disabilities to use their mode of communication with you and with their peers. For example, a child might use a picture exchange system (PECS; a system of pictures that allows for a conversation, requests, and responses); an augmentative and alternative communication device; or sign language. Facilitate communication between a child using a system and their peers. Peers are curious about such alternative communication modes. Invite their questions and answer them directly. Teach peers that the device or system is not a toy but a tool the child uses to communicate with them.

> Encourage children to use their voice instead of relying on gestures. Humor is a good way to get them to talk or point without forcing them to do so. Consider this example:

> **Child:** (*Hands adult a book.*)
>
> **Adult:** You have a book! What should we do with it?
>
> **Child:** (*Looks at the book.*)
>
> **Adult:** (*Replies playfully.*) Hmm, should we put it in the aquarium for the fish? (*Points to the nearby fish tank.*)
>
> **Child:** (*Giggles.*)
>
> **Adult:** Or maybe we should wear it as a hat? (*Places the book on their head.*)
>
> **Child:** (*Laughs and shakes their head.*)
>
> **Adult:** No? Okay, what do you think we should do with the book?
>
> **Child:** Read me. (*Points to self.*)
>
> **Adult:** Ah, you want me to read the book with you! Let's find a cozy spot to read together.

In this exchange, the child only achieves the desired result by speaking. Also, the teacher uses this as an opportunity to expand the child's two words ("Read me") into two sentences that the child easily understands.

> Use questions appropriately and not to excess. Bombarding children with questions tends to end dialogue, whereas making comments often invites further talk. When you do use questions, make them applicable to what the child is focused on, and ask open-ended questions to invite thoughtful and expanded answers (for example, ask, "How will you make your soup?"). (See "Questions and Comments That Open—or Close Down—Thought" on page 138.) Avoid questions that have a single or brief correct answer (for example, do not ask "Will you put beans in your soup?").

> Talk to parents and coworkers in the presence of children. Hearing adult conversations helps children expand their own vocabularies and syntax.

Questions and Comments That Open—or Close Down—Thought

Convergent or close-ended questions, to which the adult already knows the answers, tend to discourage children from expanding on their answers. Divergent or open-ended questions and comments, used when adults want to learn what children think, are more likely to open up conversations. The following are examples of questions and comments that encourage children to think and to share what they are thinking and that also permit adults to introduce new vocabulary words.

Encourage children to think, reason, and use expanded language:

"How can you tell?"

"What do you think made that happen?"

"Can you tell me how you did/made that?"

"I wonder what would happen if . . .?"

"What does this remind you of?"

Introduce vocabulary words and concepts:

"How can we move the truck [or ball or sand] *without* using our hands?"

"I love pumpkin seeds because they are *flat*, have *pointed* ends, and after I bake them in the oven, they're *crunchy*. What else do you notice about them?"

"I wonder how those rocks got to the bottom of the bucket?"

"What things in the science area [or house area or block area] are *heavy*? Which do you think is the *heaviest*? How could we find out?"

When multilingual learners answer your open-ended questions with sentences you don't understand, appreciate the fact that they are practicing their oral language even if you don't know everything they are saying. By keeping a recording device handy, you can capture these episodes of expanded language and find a parent or colleague to translate them for the child's portfolio.

Building on children's home languages is important for a number of reasons, one of which is that skills developed in the home language often transfer to English. The stages of language development for multilingual learners can vary widely, depending on factors like the strength of their first language and its transferability to the second language. These stages include the following (Nemeth 2016; Sandhofer & Uchikoshi 2013; Tabors 2008):

❯ Children continue using their home language but may speak less or stop using it in the program if the environment does not support it.

❯ Children observe interactions and develop receptive language in English.

❯ Children understand English rhythms and intonations, using key phrases. They may use telegraphic and formulaic speech.

❯ Children achieve informal fluency in the new language, speaking in full sentences and engaging in conversations. They still think and understand many things in their first language and require ongoing support in both languages.

A child's progression through these stages may span from six months to two years or more. Adults should therefore hold reasonable expectations for children.

Teaching strategies. To support young children as they maintain knowledge of their first language while they acquire proficiency in a second language, try the following:

❯ Encourage children to communicate with you and with each other regardless of the language(s) they use. When possible, pair children who do not speak English with multilingual learners who do speak at least some English to help them make the bridge between languages. Children may use some words in their home language alongside English words, blending the ideas and words together in their own "linguistic repertoire," as in "More água, please!" (Wright et al. 2022, 18). This is known as translanguaging. Understanding that language "is not organized according to adult-established labels for languages (named languages)," teachers support translanguaging to encourage children's communication and positive sense of self and express acceptance of multilingual practices.

❯ Use narrative to enhance fluency. Describe actions, thoughts, and feelings throughout the daily routine, such as turning the message board into a story about the day's events, to enhance listening and speaking skills.

❯ If you do not speak a child's home language, use visuals, facial expressions, and gestures to aid the child's understanding. Use affirming strategies like smiling, nodding, and making specific comments about what children are doing to support their language development.

> Focus first on vocabulary rather than grammar or sentence structure. Nouns, verbs, and adjectives and adverbs (descriptive words) allow the multilingual learner to begin communicating with others. The success of being understood will encourage the child to continue learning and talking in English.

> Sing songs, read books, and tell stories in children's home languages as well as English. Invite families to share the songs and stories they enjoy and to teach them to the class. Ask family members to record stories in their home languages and add them to your listening center. Listening to stories in their home languages—especially those read by people they are very familiar with—supports children's language development and cultural identity.

> Encourage families to share materials written in their home languages to use at school. These materials might be magazines or newspapers written in the home language as well as food or other packaging materials for use in the dramatic play area.

> Encourage dramatic play to expand English vocabulary. Using props and actions during play enables multilingual learners to supplement their use of words with gestures and materials, reducing their frustration in trying to communicate. Their peers will often spontaneously fill in the words, providing a natural learning opportunity. Dramatic play also allows multilingual learners to pick up the rhythms and intonations of English dialogue. They may stand on the sidelines, listening and watching, until they feel ready to join in and try out their new words.

> If you use both English and a child's home language, be selective about when you do this (Nemeth 2016). For example, decide which language to emphasize at different times of the daily routine (perhaps the home language during meals but English during small group). Using both languages all the time can not only be overwhelming for multilingual learners but can also make other children impatient.

> Create picture cards showing common objects or frequently used words that are captioned in both languages to help both children and adults learn more than one language.

Listening and Speaking   **Enhancing sound awareness and production**

This skill area refers broadly to awareness of sounds (including nonwords) and is the simplest level of phonological awareness (more on that on pages 142–144 in this chapter). It also includes being able to produce various sounds with the vocal cords. Early and frequent exposure to sounds, especially the sounds of language, is crucial for a young child's development of language and literacy skills. By interacting with children as they create and play with these sounds, adults support and extend early language and literacy learning.

Teaching strategies. To ensure that young children are exposed early and often to a variety of sounds, consider and elaborate on the following ideas:

> Provide many noisemaking items inside the classroom, including musical instruments; tools and a workbench; timers that tick and ring; noisemaking toys; music players; interactive media with appropriate noisemaking software or apps; things that make noise during filling and emptying, such as pea gravel, stones, buttons, and running water; and beanbags or bags filled with these or other types of materials.

> Ask children to vary the sounds they make with instruments, other materials, or their voices. For example, ask them to make sounds that are loud and soft, fast and slow, high and low, long and short, or continuous and interrupted. Prepare a child who is sensitive to sensory input by, for example, doing this activity with the child individually before introducing it to the entire group.

> Call children's attention to a wide variety of sounds inside and outside the classroom, including those in nature (wind, birds, running streams), throughout the building (bells, buzzers, doors opening and closing, footsteps in the hall), and in the neighborhood (cars, construction vehicles, sirens, animals). Comment on what you hear and encourage children to be alert to different sounds.

> Ask children to identify the sounds they hear. At group time, have them close their eyes as you or a child make different sounds with tools and materials, and ask the children to guess the source of the sound. This game promotes language development and sets the stage for recognizing differences between the sounds of the letters of the alphabet. Record sounds to use in this game, such as whistles, clapping, stomping of heavy boots, a baby's crying, crackers (or other crunchy food) being eaten, hammering or sawing, a cat's meowing. Invite families to record sounds they hear indoors and out, and then play them back for all the children to guess what made each sound.

> Use nursery rhymes, fingerplays, and songs that play with sounds. Together, enjoy making up nonsense words.

> Provide puppets and other props that encourage children to play with sounds and try out different voices in dramatic play.

> Read books and tell stories that include sounds (*grrr, whoosh, waa, mmm*). Add your own sound effects. Encourage children to imitate and make up sounds that go with the story.

ADULT-GUIDED experiences are especially important for learnings such as:

| Listening and Speaking | Promoting phonological awareness |

Phonological awareness, or knowledge, is the ability to attend to the sounds of language as distinct from its meaning. At its simplest level, it includes the awareness of speech sounds and rhythms. It also extends to rhyme awareness (word endings, also known as *rimes*) and sound similarities (such as the initial sounds of words, also known as *onsets*, emphasized in alliteration). Phonological awareness is crucial to the development of literacy.

Phonemic awareness is one type (or subset) of phonological awareness, an important skill for preschoolers to develop. A phoneme is the simplest unit of sound, such as the /b/ sound in *bat*. Phonemic skills involve blending—that is, combining individual sounds to make a word, such as putting together the sounds /b/, /a/, and /t/ to make *bat*. Phonemic skills also involve a "reverse" process called segmentation—separating the sounds within a word, such as breaking *bat* into /b/, /a/, and /t/.

Teaching strategies. When teachers introduce children to multiple experiences with oral language and systematically engage them in activities such as alliteration and rhyming, they help children develop the skills to become readers and writers. When planning these activities, include aspects of children's social and cultural contexts, such as words in a child's home language and a nursery rhyme or story that is part of a family's culture (Gritt & Standish 2024). Consider the following strategies to support phonological awareness:

> Point out language sounds that are meaningful to children. For example, say, "I'm throwing the ball to Benjamin. *Ball* and *Benjamin* start with the same /b/ sound." For children with developmental delays or disabilities, provide visuals for sounds, letters, and/or words.

> Share songs, poems, stories, nursery rhymes, and chants that feature rhyming. Ask children to supply the rhyming words, especially once they are familiar with the verse or text. Substitute a different word at the end of a familiar rhyme and ask children to come up with a next line. For example, you might set an example by saying "Hickory, dickory, door. The mouse ran up the floor." When children grasp the idea, invite them to make their own substitutions ("Hickory, dickory, pear. The mouse ran up the _____.") Accept children's rhymes, even when they contain nonsense words. Encourage multilingual learners to think of a rhyming word in their home language if they cannot think of one in English (as in the opening vignette for this chapter). To support children who need more repetition, use rhyming activities with words they know and slowly add others.

> Share songs, poems, stories, nursery rhymes, and chants that feature alliteration, in which there is repetition of the initial or beginning sound of words, such as "Baa, baa, black sheep." Substitute a different sound at the beginning of the words in a familiar song, poem, or chant—for example, "Willoughby, Wallaby, Woo"—and ask children to do the same. When children grasp the idea, invite them to make up their own alliterative changes and songs. (See "Playing Alliteration Games.") Asking families to share nursery rhymes from their own cultures may yield interesting new options for alliteration in a language that is new to your classroom but dear to some of your children.

> Use rhymes and alliterations throughout the day. For example,

It's snack time; it's snack time.

Everyone gets a treat.

It's snack time; it's snack time.

I wonder what we've got to eat!

Playing Alliteration Games

Because alliteration highlights phonemes that start a word, it helps young children develop phonemic awareness. Here are some alliteration games you can use to have fun and promote learning.

Who Is It?: Ask children to guess who in the group has a name beginning with a certain phoneme. You can also play this game with the names of characters in a book familiar to the children.

- "I'm thinking of a person in this room whose name starts with /sh/. Guess who."

- "I remember someone in [book title] whose name begins with an /r/ sound. Who do you think it is?"

Doing the Names: Combine the initial sound of children's names with the initial sound of actions for them to perform. "Anyone whose name starts with the sound /w/, let's see you wave. Wen and Waseem are waving. Everybody wave with Wen and Waseem. Now let's see everyone wiggle."

Word Starters: Ask children to think of words that begin with the same sound.

- "Let's think of words that start like *car*, *cat*, and *call*."

- "How many words can you think of that start with a /p/ sound?"

> Play games that encourage children to segment the sounds in words. For example, "I'm going to say some words, and I want you to say back just the first sound you hear at the beginning. Can you say the beginning of *sand* [*sink, sun,* etc.]?" Do the same thing for the endings of words. For example, "Tell me what's left if I take off the first part of *coat* [*cup, carrot,* etc.]." Play these games with common non-English words, especially words multilingual learners use with one another or have taught to their English-speaking peers (such as the beginning or end of *casa*, which is Spanish for *house*).

> Lead guessing games that encourage blending sounds in words. For example, "I'm thinking of someone whose name begins with the /k/ sound and ends with an /ade/ sound. Who do you think it is?"

> Respond to children's requests for help with spelling a word by saying the sound of each letter aloud as you (or they) write it.

Listening and Speaking ❭ **Expanding vocabulary**

Vocabulary is the sum of words understood or used by a person. Receptive, or listening, vocabulary is the number of words a child understands. It is generally greater than productive, or speaking, vocabulary, which refers to the number of words a child can say and use correctly.

Multilingual learners may not know as many words in English as their monolingual peers, but their combined vocabulary—the number of words they know in either or both of their languages—is generally comparable (Zero to Three 2023). A review of research by Banse found that vocabulary instruction for multilingual learners is effective when it is "intentional, explicit, sustained, and occurs throughout the day" (2021, 1352).

Teaching strategies. Children's vocabularies do not get larger by emphasizing isolated or stand-alone words. The best way to grow vocabulary is to build on what children are talking about by adding synonyms and other words related to the topic of conversation, including during reading (Christ & Wang 2012; Collins 2012). For children to learn new words, including their meaning and how to use them, they need repeated exposure and practice (once or twice is not enough!) in one or more "communities of speakers." The early learning program is one such community. Here are some strategies you can use to accomplish this:

> Talk with children—a lot! Talk to them during routines and during play. Make sure the conversation is reciprocal; listen as well as talk. For children with developmental delays or disabilities, provide extra time, visuals, and multiple ways of communicating for them to convey their thoughts and ideas and the words they are learning.

> Use words that build on children's interests. When one child asked, "Why is Sniffy [the class guinea pig] eating the tube?" the teacher replied, "He gnaws on cardboard and wood fibers to wear down his teeth. Otherwise they would grow too big for his mouth."

> Read books that are rich in vocabulary words and interesting ideas that will spark children's questions and engage them in conversation.

> Offer your own definitions when reading a book with unfamiliar or specialized vocabulary. This can both build vocabulary and facilitate comprehension of the text. When reading "The bear lumbered toward the mitten," you can say, "'Lumbering' is a way of moving that a heavy animal might do. Show me what you think 'lumbering' might look like if you were a big bear." You can also provide information to help children know what category something is in, such as "This is a tortoise. A tortoise is a reptile that lives on land and looks like a very large turtle." Provide familiar synonyms when you use words that are new to children. This strategy is especially helpful for multilingual learners as they build their repertoire of English words while continuing to master new vocabulary in their home language.

> Vary experiences to introduce new and unusual words. Field trips are good sources, and dramatic play also helps to illustrate a variety of words. Humor is another way to encourage exploring and having fun with language. Young children enjoy jokes and silly names and rhymes.

> Create learning experiences in which children organize and relate concepts by using vocabulary words in classification (sorting and matching), seriation (ordering objects and making patterns), and spatial and temporal (space and time) phenomena. For example, give children items to sort and ask them to describe the items to one another using the traits by which they did the sorting (see "Geometry and Spatial Sense" on pages 182–188 in Chapter 7 for more examples). Doing these activities in small groups not only helps children use their own vocabulary but also allows them to hear and learn the words used by their peers.

> Show children how to use words to give one another directions during group projects or games. For example, during a Follow the Leader activity, encourage children to give creative directions like "Jump like a frog to the sandbox" or "Hop on one foot to the tree." This introduces interesting words and actions (jump, frog, hop, sandbox) in a playful way. Even children who are not familiar with those terms (including multilingual learners) will see and imitate those who do (or watch the teacher demonstrate), which facilitates acquisition of the new words.

> Announce your motivations and intentions: "I'm going to the house area to see what Bessie and Vinod are cooking. It smells like they're making something spicy for lunch."

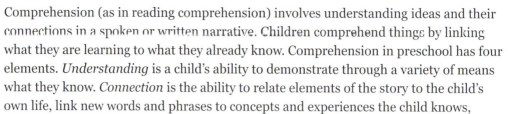

Comprehension (as in reading comprehension) involves understanding ideas and their connections in a spoken or written narrative. Children comprehend things by linking what they are learning to what they already know. Comprehension in preschool has four elements. *Understanding* is a child's ability to demonstrate through a variety of means what they know. *Connection* is the ability to relate elements of the story to the child's own life, link new words and phrases to concepts and experiences the child knows, and discover new relationships, ideas, and knowledge. *Prediction* is the capacity to imagine what will happen next based on what has already happened in the book. (Children often answer the question "What do you think will happen next?" with what they *want* to happen next rather than what is likely based on the story arc or pattern. For example, a child might guess that Santa will come, when, up until that point, the book was about a family of rhinos in Africa.) *Retelling* is recounting the story in sequence and with an increasing level of detail.

Teaching strategies. Think of comprehension as the steps between what goes in and what comes out when children encounter text. As young children develop, their brains are increasingly able to build the mental structures necessary to process this material, but they need explicit guidance from adults to establish connections and make sense of the books they hear and read. Reading comprehension improves when oral language in general is better developed. That is why it is so important to talk, sing, and read with children from birth to create a language-rich context for learning. The more they hear, the more they learn. Try strategies such as the following:

> Read children's favorite stories again and again. Repetition enhances children's awareness of character and narrative sequence, enables children to learn something new on different readings, and makes it easier to recall and use information. Repeated practice is particularly helpful for children with developmental delays or disabilities and multilingual learners.

> Answer children's many questions by finding informational books or digital sources on the topic. Ask them what they think about the book. Does it match what they already know about the topic? Was some information new? Make connections to other books on that topic you have read.

> Examine and discuss the pictures in books. Encourage children to tell or "read" the story in familiar books by looking at the pictures. Ask them to describe what they see. Converse about how the characters and situations depicted relate to objects, people, events, and ideas in children's own lives, both at home and in the classroom.

> Engage children in reviewing and predicting as you read. Stop occasionally to encourage children to recall what has happened so far. Rather than asking close-ended questions (such as "What did the duck say?"), invite comments by saying, "Let's see what we can remember so far" or "Can you help me remember what happened at the very beginning?" Ask children what they think the picture or words on the next page will be, or how they think a character will solve a problem. Encourage them to look and listen for clues that suggest what might happen next. Relate the picture and text at the end of the book to the title and first page.

> Encourage children to represent stories in various ways during art, dramatic play, block play, movement, and other activities. Suggest ideas such as moving to the next activity like a character in a book or drawing a series of pictures to show the sequence of events in a story. Nonverbal representation is especially encouraging for multilingual learners; their engagement also provides teachers with insight into how much of a story they understand. Offering the opportunity to create something through art can also serve as a "first draft" to help the child get their thoughts together before orally sharing what they're thinking about—again, this can be particularly helpful for multilingual learners.

> Recall and talk about stories and informational books at times other than when you are reading the books—for example, during snacks or related field trips. Listen for children's comments that can lead naturally into discussions of familiar and favorite narratives.

> Provide audio versions of books as another way to listen to familiar stories and to accommodate auditory processing difficulties.

Reading

Of the key knowledge and skills in the area of reading, child-guided experiences seem particularly important in the following:

> Acquiring visual discrimination skills

> Learning about environmental print knowledge

> Developing print awareness

> Gaining motivation to interact with printed materials

Adult-guided experiences seem especially significant in the following:

> Understanding the relationship between spoken and written language

> Gaining alphabet knowledge: letter identification and letter-sound knowledge

---

CHILD-GUIDED experiences are especially important for learnings such as:

Reading | **Acquiring visual discrimination skills**

Reading depends on the ability to visually distinguish the structural features of letters and punctuation and to understand how they form words, sentences, and paragraphs. To become readers, children must recognize the types of marks that make up print, such as lines, dots, and closed shapes. They have to further distinguish between types of lines—straight and curved, vertical and horizontal. Finally, children have to perceive how printed marks are arranged on a page and in relation to one another. Notice children's interest in these features and expand on that interest with intentional support, as illustrated in this vignette:

A kindergarten class is enjoying playing outside. A little boy quietly picks up a piece of chalk and begins to draw a straight line across the middle of the play yard. When his line reaches the wall, he changes course, crawling and ducking through balls and jump ropes to extend the line around the perimeter of the yard. Another child grabs a piece of chalk and draws a wavy line next to the straight one. Soon the ground is streaked with lines of all shapes and sizes. A chorus of scuffling footsteps and giggles permeates the air. The teacher begins to document with photographs and notations, asking the children to describe their lines. They offer complex names—*zigzag, loop-dee-loop, rollercoaster, squiggly slide.* The children also comment on the lines' attributes: whether or not they are wavy, pointy, or a little of both.

Ms. Fine continues the conversation about lines and curves into the classroom with an ongoing hands-on activity during morning and afternoon choice time. She creates an "interactive line" center and fills it with materials the children can manipulate—flexible sticks, pipe cleaners, aluminum foil, tape, and string.

"Can you make a line?" Ms. Fine asks each child as they visit. After several days, she notices that most children are making connections between the shapes of the lines and the letters of the alphabet:

"This one curves like the letter *C.*"

"This one looks like the letter *O.* It's a circle."

"I made the *A, U,* and *D* in my name."

Building on their emerging knowledge, Ms. Fine reads the class *The Line,* by Paula Bossio, and *Lines that Wiggle,* by Candace Whitman and illustrated by Steve Wilson. These books help demonstrate how a line can be turned into anything with just a bit of playfulness and imagination. (Adapted from Fine 2022)

Teaching strategies. Children's visual discrimination comes with physical maturation, but there are specific teaching strategies that can help young children acquire the particular visual skills needed for reading. Some of these ideas will seem obvious; others may inspire your creativity. Here are some recommended strategies:

> Provide a visually rich environment that includes not only many examples of print but also nonprint materials with diverse features. Most teachers know that having lots of printed materials in the classroom is important for early reading. (See "Developing Print Awareness" on pages 150–151 for more information on this topic.) However, there are many things without letters that can also help young children become aware of the lines, marks, and contrasts they will find in print. Examples include artwork and reproductions of artwork (representative of many cultures, especially distinctive visual patterns and motifs), maps and diagrams, plants with flowers and variegated leaves, patterned fabrics, and wood with distinctive grains.

> Use vocabulary words related to print's visual features, such as *straight, curved, circle, long, tall, short, blank, empty space,* and *line.* Call attention to visual features of objects indoors and outdoors, such as size, shape, form, color, foreground, and background. As noted in the vignette above, children will start to incorporate this vocabulary into their play if supported throughout the day.

> Encourage children to describe the visual attributes of materials, tools, artwork, and so on in their environment. Talk about the features that make things look the same or different.

> Play games and plan art activities that focus on visual characteristics. For example, partially hide objects and encourage children to find them; then ask them what features helped them find the object. Make imprints and rubbings (such as with sneaker soles, tree bark, keys, hands, and feet), then ask children to match these to the actual objects, discussing how they did so.

Reading > **Learning about environmental print knowledge**

Children and adults encounter environmental print in the context of everyday life. Examples include company names, logos, and advertising copy in stores and on television, web pages, and vehicles; apps; product labels; menus; street names and traffic signs; storefronts; billboards; and text and captions in magazines and catalogs.

Teaching strategies. Although children encounter environmental print all the time on their own, teachers play a significant role in calling it to their attention. Keep in mind that until text has meaning for children, any other visual input seems equally important to them. Pointing out text and modeling its use, such as writing a message to someone in the office to tell them who is absent today, helps children discern the difference between letters and, say, variegation on a plant or stripes on shells. Try strategies such as these:

> Create a print-rich classroom environment that includes environmental print materials: photo albums, magazines (for children and adults), catalogs, brochures, flyers, junk mail, instruction manuals, calendars, greeting cards, ticket stubs, business cards, and empty seed packets. Include materials with languages used by the families in your class and, if possible, materials used by people with varying abilities, such as braille magazines or menus. Digital text such as ebooks that can "read" to the listener in various languages can be included on classroom devices.

> Set up learning centers that incorporate reading and writing materials. For example, the house area can include empty food boxes and cans with labels (foods should include those the children are familiar with), store coupons, play money, cookbooks, message pads, and pencils. A restaurant center could be equipped with menus, wall signs, and notepads for taking food orders.

> By changing the dramatic play area's contents regularly, you will also be able to change out the functional print included in the area. A fire station can have maps, phone directories, and memo pads. A doctor's or veterinarian's office will have medical charts, posters of the human body (or animal's body), and magazines in the waiting room.

> Ask families to contribute materials. This can be a wonderful source of materials in multiple languages and brings materials that are familiar to the children into the classroom.

> Affix labels and captions on interest centers and materials throughout the classroom. Post signs and lists, such as weekly snack menus, the daily routine, or the names of children in each small group. Consider having multiple labels in each language represented in your classroom. Color-code the print and/or the label so the language is consistent throughout the room (Spanish text in red, Arabic in blue, English in green, etc.). Invite families to help you in getting it right.

> Put printed materials at children's eye level and make them accessible.

> Visit places in the community that feature print (library, sign shop, bookstore, supermarket). Look for large print at the children's eye level. For example, product signs on shelves are easier for children to see than aisle signs hanging from the ceiling.

> Support multilingual learners by translating between non-English and English words and phrases commonly found in your community (for example, on storefronts and product packages). Take walks around the neighborhood. Encourage families to bring in empty containers of products representing their language, and add the corresponding English word(s) to the labels. Invite parents to help with this labeling activity. When possible, add phonetic spellings so adults who are unfamiliar with the words can say them to the children in their home language.

> Provide materials for children to create their own printed resources as they play. For example, having paper and markers or pencils in the dramatic play area may serve as inspiration for a group of preschoolers to make tickets and signs for their pretend train trip.

Reading ⟩ **Developing print awareness**

Print awareness, or concepts of print, includes general knowledge about the conventions of print and how books work. For example, young children learn that books have distinctive parts (cover and pages, beginning and end), an author or illustrator or both, and a written message separate from (though related to) the pictures. Through repeated experiences, they master directionality—that is, knowing books are held right side up (orientation) and read front to back (turning pages in order), and each text page in English is scanned from top to bottom and left to right. Remember that some families read to their children in a language that uses print from right to left. Acknowledging to children that English works one way and other languages may work in different ways can be validating for all. Inviting children to share books or other texts from home can help illustrate this.

Teaching strategies. The logical structure of books is so well known to adults that they take it for granted. Although repeated exposure to print helps bring about children's awareness of it, adults can play an intentional role in pointing out the main features of books with strategies such as these:

> Provide many different types of books—illustrated storybooks, controlled vocabulary books (which use a limited number of words repeatedly, adding new words gradually, and encourage sight reading), picture dictionaries, and informational (nonfiction) books—for children to hold, carry, look at, listen to, and talk about to aid in their understanding and application of the general rules of print.

> Provide lots of other printed products children can interact with, such as the environmental print materials discussed in the previous section, dictated stories, and stories children have written (and illustrated) themselves.

> Ask children to hand you a book so you can read it. Accept or reorient the book as needed. Occasionally pick up or hold a book the wrong way and see how children react. Make a visual and vocal point of turning the book right side up.

> Point out book and print features while looking at books with children. For example, say, "This is the front cover, and this [turning it over] is the back cover. This is called the 'title page' because it has the name, or title, of the book." Explain the concepts of author and illustrator and read these names before you read a book. Encourage children to turn the pages as you read. When you're done, you might say, "That's the end of the story." After finishing the book, go back and point out page numbers in sequence. (Once you begin reading, don't interrupt the story to point out book features. It can destroy the pleasure of reading. Also, children need narrative continuity to build comprehension skills. You can mention print attributes occasionally, but for the most part, point these out before and after reading the book.)

> Make books with children that include all the parts (front and back covers, title page with their names as authors and illustrators, drawings with words). Leave commercially produced books on the table so that children can refer to them while they make their own books. Display the children's finished books; put them in the reading area so they can look at their own and their classmates' books.

> Favor print books, which children can manipulate, over ebooks. However, as ebooks (and other forms of print on electronic devices) have become increasingly common, demonstrate basic practices to children who are not familiar with them, such as how to scroll down or "turn" the page. Children who have experience with these devices and programs will often provide instruction to children who are less familiar with them.

> Share resources for quality beginner books with families. Sources such as the Barbara Bush Foundation for Family Literacy provide free eBooks for families and communities that have few actual books (www.barbarabush.org/family-resources). Storylineonline.net has celebrities reading wonderful stories.

This area refers to children's interest in—or disposition toward—engaging with printed materials and the things that are represented in print, such as stories and information.

Teaching strategies. Interest in reading cannot be forced on children. Fortunately, if they have positive reading experiences with adults, children will be motivated to want to read themselves. To foster positive attitudes toward reading, try these strategies:

〉 Read to children frequently, both individually and in small groups.

〉 Create cozy and comfortable places where you can read with children and they can look at books by themselves. Provide stuffed animals and dolls for children to read to. Add page fluffers (temporary or permanent materials attached to the corners of the pages) to book pages to make them easier for children with physical disabilities to turn.

〉 Display books on open shelves, with attractive and colorful covers facing outward.

〉 Include books in each activity area. Place books about construction in the block area; books about farms near the barn set; and books about colors, art, or shapes in the art area.

〉 Encourage children to select which book(s) to read. Let them know you expect them to succeed at reading.

〉 Make sure there are enough books for all children to choose from. If you're short on books, try using bonus points from book clubs to order more. Accept books from retiring colleagues or families of older children who no longer need them, or go to thrift and consignment shops or yard sales.

〉 Choose books that interest the children. Remember that they are curious, so virtually any subject, well presented for their age, can intrigue them. This includes stories, informational text, books about people, rhyming books, alphabet books, children's magazines, "how-to" books like cookbooks (procedural text), books in the children's home languages, and books made by the children themselves.

〉 Provide books that children will have success "reading" themselves, such as wordless books and easy-to-read books (with predictable word sets).

〉 Let children see you reading for enjoyment and information.

〉 Encourage parents to read to children at home. Start a lending library in the classroom. Make book backpacks for each child so they can choose books to take home and return.

〉 If your program uses ebooks or other digital texts, choose appropriate titles and read them with children the same way you would a print book (that is, using the interactive procedures described in the previous section of this chapter). Provide this same guidance to families, emphasizing the importance of parents reading ebooks *with* their children.

ADULT-GUIDED experiences are especially important for learnings such as:

| Reading | Understanding the relationship between spoken and written language |

This area involves connecting what people say with the same words when written. It requires children to understand the one-to-one correspondence between the two modes of expression.

Teaching strategies. The relationship between spoken and written words may seem self-evident to adults, but grasping this abstract connection is a notable achievement for young children, whose concrete minds are just beginning to form mental representations. Here are some strategies:

> Take children's dictation and read it back to them verbatim. (When you take dictation on paper, ask children where on the page to begin writing, to reinforce that print concept.) The power and pleasure of seeing their words in print—provided it's voluntary and not coerced— encourages children to invent additional occasions for dictation. Opportunities for taking individual dictation include labels; captions on artwork; role-playing props (such as menus, traffic signs, party invitations); and original songs, rhymes, and chants. Opportunities for group dictation include original stories, songs, rhymes, and chants; rules for a game children have invented; lists and graphs (such as favorite foods, toys, and colors); shared experiences ("Our trip to the pet shop"); and small group problem-solving discussions ("How can we stop fighting over the red wagon?"). Encourage multilingual learners to dictate stories and captions in their home language and/or a combination of their home language and English. Refer to children's dictated pieces as an occasion arises: "Hmm, I think Johann and Bea included a rule about that in their list of rules for this game. Let's go look at it."

> When you read to children, run a finger along the lines of print, point out and enunciate individual words, and model intonation. Do the same whether you are reading a print book or an ebook. Ebooks with narration in different languages can help both teacher and child learn to pronounce the words in each other's language.

> Engage children in speaking and acting out written stories from books of their own creation as well as commercial books.

> Make picture cards and write appropriate words (nouns, verbs, short sentences) underneath. These can be about individual items and actions or use related word sets (such as buildings or planting a garden). Point to the pictures and words as you read the text aloud. Encourage children to look at the cards on their own, as well as with partners, and to say the written words aloud. Again, encourage multilingual learners to use whatever language, or combination of languages, they are comfortable with.

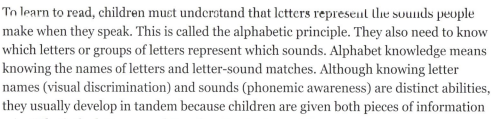
To learn to read, children must understand that letters represent the sounds people make when they speak. This is called the alphabetic principle. They also need to know which letters or groups of letters represent which sounds. Alphabet knowledge means knowing the names of letters and letter-sound matches. Although knowing letter names (visual discrimination) and sounds (phonemic awareness) are distinct abilities, they usually develop in tandem because children are given both pieces of information together, as in, "That's the letter *m*, and it makes the /m/ sound."

With informed guesses, as well as continued explicit instruction, children come to understand that other words they are interested in saying and writing begin with the same letter—for example, that *mom, me, mud,* and *motor* all begin with the /m/ sound. Children find it easier to identify letters at the beginning of words, especially if the letters are capitalized. For example, the initial *b* in the word *bubble* is easier to find (and hear) than the embedded *b* in the middle of the word.

Teaching strategies. Like phonological awareness, alphabet knowledge is critical in early literacy. The alphabet is an arbitrary code of letters and sounds unique to one or more related languages. Children must learn the rules and conventions of their language(s); they cannot make them up. Adults, therefore, play an explicit role in transmitting this body of information in ways that are meaningful and engaging for young children. At the same time, children need ample opportunities to experiment and practice the alphabet on their own. Try the following strategies:

> Display alphabet letters where children can see them, at eye level. Provide alphabet letters and blocks children can hold, copy, trace, and rearrange, such as cutout letters and letter stencils; magnetic letters; letter-shaped cookie cutters that children can press into sand and playdough; and alphabet puzzles.

> Provide alphabet knowledge in context. Call attention to letter names and sounds when they are relevant to children's playing, reading, and writing. This strategy is more effective than offering such information isolated from children's ongoing and meaningful activities.

> Say the names of letters and sound them out in words children read, write, and dictate. Sound out letters, letter strings, and letter combinations in the words children dictate. For example, if they dictate a party menu, write and enunciate, "/c/ /a/ /k/." That makes the word *cake.* I like chocolate frosting on my cake!" Include the letter strings and combinations at the beginning, end, and (later) the middle of words.

> Connect sounds to the letters children write to stand for whole words. For example, if a child writes *HB* and reads, "Happy Birthday," say, "Yes, I see the *H* for the /h/ sound in *happy* and a *B* for the /b/ sound at the beginning of *birthday.*" Sound out the (invented) "words" children spell. If they ask, "What word is this?" or "What does this spell?," pronounce the

word as it is written or arranged. For example, if a child arranges the letters KRGMS, say "This word sounds like /k/ /r/ /g/ /m/ /s/. You wrote *krgms*. I think you made up a new word. I don't know that one. What do you think it means?"

> Involve children in searching for letters by their sounds: "I'm looking for a letter that makes the sound /s/. Can you find one?"

> Identify initial letter sounds in children's names and other familiar words. Often the first letter and sound that children learn is the one that begins their own name, or it's a word they use often and find important, such as *Mom*, their dog's name, or a favorite food.

> Link the remaining sounds of a word to the first letters in children's names. For example, while writing and spelling *cat,* you might say, "It begins with *c* like the /c/ in Carla. It ends with *t* like the /t/ in Tomas. In the middle is an *a* just like the /a/ in Alex."

> Make sure any technology programs you use with children are interactive, not simply drill and practice. (Use resources like Common Sense Media to find apps and games that educators have reviewed.) For example, look for game-like software and apps that allow children to choose the letters and manipulate (move) them around the screen. Make sure the auditory component (pronunciation of the letter sounds) is clear and that the letters are large and distinct so that children can read them easily.

Writing

Just as is true for other areas of development, writing becomes important to children when they find a personal use or connection to it. Not surprisingly, name writing is highly motivating to children. Like most other aspects of literacy, children learn best through meaningful modeling of engaging, authentic uses of the practice, such as signing their name for a package delivery in the dramatic play area, captioning a piece of artwork, or writing a thank-you note to the children's book illustrator who visited the class. Byington and Kim (2017) discuss writing development more specifically, including the stages of emergent writing and suggestions for writing materials and literacy props to include in learning centers.

Of the key knowledge and skills in the area of writing, child-guided experiences seem particularly important for the following:

> Acquiring fine motor skills

> Gaining awareness of the purposes and functions of written words

Adult-guided experiences seem especially significant for the following:

> Developing letter- and word-writing skills

> Improving awareness of the conventions of spelling, grammar, syntax, and punctuation

CHILD-GUIDED experiences are especially important for learnings such as:

| Writing | Acquiring fine motor skills |

Writing, like reading, is dependent on children having certain perceptual motor skills. Prerequisite fine motor skills for writing include being able to grasp writing materials and the eye-hand coordination to make certain types of marks in specific locations on the writing surface.

Teaching strategies. The development of the fine motor skills needed for writing is, to a great degree, maturational. However, as with the visual acuity skills necessary for prereading, children depend on adults to provide materials and opportunities to practice their developing fine motor skills. Here are some examples:

› Provide manipulative materials in all areas of the classroom to develop children's manual dexterity and eye-hand coordination. Examples include items to assemble and take apart; things to copy and trace; tweezers and beads; dress-up and doll clothes with various types of fasteners; moldable art materials; drawing and painting tools; paper to manipulate and transform; scissors; hole punches; staplers; tape; cooking utensils; safety knives for cutting snacks; carpentry tools and materials such as nails and wood (use appropriate safety precautions, including safety goggles); and interactive technology.

› Provide writing materials of all kinds throughout the room. (See the suggestions in the next section, including those for children with visual or physical impairments.)

› Encourage children to play simple games of eye-hand coordination, such as aiming at a target with a beanbag or ball. (Remember that preschoolers need a large target and short throwing distance.)

› Model how to hold writing tools, scissors, and so on, especially for children who are having difficulty mastering these techniques on their own. Be sensitive to children's frustration levels. If you wait too long to intervene, children may simply become averse to writing.

| Writing | Gaining awareness of the purposes and functions of written words |

Like reading, writing is done for functional reasons (such as to communicate an idea, share information, remember to do something, or give directions) and for pleasure (such as to extend an invitation, express appreciation, tell a story, or preserve a memory). This area refers to knowing the different ways and reasons people write.

Teaching strategies. Young children want to do things for themselves and share their ideas and accomplishments with others. Writing helps them achieve these personal objectives. Strategies such as the following build on children's inherent motivation to write:

> Provide a wide variety of writing tools and materials throughout the classroom. Include materials for recording ideas (writing software, text-to-speech) and transmitting them to others (email services, envelopes and stamps).

> For children with limited visual acuity or motor control, provide appropriate assistive technology, such as magnifiers, wide crayons and markers, rubber writing grips, adjustable writing platforms (for example, those that can be affixed to wheelchair trays and raised or lowered), large-type keyboards, and voice-recognition software.

> Provide contextualized examples of print that serves a here-and-now purpose. Examples include labeled centers and materials, rules created by children, a daily schedule, cookbooks in the house area, and instructions for equipment in the woodworking or science area.

> Model the use of written language for different purposes and call it to children's attention. Point it out to them when you write things and when you use existing writing (for example, to look up information in a book or on the internet).

> Encourage writing in journals that children make themselves or in a class journal. With the children's permission, read entries at morning greeting time.

> Display children's writing where children and families can see it.

ADULT-GUIDED experiences are especially important for learnings such as:

Writing **Developing letter- and word-writing skills**

Literacy includes the ability to write letters and combine strings of letters into words. Children make letter-like forms before they write conventional letters. Letter writing usually begins with writing one's own name, starting with writing the initial letter.

Because children's experiences with writing are different, their writing skills vary widely (Collins & Schickedanz 2024). Between the ages of 3 and 6, children's name writing progresses from continuous horizontal scribbles to separate and recognizable letters arranged in the correct order (Bloodgood 1999; Hildreth 1936; Puranik & Lonigan 2011). Although children are highly motivated to develop this ability, they do so only when families and teachers continually make a connection between the sounds in their names and writing the associated letters. Adults need to call attention to environmental print that uses the initial letter in a child's name, or they can write the letter: "That's a *P*, just like the beginning of your name, Paco."

Teaching strategies. Like alphabet knowledge, letter and word writing are highly dependent on explicit instruction, but to be effective, this instruction must be provided in relevant and developmentally appropriate ways. Try the following strategies:

> Call attention to how letters are formed, particularly the lines and shapes that compose them.

> Engage children in writing and reading their writing. Write down children's dictation; then read the words back yourself, and ask children to read back the words you have written for them.

> Engage them in name writing each day—for example, writing their name on a sign-in chart, task list, bookmark, or art project (as artists do). Comment positively no matter how children write their names. For example,

>> **Soriya:** (*Writes her name with linear scribbles.*)
>>
>> **Miss Keisha:** Soriya, I see you're using lines to write your name.
>>
>> **Soriya:** (*Beams with pride.*)
>>
>> **Sam:** (*Writes his name with inverted letters.*)
>>
>> **Miss Keisha:** Sam, I see you're using some letters to write your name. You wrote an *s*. That's exciting!
>>
>> **Sam:** (*Smiles, pleased with his effort.*)
>>
>> **Miss Keisha:** It looks like you're both really happy with your work. You've been practicing writing your names many times, and you're getting better and better at it. You can be proud of your persistence!

> Some children with developmental delays or disabilities may require accommodations or adaptations when it comes to writing materials, along with ample opportunities for practice. Provide visuals as they learn letters and words. Include letters in tactile form, such as having a letter raised by dry glue so that children can feel as well as see the letter.

> With many more people tapping out messages on their phones, there is less text production around for children to observe. Act as a writer as well as a teacher. When children see adults write, they want to write too. Label what you are doing as "writing" and explain to children both its purpose and the actual letters, words, and sentences you are writing.

| Writing | **Improving awareness of the conventions of spelling, grammar, syntax, and punctuation** |

The conventions of print include a culture's correct or accepted rules of written expression. As children become literate, they often construct unconventional rules first and then gradually move toward conventional ones. For example, they may invent spellings with the most salient sounds in words, such as *DG* for *dog*. Or they might understand the ideas of "past tense" and adding *-ed* but misapply those ideas to an irregular verb (as in "I goed to the store"). (Multilingual learners will do the same with the conventions of their home language.) As adults raise children's awareness, children will begin to use the rules as they are ready. (Multilingual learners might apply the conventions of their home language to English, such as the way plurals are formed, before they master the conventions of English). Your task is to build on what children know; that is, young children's understanding is more important than whether *goed* is correct or adding *-s* rather than *-en* at the end of a noun makes it plural.

Teaching strategies. Be careful not to stifle children's spontaneous and joyful writing by repeatedly correcting them or insisting that they follow rules. Strategies such as the following help make children aware of writing conventions and their application without discouraging their impulse to write:

> Spell words aloud as you write them (whether in English or the child's home language) when you take dictation from children. Emphasize middle letters and especially vowels. Children tend to get initial letters and consonants first, so linger on other letter types to fill in the "blanks" in their spelling.

Introducing the Idea of Punctuation in Context

Punctuation is too abstract for young children to learn and apply its rules. However, they are often interested in punctuation marks and how they are used when the topic comes up in meaningful contexts. In the following anecdote, some children are impressed when their teacher uses an exclamation point to convey her feelings.

> Miss Kameko is cowriting a morning message with the whole class. She invites the child of the day, Jemar, to join her as she writes on chart paper.
>
> **Miss Kameko:** Okay, how shall we start our message? Do you want it to be Good Morning or Hello, Friends?
>
> **Jemar:** Hello, Friends.
>
> **Miss Kameko:** (*Turns to the group.*) Okay. Hello, Friends. Where do I start?
>
> **Class:** (*Point toward the upper left-hand corner of the chart paper.*) Up there!
>
> **Miss Kameko:** Okay, what should I write first? (*Moves her hand to write in the left corner.*)
>
> **Class:** Write Hello, Friends!
>
> **Miss Kameko:** (*Works with children to sound out and write the letters in Hello, Friends.*) Now we have to decide what to put at the end of Hello, Friends. Should we put a period like this? (*Holds up a picture of a period.*) Or an exclamation point, like this? (*Holds up a picture of an exclamation point.*) Jemar, what do you think?
>
> **Jemar:** (*Points to the exclamation point.*) Use the excited mark.
>
> **Miss Kameko:** You want me to use the exclamation point today. Is it because you're excited to say hello to your friends?
>
> **Jemar:** (*Nods.*)
>
> **Miss Kameko:** Okay, let's read this together. (*Runs her finger under the line as everyone reads.*)
>
> **All:** Hello, Friends!
>
> **Miss Kameko:** Oh, did that sound excited to you?
>
> **Class:** No!
>
> **Miss Kameko:** How about we try it again? (*Runs her finger under the text and all read together, this time shouting the words.*) Well, that sounded much more excited! These marks help us know how to sound when we read a word or a sentence. We call those punctuation marks. This mark that Jemar called an excited mark helps us know to read as if we are excited. It's really called an exclamation mark, but I like Jemar's name better!

Later, Miss Kameko observes Molly and Sagar playing store in the dramatic play area. Molly announces, "The store is open. You should make a sign." Sagar, who has a reputation among the children as being a good speller, grabs a paper and pencil and spells as she carefully writes *Open.* "O-P-E-N. There." "No," Molly shakes her head. "We're excited that we're open. Put a excited mark." Sagar adds the punctuation and shouts to some nearby children, "We're open!"

Adapted from Damico & Bennett-Armistead 2003.

> Respond to children's requests for help to spell words correctly. Have children stretch the word out as they say it so they can hear each sound better. This can also be done by syllables if the word is longer. Called segmenting, this strategy helps children take the word down to its smallest parts, phonemes. For example, with the word *sunny,* we can stretch the word to "ssssss-uuuuu-nnnnnnn-eeeee" so the child can hear the sounds. Once they realize that letters represent sounds, help them write the sounds they hear in words. As they get better at sounding out words, help them make the transition to conventional spellings. In the case of *sunny,* you would talk about how the /e/ sound is actually spelled with a *y.*

> With older preschoolers, provide word banks, word walls, and books with words that share spelling features. Post lists of "hard-to-spell words." Ask children to suggest words for the lists, and encourage them to add words throughout the year.

> Make comments to highlight writing conventions as you read or write with children, such as "This is a new sentence, so it begins with a capital letter" or "We're making a list of questions to ask Bennett's dad when he comes to make bread with us tomorrow, so I'm writing a question mark at the end of each one."

> When children make spoken errors in grammar and syntax, repeat back their ideas using conventional language rather than correct the mistakes. For example, if a child says, "I goed to the barbershop yesterday. He cutted my hair," you might say, "Oh, you went to the barbershop yesterday and the barber cut your hair." This is called *recasting*. It models the correct language for the child without embarrassing them. Do the same when children apply the rules of their home language to English. For example, if a child whose first language is German asks you to read two *buchen,* you might say, "You want me to read both books, buchen."

• • •

Teachers play a critical role in establishing a community of literacy learners through their interactions with individual children and the collaborations they foster among peers. Intentional teachers use their knowledge of child development and literacy learning to supply materials, provide well-timed information, guide discussions, make thoughtful comments, ask meaningful questions, and pose calibrated challenges that advance children's learning. Young children's motivation to learn to read and write comes from an intrinsic desire to communicate, but they need adult guidance and support to begin the journey toward full literacy with competence and enthusiasm.

For Further Consideration

1. What basic language and literacy skills should early childhood educators teach young children? Who determines basic requirements, and how should they be assessed?

2. In your program, how do you balance time for literacy learning with other content areas in a comprehensive curriculum? How do you integrate literacy learning with early learning in other domains? If you are not yet teaching, how do you expect that you will do these things?

3. What can teachers do to help children build varied vocabulary?

4. How might systematic reading instruction take away from—or add to—the joy of reading?

5. How can you use children's knowledge of their home language to help them learn English? How can you involve and support parents whose first language is a language other than English?

Learning Objectives

1. To reflect on your own attitudes about mathematics and how you might be conveying your attitudes (positive or negative) to the children in your classroom

2. To explain why young children are developmentally ready to engage in math learning

3. To explain why young children require intentional mathematics learning experiences despite having intuitive understanding of some math concepts and to evaluate when child-guided and adult-guided experiences are each appropriate for mathematics learning

4. To identify and explain the five content standards of mathematics set forth by the National Council of Teachers of Mathematics (NCTM)

5. To identify culturally, linguistically, and developmentally appropriate materials and everyday activities that facilitate children's math learning, including manipulatives, games, books, real-world objects, and investigative activities

6. To identify ways to differentiate early math learning for children, including multilingual learners and children with developmental delays or disabilities

CHAPTER 7

Mathematics

Holland Banse

Gretchen, nearly 5, says, "I need a big circle for the bottom of my snow lady." She finds a large wooden circle in the block area and brings it to the art area, where she traces it onto a piece of construction paper, cuts out the circle-shaped sheet, and tapes it on the lower edge of her paper. She asks her teacher, Mrs. Torres, for help finding a "medium circle for the middle." Mrs. Torres suggests that she look for round items in the house area. Gretchen goes there and chooses two lids, one from a coffee canister and one from a yogurt container. "I found a medium and a small circle!" she tells Mrs. Torres.

• • •

On a tablet, Sheldon, 4, uses his finger to drag pictures of pizza slices onto pictures of some plates. He drags two of the four pieces onto each of two plates. "Look," he tells his friend Atef. "I made two plates of pizza, one for me and one for you. We have the same! Pizza time!" Atef (nearly 4) uses his finger to drag his slice off the plate, and the friends pretend to chomp the pizza.

Mathematical thinking emerges in infancy, but its ongoing development takes time. Infants seem to intuitively recognize features such as quantity (Feigenson et al. 2004; Wang & Feigenson, 2021), shape (Dillon, Izard, & Spelke 2020), and size (Sensoy, Culham, & Schwarzer 2020). In addition, researchers have found that a knowledge of precursor math concepts—such as attribute, comparison, change, and pattern—contributes to mathematical understanding during the first three years of life (Hynes-Berry, Chen, & Abel 2021). As children grow, they continue to develop these and other intuitive ideas about mathematics naturally and with curiosity. This intuitive knowledge is the foundation for deeper understanding of mathematical concepts and vocabulary (Feigenson et al. 2004; Purpura et al. 2017), both of which benefit from intentional learning opportunities.

The chapter's opening vignettes reflect these ideas. The children's remarks reflect an interest in mathematical subjects that matter to them—including shape (geometry) and relative size (big, medium, small); number and operations, such as division; and the use of number words to describe length, width, and operations. The children's remarks illustrate that "prekindergarten children have the interest and ability to engage in significant mathematical thinking and learning" (Clements 2004, 11). Yet, the vignettes also illustrate that the teacher shaped the context in which each child generated a mathematical idea, either by responding to or initiating children's mathematical thinking. Children acted on materials set up to engage their learning, received input and experiences that extended their ideas, and, in some cases, were introduced to vocabulary that describes those ideas.

Adult guidance, ranging from well-planned learning environments to modeling to adult-guided activities, contributes to growth in children's mathematical thinking. It is therefore not surprising that the National Center for Education Evaluation and Regional Assistance (NCEE) recommends that preschool teachers "provide intentional instruction to build children's understanding of mathematical ideas and skills" (Burchinal et al. 2022, 23). This instruction includes guided play and meaningful small group experiences that provide choice and hands-on exploration, with a focus on both basic skills and more advanced mathematical ideas (such as moving beyond counting strategies to reasoning strategies). Understanding that mathematical development is gradual and aligns with well-described developmental trajectories (Clements & Sarama 2020; Sarama & Clements 2019) helps teachers choose learning experiences that are appropriately geared to individual and group developmental levels and interests. Small group and whole group activities also give teachers information about children's knowledge, thinking, and skills so that they can help advance children's learning (Stipek 2017). Burchinal and colleagues explain:

> Developmental progressions in mathematics are the order in which mathematical skills and understanding typically develop. For example, children learn to recognize and name shapes before they can combine or separate shapes to form new ones. . . . Teachers can use learning trajectories to decide which instructional activities to do with children and in what order. (2022, 28)

Although we now know that young children are more capable of learning mathematical concepts than previously thought, many children in the United States experience persistent challenges in formal mathematics achievement throughout the school-age years (US Department of Education 2024), and these challenges have implications for lifelong academic, social, and personal outcomes. Associations between early mathematics skills and both later mathematics achievement (see, for example, Geary & VanMarle 2016; Jordan & Dyson 2016) and reading skills (Duncan et al. 2007) highlight the importance of providing preschool children with rich opportunities for early mathematics. Unfortunately, observations of US preschool classrooms show that very little, if any, time is devoted to mathematics learning opportunities, with mathematics activities occurring for less than 6 minutes on average per classroom during a two-hour observation period (Mazzocco et al. 2024). When teachers do present math activities, they are more likely to be teacher-led large group activities rather than small group or individualized activities and more likely to focus on number knowledge rather than other domains of mathematics.

In addition, the typical early childhood curriculum incorporates few sustained early mathematics experiences (Claessens et al. 2021), and those that are included focus heavily on number knowledge, particularly counting, rather than operations or geometry. Yet, children spontaneously explore topics such as patterns, shapes, and the transformations brought about by processes like adding and subtracting (Ginsburg et al. 2006). A limited focus on the counting sequence is unfortunate because additional domains of mathematics are also critical for later mathematical understanding (Gilligan, Flouri, & Farran 2017; Mix 2019).

Researchers and practitioners have developed systems for categorizing the mathematical areas in which young children demonstrate interest and ability (see, for example, Campbell 1999; Greenes 1999; Levine & Pantoja 2021). NCTM's (2000) *Principles and Standards in School Mathematics* includes standards for pre-K through grade 2. NAEYC's (2002) joint position paper with NCTM (updated in 2010) supports those standards and offers recommendations for early mathematics education. NCTM's (2000) standards, as well as the organization's follow-up publication, *Curriculum Focal Points for Prekindergarten Through Grade 8 Mathematics* (2006), continue to be widely cited in the field and used by many state departments of education and local school districts to develop comprehensive early mathematics curricula in preschool programs and the primary grades.

NCTM (2000) defines five content standards: number and operations, geometry, measurement, algebra, and data analysis and probability. The standards are described in this chapter, along with their application in the preschool years. NCTM also defines five process standards, consistent with the strategies suggested in this chapter: problem solving, reasoning and proof, connections, communication, and representation. Early mathematics learning opportunities, particularly problem solving and reasoning, are at the heart of equitable mathematics learning, as the NCTM 2022 position statement explains:

> Mathematics includes a wide range of concepts and ideas that are intricately connected and should be taught through strengthening children's problem-solving and reasoning processes. Implementations from a one-size-fits-all developmental framework are harmful, leading to the labeling and sorting of children, resulting in segregation, marginalization, and privilege that is strongly correlated with race, language, class, and ability status (Annamma, Morrison, and Jackson 2014; Mazzanti and Allexsaht-Snider 2018), and to the narrowing of mathematics experiences to rote counting, number recognition, and procedures and answer-getting activities (NAEYC/NCTM 2010; NCTM 2020). Young children are intuitive problem solvers (Carpenter et al. 2017). We must not withhold problem-solving opportunities or assume that learning to count precedes problem solving. (NCTM 2022)

Strategies for developing the following content standards into practice with children appear in "Fitting the Learning Experience to the Learning Objective" later in this chapter, where they are considered separately as child-guided and adult-guided experiences.

> Number and operations involves recognizing quantities, counting objects, and engaging in basic addition and subtraction. This builds the foundation for understanding the relationships and properties of numbers.

> Geometry and spatial sense involves identifying and describing shapes, positional relationships, and an awareness of space. This fosters skills such as mapping, orientation, and recognizing patterns in the environment.

> Measurement involves comparing lengths, weights, and capacities and understanding basic concepts of time. Children develop measurement understanding through exploring and expressing quantities in the context of their everyday experiences.

> Patterns, functions, and algebra involves exploring patterns through repeated sequences. As children identify, extend, and create patterns in various contexts, they are building a foundation for understanding functions and algebraic thinking.

> Data analysis involves simple data collection, representation, and interpretation. This fosters children's learning of how to organize and make sense of information as well as skills for understanding and analyzing data in a variety of forms.

Young Children's Development in Mathematics

Young children, like those quoted in the vignettes at the beginning of the chapter, start with only an intuitive or experiential understanding of mathematics. They don't yet have the concepts or vocabulary they need to be able to *use* what they intuitively know or to connect their knowledge to formal mathematics. For instance, a child may intuitively understand that one pile of blocks has more blocks than another pile, but to describe this idea, the child has to learn quantity words like *more,* ideas about counting, and eventually, number words like *ten* and *five.* Similarly, children learn how their earlier mathematical knowledge is connected to mathematics ideas they learn later, such as when adding or subtracting. The preschool teacher's role, therefore, is to have a good conceptual understanding of early mathematics, identify children's current mathematical understanding, nurture the accurate use of mathematical language, and tailor experiences and activities to meet the needs of the children. Turning children's early and spontaneous mathematics play (child-guided experiences) into an awareness of their own mathematical thinking, in ways that follow logical sequences, is at the heart of intentional teaching in this area.

Developing a Disposition for Mathematics

The goals of early mathematics education are to do more than just build factual content knowledge. Another important goal is to foster children's positive disposition toward learning and using mathematics. A positive disposition reflects an individual's understanding and appreciation for the importance of mathematics, seeing mathematics as interesting and useful, and believing that mathematics success can be achieved with effort. Teachers seeking to help children build a positive disposition toward mathematics may wish to reflect on their own outlook. Teachers who experience mathematics anxiety may limit mathematics learning opportunities for children (Geist 2015). An intentional teacher can help children's mathematics learning by demonstrating interest and joy while engaging in mathematics (Solarski 2024). That is, teachers of young children who learn to love teaching mathematics will help children realize that they, too, can be competent young mathematicians.

The following components are instrumental in helping children develop their mathematical disposition:

> Engaging early mathematical experiences: Young children benefit from engaging in a variety of play-based mathematical activities. Opportunities for choice, creativity, and social engagement during mathematical play have high value (General Education Leadership Network 2019). Math play lays the foundation for more formal mathematical understanding (NCTM 2022).

> Intentional adult interactions: In early mathematics, free exploration is important yet insufficient for deep learning. There are concepts, principles, and vocabulary that children can only construct through consistent and purposeful interactions with adults. Even for those areas in which their investigations are key, children do not always construct mathematical meanings from them (Trawick-Smith, Swaminathan, & Liu 2016). As Baroody, Clements, and Sarama note, "Self discovery learning and then explicit teacher scaffolding helps ground instruction in children's existing informal knowledge and fosters sense making of new problems and solution strategies" (2019, 339). In this way, adult-guided experiences supplement child-guided exploration.

> A focus on foundational concepts: As children encounter more challenging and complex mathematical concepts, they will benefit from a strong foundation in basic mathematical concepts such as counting (Franke, Kazemi, & Turrou, 2023), number knowledge, operations, patterns (Fyfe, McNeil, & Borjas 2015), shapes, and spatial reasoning (Gilligan et al. 2017; Mix 2019; Verdine et al. 2017).

> Opportunities for problem solving and critical thinking: Activities that prompt children to think mathematically and apply their knowledge to solve problems contribute to a deeper understanding of mathematical concepts.

Teachers may worry that mathematics education is developmentally inappropriate for children, because they perceive it is too academic, can be overly didactic, and takes away from time that could instead be spent on other important areas of development, such as social and emotional development and language and literacy. However, like all high-quality early childhood activities, early mathematics can and should be integrated into engaging, play-based, and meaningful learning experiences, as the teaching strategies discussed later in this chapter will demonstrate. Further, teachers must "recognize that *everyone* is capable of learning math, regardless of age, gender, ability, interests, culture, or home language" (Solarski 2024, 131).

Teaching and Learning in Mathematics

Young children need many opportunities to represent, reinvent, quantify, generalize, and refine the understandings they gain from their experiences and intuitive ideas. To provide meaningful and effective mathematical experiences, intentional teachers design programs so that children encounter concepts in depth and in a logical sequence. They use a variety of approaches and strategies to achieve this focused emphasis. They integrate mathematics into play and daily routines and across other domains in the curriculum, and they do so in a coherent, planned manner. As NAEYC and NCTM (2010) explain, this means that mathematics experiences "follow logical sequences, allow depth and focus, and help children move forward in knowledge and skills"; it does not mean "a grab bag of experiences that seem to relate to a theme or project" (2010, 8).

In addition to integrating mathematics into children's play, classroom routines, and learning experiences in other parts of the curriculum that do not focus exclusively on mathematics, intentional teachers provide carefully planned experiences that focus children's attention on a particular mathematical idea. Small groups are particularly effective for this, allowing teachers to guide children toward a learning objective while also providing child choice and agency.

Research points to the materials and activities that foster the development of mathematical concepts, as well as the criteria that may influence the effectiveness of those materials as learning tools. For example, many teachers use manipulatives, such as counters, Unifix cubes, craft sticks, attribute blocks, three-dimensional shapes, and floor graphs, when engaging children in mathematics learning opportunities. However, using manipulatives doesn't guarantee children are learning mathematics. How teachers and children use the manipulatives matters more for children's learning (Björklund et al. 2022; Laski et al. 2015). For example, young children may become distracted when working with manipulatives to solve mathematical tasks, and teachers may need to suggest they use alternative representations (such as drawings) to remain focused on the task. Nevertheless, manipulatives can be a valuable teaching tool. With many opportunities to manipulate countable sets of objects, children can develop concepts about discrete numbers (such as "how many," "more than," and counting principles). To construct ideas related to continuous quantity (something is "more" or "less" along a scale), children need opportunities to manipulate noncountable materials such as sand, water, or clay (Ginsburg et al. 2006). Interactive media may also play a role in early mathematics education if the technology is used appropriately, especially for children with developmental delays or disabilities (Clements & Sarama 2016; NAEYC & Fred Rogers Center 2012; Wickstrom, Pyle, & DeLuca 2019). (See also "Learning About Technology [Including Traditional and Digital Tools]" on pages 230–234 in Chapter 8.)

Preschoolers' mathematical thinking may also be fostered by cooperative interaction among peers (Clements 2022). Franco, Orellana, and Franke (2021) found that when kindergartners collaborated, asked questions, and observed each other, they extended their numerical knowledge and engaged in spatial reasoning and problem solving. Cooperative learning may also be useful for children with developmental delays or disabilities, who can thrive with structured practice, repetition, and reinforcement of math skills in a supportive environment that promotes math learning interactions with their peers. Of course, intentional teachers can facilitate instruction in a way that promotes reflection and problem solving.

When teachers understand what and how children think and learn in the areas of early mathematics, they recognize the value of daily reliance on mathematics learning opportunities. The strategies listed below are organized around ideas that support intentional efforts to devote *time* to mathematics learning opportunities in meaningful contexts, provide *materials* that promote mathematical thinking and exploration, and *respond* to children in ways that support their development as mathematical thinkers:

Strategies for including mathematics throughout the day (Frye et al. 2013):

> Ensure that children have frequent, focused opportunities to explore mathematics by regularly providing mathematical small groups and one-on-one learning experiences. Extend mathematics learning opportunities throughout each day by embedding mathematics activities or prompts into daily classroom routines.

> Integrate mathematics into the curriculum by introducing mathematics concepts into other areas of the curriculum related to language arts, science, and art.

> Introduce mathematical content through books. Children can be exposed to ideas about counting, operations, shapes, patterns, and all areas of mathematics through books, especially when invited to engage with the books. Storybooks and nonfiction texts are also a wonderful way to introduce real-life problems whose solutions depend on mathematical reasoning (Ginsburg et al. 2019; Heroman 2016; Onesti, Uscianowski, & Mazzocco 2022), and meaningful stories can help children focus on and learn mathematics concepts. Look for books that support mathematics learning in children's home languages. (For a list of suggested storybooks involving math concepts and ideas for using them with children, see Onesti, Uscianowski, & Mazzocco 2022. To find books featuring a wide variety of cultures and languages, see leeandlow.com.)

Strategies for providing math-related materials:

> Create a mathematics-rich physical environment. Provide mathematics materials throughout your classroom. For instance, include Unifix cubes in the block area, where they can be incorporated into children's play. Display numerals and shapes meaningfully on walls and also on materials that children will see and use, such as in the dramatic play area. Be sure all mathematical materials are visible, accurate (a diamond is not a mathematical shape, for example, and yet is often listed as such), and accessible to children so that they can see, manipulate, and discuss these materials easily.

> Encourage exploration. Provide materials that have diverse sensory attributes, and allow children sufficient time and space to discover their properties (see "Materials to Use for Mathematical Exploration" on pages 178–179). At the same time, understand that children may see or use objects in ways that differ from adults' intentions. Teachers might not see the mathematical principles children identify in art materials or dramatic play props, but children might, for instance, count the Velcro strips on a smock; count the rooms of a dollhouse and categorize them by shape or size; or identify symmetries or patterns in materials, books, or even the classroom itself. McClure et al. explain that they might

> line up acorns on a table to take stock of what they have collected on the playground (say, eight big acorns and two small ones) and then determine whether they have more or fewer of a particular size. With guidance from a teacher, they can start solving problems using mathematical reasoning, such as how many more small acorns they would need in order to show equal numbers of small and big ones. (2017, 15)

> Play games with mathematical elements. Games invented for or by children offer many opportunities to address such concepts as (non)equivalence, spatial and temporal relations, and measurement. For instance, when teaching about numbers and counting, have children explore dominoes or dice, and encourage them to match quantities. Many such games (for example, throwing beanbags and measuring their distance from the baseline) are not language dependent and can be adapted for children with developmental delays or disabilities, enabling them to participate with their peers. Ask families to share math games they know from their own childhood or they play in their homes, and share the math games from your classroom to encourage families to play these games at home.

Strategies that focus on teachers' behaviors involve observing, assessing, and responding:

> Individualize teaching. Use observational data captured via checklists, work samples, and anecdotal records to help inform your teaching strategies.

> Model using language for mathematical properties, processes, and relationships. Multilingual learners can pick up these terms along with their peers.

> Model mathematics activities after giving children opportunities to explore the materials in their own ways. This helps to avoid constraining their creative use of the objects (Bonawitz et al. 2011).

> Challenge, coach, and support mathematical thinking. Use facial expressions and gestures as well as drawings to depict math tasks or break down math tasks into smaller steps.

> Encourage reflection and self-correction. Provide hints to help children reconsider their answers and figure out solutions on their own. For example, when a child remarks that a puzzle piece "doesn't fit," say, "I wonder how we can figure out where that piece might fit." Challenge their thinking by asking questions like "Is it a triangle if I turn it this way?" or "If we counted those gems again, do you think there would still be seven?"

> Encourage peer interaction. Children can sometimes explain mathematical ideas to their peers more effectively than adults can. Doing so also solidifies their own understanding of the concepts.

> Draw on children's everyday experiences and home life. For multilingual learners and children of color in particular, these connections signal that their daily experiences are valued (Negrette & Karabon 2023).

In general, an investigative approach promotes exploration and learning over a purely didactic one. As McClure and colleagues (2017) note, "Many early childhood classrooms focus on extremely limited objectives—for example, fostering the memorization of the counting sequence, basic addition facts, and shape names by rote—and, as a result, have minimal impact on children's overall mathematical proficiency." Engaging in open-ended tasks by using investigation and inquiry provides more meaningful opportunities for math learning.

Connecting Teaching to Children's Lives

By Amy Schmidtke

Three kindergartners, Flor, Jorge, and Myra, are playing restaurant in the house center with teacher-created menus featuring photos of traditional Mexican food. Toy versions of the food as well as a cash register are available in the center.

Flor: Our restaurant is open!

Miss Jasmine: (*Walks over and sits at a small table.*)

Flor: Welcome to our restaurant! What do you want to eat? (*Hands Miss Jasmine a menu.*)

Miss Jasmine: Hmm...let me see. Which costs more, the enchiladas or the tacos?

Flor: The tacos are 5 pesos, but the enchiladas are 3 pesos.

Miss Jasmine: So which one costs more?

Flor: (*Thinks.*) The tacos are more money.

Miss Jasmine: Can I please have the combo with two enchiladas and flan? And then I'll have a glass of horchata.

Flor: Yes!

Flor tells Jorge and Myra what Miss Jasmine ordered. They make the food. Within a few minutes, Flor returns to where Miss Jasmine is seated with a plate with two enchiladas, a small saucer with flan, and a plastic cup. She also brings a plastic fork.

Miss Jasmine: (*Pretends to smell the food.*) Oh wow, this smells amazing! Thank you so much! It smells like it has some spicy peppers in it. I love spicy food. How many peppers did you put in my food?

Flor: Three!

Miss Jasmine: (*Pretends to take a bite of an enchilada.*) So delicious! Yum!

Flor brings the toy cash register to the table. In it, there are different denominations of laminated Mexican pesos. Flor hands Miss Jasmine several bills. Miss Jasmine opens the menu.

Miss Jasmine: Let's see how much I owe you. The horchata costs 1 peso. (*Puts down 1 peso.*) And the enchiladas with flan cost 3 pesos. (*Puts down 3 pesos.*) How many pesos do I owe you?

Flor: (*Counts the number of pesos.*) One, two, three, four. Four pesos!

Miss Jasmine: (*Hands over the 4 pesos to Flor.*)

Flor: (*Opens the register and puts the bills inside.*) Thank you!

Miss Jasmine: Thank you!

This vignette exemplifies the concepts of counting, adding, recognizing and naming numerals, and other aspects of number sense, all in a meaningful context. Miss Jasmine taps into the children's funds of knowledge by picking dishes that the children are familiar with. Her goal is to highlight the foods that her children eat, giving them a place of importance in their classroom—something familiar for the Mexican American children as well as exposure to something new for the children from other cultural backgrounds. She also uses the name of the currency that Flor is familiar with (pesos).

Fitting the Learning Experience to the Learning Objective

The rest of this chapter describes what preschoolers learn as they begin to acquire mathematical literacy across NCTM's (2000) five content standards: number and operations, geometry, measurement, algebra, and data analysis and probability. Some of NCTM's standards may seem too sophisticated for preschool mathematics. That is, are young children *really* doing what older children and adults know as geometry, algebra, or probability? In writing its standards document, NCTM opted to use one label for each area across the entire age range, from pre-K to grade 12, to emphasize that for each content standard, children at *every* age are learning aspects of math that relate to that standard. However, in this chapter the labels are modified slightly for three of the areas to be more descriptive of the specific learning occurring at the preschool level; those are geometry and spatial sense; patterns, functions, and algebra; and data analysis. Number and operations as well as measurement remain labeled the same. Of those five areas, number and operations, geometry and spatial sense, and measurement are areas particularly important for 3- to 6-year-olds because they help build children's foundation for mathematics learning.

Each section of this chapter is organized into those concepts and skills that children are most likely to learn through exploration and discovery (child-guided experiences) and those that may require adult-guided experiences to supplement what children learn through their independent efforts. As with every domain in this book, this division is not rigid.

Number and Operations

In the preschool years, number and operations focus on seven elements or goals for early learning: subitizing, counting, composing and decomposing, adding to and taking away, grouping, equal partitioning, and ordinality. (For further explanations and examples, see Clements & Sarama 2020.)

Subitizing is the immediate and accurate recognition of very small quantities (up to four or five) *without* counting. Subitizing is an intuitive skill that teachers can further support by gradually reinforcing children's ability to recognize quantities in groups, thus laying the foundation for later mathematical concepts like multiplication (Clements, Sarama, & MacDonald 2019). This type of subitizing is known as perceptual subitizing; in kindergarten, children move to conceptual subitizing, in which they join two sets of objects.

In contrast to subitizing, *rote counting* involves learning a sequence of number words and reciting those number words. Rote counting is then used to count objects (known as *object counting*) to identify the quantity of items in a collection. Young children rote-count before they master the object counting, but the accuracy of their counting improves as they gain mastery of the principles.

Composing and decomposing of number are complementary processes: Composing is mentally or physically putting, or joining, small groups of objects together (for example, two stones plus three stones makes five stones) and understanding that the combination of smaller numbers leads to another (specific) larger quantity. Decomposing refers to breaking, or separating, a quantity into two or more smaller quantities (for example, five spoons is two spoons plus two spoons plus one spoon, or it is the same as three spoons and two spoons).

Adding to and taking away is knowing that adding to a collection makes it larger and subtracting makes it smaller. When this understanding is combined with counting and (de)composing, children can solve simple problems with increasing efficiency.

Grouping is related to composing/decomposing and addition/subtraction. Sets of objects with the same quantity are groups, and groupings of 10 are the basis for understanding place value later (that is, making groups of 10 and then counting the objects left over). *Equal partitioning* is dividing a collection into equal parts, a prerequisite to children's understanding of division and fractions.

Aside from numbers revealing how many or how much of something exists, numbers also reveal ordinality—for example, which items or groups have more or less of some object attribute such as size, age, or sweetness; the order of objects in a series according to some attribute (such as length, color intensity, loudness); or sequence in position (first, second, and last in line, for instance).

To develop the mathematical understanding and skills encompassed in these areas, preschoolers need an optimal blend of child- and adult-guided experiences. These skills extend far beyond intuitive ideas. Therefore, it is important that young children have ample opportunities to work with materials that lend themselves to ordering, grouping and regrouping, and so on, but it is also important for them to have conversations that build mathematics vocabulary around these ideas (Purpura et al. 2021). Be sure to include materials representative of the children's homes and cultures (for example, nesting dolls), being careful to use materials that are meaningful to the children you work with. Children may intuit certain properties and processes from their spontaneous explorations, whereas adults provide conventional labels to describe the numerical properties and transformations children observe. Adults also challenge children to try additional transformations and reflect on the results. These experiences and the role of the intentional teacher within these experiences are described in the sections that follow.

Of the key knowledge and skills in the area of number and operations, child-guided experiences may be particularly important for the following:

> Intuiting number and its properties

> Performing informal arithmetic

Adult-guided experiences seem to prove helpful for the following:

> Counting and numeration

> Performing simple arithmetic

CHILD-GUIDED experiences are especially important for learnings such as:

Number and Operations	Intuiting number and its properties

Even before they learn how to count, young children intuitively understand quantity and equivalence. For example, they can instantly recognize small quantities (subitizing sets up to four) and can assess which of two small sets contains more or if they are the same (Feigenson et al. 2004). When children learn number words, they may learn to subitize up to five (Clements Sarama, & MacDonald 2019) without counting, specifying how many they detect, especially when prompted by an adult (MacDonald & Wilkins 2016). Children eventually learn to use one-to-one correspondence to establish equivalence (for example, putting one stone on each leaf to see that there are equal quantities). Children may be able to make equal sets (that is, make groups) by putting one in each pile, then another in each pile, and so on (for example, to distribute an equal number of crackers to each person at the table). Although lacking a formal knowledge of sets in a strict mathematical sense (defined as a collection of distinct elements, such as a set of squares versus a set of triangles), young children may also create groups and recognize when items share all or some attributes with other items in a group.

A central objective of early mathematics education is developing children's number sense. This term can refer to intuitive, preverbal skills (such as subitizing) or very broadly to learned skills and knowledge related to numbers and their magnitude, the relationship between quantities, and the operations that can be performed on numbers (Chen, Paul, & Reeve 2022).

Some counting principles are essential to understanding number, such as establishing one-to-one correspondence (linking a single number name with one, and *only one,* object), cardinality, and number constancy. The cardinality principle refers to the understanding that when counting, the last number word in the counting sequence specifies the quantity of a set. Number constancy reflects understanding that moving items around (within a set) does not change how many items there are, as long as none are removed (or added to) during rearrangement. An ability to identify equivalence is also fundamental to understanding number. Three-year-olds may recognize equivalence between collections of one to four objects (for example, two hearts and two squares) without actually enumerating the items. They may also recognize equal collections in different arrangements as being the same (for example, three squares on the top and two on the bottom has the same number as one square on top and four on the bottom). Four-year-olds may make auditory-visual matches, such as equating the sound of three dings with the sight of three dots. These findings suggest that by age 3, children have already developed a nonverbal representation of number, although it's unclear what this mental representation is like or how accurate it is. Regardless, they can clearly represent and compare objects even before they can count them (Baroody 2004; Clements & Sarama 2020). In addition, older preschoolers may also demonstrate comfort with the *part-part-whole* concept, which describes the understanding that a whole number is made up of parts (Richardson & Dolphin 2020). For example, the number 5 is composed of 4 and 1 or 3 and 2. This understanding supports children's later ability to add and subtract.

Teaching strategies. Intuition develops with experience. You can help young children develop their number sense by surrounding them with a number-rich environment that offers many opportunities to work with materials and processes that rely on numbers and their operations, as shown in the following examples (see "Materials to Use for Mathematical Exploration" on pages 178–179 for further suggestions for materials):

> Label and describe number phenomena that occur naturally in the children's play (for example, "There are four wheels on Katie's truck and two more, or six, on Darnell's" and "You found the second mitten for your other hand"). Occasionally recite numerals both in children's home languages and in English. Keep in mind that while reciting numbers helps children talk about math, learning how numbers work is much more important.

> Provide materials that allow children to explore one-to-one correspondence, such as nuts/bolts and seeds/holes in the dirt. Children will also make one-to-one correspondences with any sets of materials they are playing with; for example, they might give each stuffed bear a plate or ball. Here again, the one-to-one concept can be explored independent of the child's proficiency in English or verbal skills.

> Include materials that can be broken down and divided into smaller parts, such as a lump of clay that can be divided into smaller balls or a piece of fruit that can be sliced or separated into sections. Unit blocks, LEGOs, and other toys with equal-size parts that children can build up and then break down into components also work well. Be sure to provide larger manipulatives for children who struggle with fine motor tasks.

Number and Operations > **Performing informal arithmetic**

Informal arithmetic is something similar to adding and subtracting nonsymbolically—that is, without using symbols like numerals, number words, or other written symbols. Even before receiving formal instruction, preschoolers often can solve simple nonverbal addition and subtraction problems (for example, two children are drawing at the table when a third child sits down, and then one child fetches "another" piece of paper for her). Children begin by acting out the problems with objects (such as by setting out two beads and then "adding on" one more). Later they can substitute representations (such as marks on paper) for the physical objects and form mental representations (such as visualizing two beads, then adding one more). This understanding is fundamental to later success in school mathematics. You can help children learn that quantities can be represented by symbols like number words or numerals (Fyfe et al. 2015).

Teaching strategies. Because preschoolers tend to think concretely much of the time, handling objects and working with visual representations like pictures or drawings help them carry out and understand operations. The following are examples of strategies teachers can use:

> Provide many small items that children can group and regroup by adding and subtracting units. Include toys, cooking and eating utensils, items of clothing, and other objects related to children's cultures or parents' occupations that might be found at home (such as spools, thimbles, fasteners). When multilingual learners work with items they have seen at home rather than items they are not familiar with, they can spend less time trying to figure out what an object is and more time focusing on learning the concept or skill.

> Pose simple addition and subtraction problems during everyday experiences. For example, after a child sets the table, say, "Remember that Micah is out sick today" or "Mrs. King is going to join us for snack" and see whether they subtract or add a setting.

> Pose simple multiplication or division problems that children can solve using concrete objects. For example, give a child a collection of objects at small group time, and say, "Give the same number to everyone," or "There are five children, and everyone wants two scarves to wave in the wind. How many scarves will we need to bring outside?"

ADULT-GUIDED experiences are especially important for learnings such as:

Number and Operations > **Counting and numeration**

For young children, counting and numeration (recognizing, naming, and writing numbers) involves understanding the following:

> Numbers: Knowing the number names and the position of each one in the sequence, ordinal numbers (such as first, second, . . .), and cardinal numbers (such as one, two, . . .)

> Notation: Recognizing (hearing number name and locating correct numeral), identifying (pointing to a numeral and saying the correct number name), and writing numerals

> Counting: Determining quantity and equivalence

> Sets: Creating and labeling collections and understanding *all* and *some*

As with learning letter names and shapes, children cannot acquire knowledge of number names and numerals unless adults give them this information. At times children will ask, "How do you write *three*?" or "What comes after ten?," but the intentional teacher also is proactive in introducing the vocabulary and symbols (numerals) children need to understand and represent mathematical ideas (Merkley & Ansari 2016). With adult guidance, children can then apply this knowledge to solve problems, including those of measurement and data analysis.

Materials to Use for Mathematical Exploration

Children can use almost any object to manipulate, sort, count, combine, and measure. The items below lend themselves to exploration and mathematical thinking.

Number and Operations

Printed items containing numbers and mathematical symbols—signs, labels, brochures, pictures of charts and graphs

Materials with numbers on them—calculators, playing cards, games with dice or spinners

Numbers made of wood, plastic, or cardboard (make sure they are sturdy so that children can hold, sort, copy, and trace them)

Discrete items children can count—beads, blocks, shells, bottle caps, Unifix cubes

Paired items to create one-to-one correspondence—pegs and pegboards, colored markers and tops, egg cartons and plastic eggs

Geometry and Spatial Sense

Materials and tools for filling and emptying—water, sand; scoops, shovels

Everyday things to fit together and take apart—LEGOs, Tinkertoys, puzzles, boxes and lids, clothing with different types of fasteners

Attribute blocks that vary in shape, size, color, thickness

Tangram pieces

Wooden and sturdy cardboard blocks in conventional and unconventional shapes

Containers and covers in different shapes and sizes

Materials to create two-dimensional shapes—string, pipe cleaners, yarn

Moldable materials to create three-dimensional shapes—clay, dough, sand, beeswax

Things with moving parts—kitchen utensils, musical instruments, cameras

Books that feature shapes and locations, with illustrations from different perspectives (for example, a farm field photographed from an aerial perspective, an apartment building observed from the sixth floor of a building across the street)

Photos of classroom materials and activities from different viewpoints

Materials that change with manipulation or time—clay, playdough, drawing apps, sand, water, plants, animals

Materials to explore spatial concepts (*over/under, up/down*) and to view things from different heights and positions—climbing equipment, large cartons

Maps and diagrams

Measurement

Ordered sets of materials—nesting blocks, measuring spoons, paintbrushes, drums

Ordered labels so children can find and return materials to their storage place—tracings of measuring spoons on the pegboard in the dramatic play center

Storage containers in graduated sizes

Materials that signal stopping and starting—timers, musical instruments, musical recordings

Materials that can be set to move at different speeds—metronomes, wind-up toys

Things in nature that move or change at different rates—slow- and fast-germinating seeds, insects that creep and scurry

Unconventional measuring tools—yarn, ribbon, blocks, cubes, timers, shoes, ice cubes, containers of all shapes and sizes

Conventional measuring tools—tape measures, scales, clocks, grid paper, thermometers, measuring spoons, graduated cylinders

Patterns, Functions, and Algebra

Materials with visual patterns—toys, dress-up clothes, curtains, upholstery

Materials to copy and create series and patterns—beads, sticks, small blocks, pegs and boards, writing and collage materials

Shells and other patterned items from nature

Original artwork and reproductions featuring patterns—weavings, baskets

Pattern blocks

Routines that follow patterns

Stories, poems, and chants with repeated words and rhythms

Songs with repetitions in melody, rhythm, and words

Mobile apps that allow children to recognize and create series and patterns

Data Analysis

Tools for recording data—clipboards, paper, pencils, crayons, markers, chalk, tablet

Materials for diagramming or graphing data—newsprint pads and easels, graph paper with large grids, poster board, floor graphs, interactive apps

Small objects to represent counted quantities—buttons, acorns, pebbles

Boxes and string for sorting and tying materials into groups

Sticky notes and masking tape for labeling

Early counting is finding out "how many," which is a powerful problem solver and essential to comparing quantities. Research (Gelman & Gallistel 1978) has identified five principles of counting: (1) stable order (two always follows one), (2) one-to-one correspondence (each object is assigned a unique verbal number name), (3) cardinality (the last counting name identifies how many), (4) order irrelevance (objects can be counted in any order without changing the quantity), and (5) abstraction (any set of objects can be counted). Adult-guided experiences help preschoolers develop these understandings.

Older preschoolers may use counting to determine if two sets of objects are equivalent. Between the ages of 3 and 4, as they acquire verbal counting skills, children are increasingly able to represent and compare sets of objects, including collections larger than four items. They recognize the "same number name" principle (two collections are equal if they share the same number name, despite any differences in physical appearance). Similarly, by counting and comparing two unequal collections, preschoolers can discover the "larger number" principle (the later a number word appears in the sequence, the larger it is). By age 4, many preschool children can name and rote-count up to 10 and compare sets of objects up to 5. When they have ample opportunities to learn the counting sequence, children often learn to count a collection of 20 objects by age 5 (Clements 2004; Clements & Sarama 2020). They are also fascinated by large numbers, such as 100 or a "gazillion," even if they only know them as number names without a true sense of their value.

Equal partitioning builds on and is related to the concept of equivalence. Equal partitioning is the process of dividing something (for example, a plate of eight cookies) into equal-size parts (for example, to serve four children). Children as young as 5 can divide a quantity into equal size groups when prompted (Björklund et al. 2022).

Teaching strategies. Children seem to be interested in counting everything. You can invent or take advantage of many situations to count objects and events in children's daily lives. Here are some examples:

> Notice things that children typically compare (such as the number of children in the room today, or their ages) and provide materials and experiences based on these observations. Think of fun and unusual things to count, such as the number of mosquito bites on someone's ankle or freckles on an arm. As children gather or distribute countable materials, engage them in counting items at cleanup, small group (handing out one glue bottle per child), and choice time (distributing playing cards).

> After children finish counting, always remember to ask "How many?" or "How many altogether?" to support children's understanding that the last counting word reflects the full quantity (that is, the cardinality principle).

> Make numerals prominent. Place numerals of different materials, sizes, colors, and fonts throughout the classroom. Provide cards with dots and numerals for children to explore, sort, and arrange in order. When you use sign-up sheets, use numerals so children can indicate not only the order in which they will take turns but also how many turns they want or for how long (such as two minutes, three flips of the sand timer).

> Use written numerals, and encourage children to write them. For example, when they play store, encourage them to write size and price labels, orders, and the amount of the bill. Writing numerals can give multilingual learners a language-free way to participate with their peers—as well as an opportunity for adults (and other children) to supply the English words for the numerals they write.

> Respond to children's own questions as the springboard for teachable moments rather than simply supply an answer. For example, if a child asks how old they will be on their birthday and whether they will be older than another child, you might ask other nearby children to help figure it out given the children's current ages.

Number and Operations > Performing simple arithmetic

Younger preschoolers perform simple arithmetic concretely—that is, by physically manipulating objects to join and separate them from a set. Some older preschoolers, however, begin to add and subtract whole numbers by using numerals to abstractly represent small collections of objects rather than physically manipulating or visualizing the objects. They can do this because they can hold a representation of quantities in their minds. For example, they may say out loud, "Two and one more is three" or "If Logan isn't here today, I only need four trays."

Teaching strategies. Arithmetic follows fixed rules or conventions. As with combining letters into words, performing operations on numbers depends on knowing these rules. With support from their teachers, preschoolers can use counting to solve simple word problems that come up in play and exploration; they do this by seeing or representing each object. Teachers can therefore readily implement strategies such as the following to enhance young children's early understanding and use of arithmetic:

> Use real objects when helping children solve word problems. For example, if a child is lining up animal figures, ask how many how dogs there would be if he added two more to make the row longer. Wonder aloud how many dogs would be left if he made it three animals shorter.

> Pose challenges that build on children's interests. For example, if a child calls your attention to the enclosures they made for their two squirrels—one for each squirrel—you might wonder aloud, "Hmm, what if two more squirrels came? I wonder how you could include them." Be careful, however, to not let your questions or "wonderings" derail the child's own intentions for the activity.

> Encourage children to use arithmetic to answer their own questions. For example, if a child says, "My daddy wants to know how many tortillas to bring for snack time tomorrow," you could reply, "Well, there are sixteen children and two teachers. Plus, your daddy and your brother will be here, too. How can we figure out how many tortillas you'll need to bring?"

> Engage children in reflecting on their arithmetic solutions rather than tell them whether they're right or wrong. When children are stumped or arrive at erroneous answers, resist the temptation to give the answer or correct them. Instead offer comments or pose questions that encourage them to rethink their solutions ("Remember in our small group how we touched each button when we counted them? I wonder if you could try that with your stickers to find out how many you have").

Geometry and Spatial Sense

In the preschool years, learning about geometry and spatial sense focuses on four elements:

> Shape: The outline or contour (form) of objects; comprises identifying two- and three-dimensional shapes

> Spatial relationships: Understanding the relationship of objects in the environment

> Transformation: The process of moving (sliding, rotating, flipping) shapes to determine whether they are the same; it also involves building larger shapes from smaller shapes

> Visualization and spatial reasoning: Creating mental images of geometric objects, examining them, and transforming them

At first, children's mental representations are static; that is, children cannot manipulate them. Later children can move and transform images mentally, such as deciding whether a chair will squeeze into a given space, how low to bend their bodies to slide under a shelf, or how to rotate a puzzle piece to interlock it with the one beside it. These shifts in mental representation ability emerge gradually.

Spatial concepts and language are closely related; words facilitate an understanding of such concepts as on top of, next to, behind, and inside. For example, where someone stands determines whether they are in front of or behind another object. Because society has specific conventions for labeling various shapes, transformations, and especially concepts of position, location, and so on, teachers need to enhance children's descriptive vocabulary in this domain. Integrating spatial language into play-based math activities will help children develop spatial reasoning (Casasola et al. 2020). Many spatial terms are new to preschoolers, so multilingual learners can learn the words together with their English-speaking peers, assisted by visual cues and actions (with their bodies and materials).

Of the key knowledge and skills in the area of geometry and spatial sense, child-guided experiences seem most helpful for the following:

> Familiarity with two- and three-dimensional shapes and their attributes

> Orienting self and objects in space

Adult-guided experiences may be especially significant for the following:

> Creating, naming, and transforming shapes

> Articulating position, location, direction, and distance

CHILD-GUIDED experiences are especially important for learnings such as:

Geometry and Spatial Sense — **Familiarity with two- and three-dimensional shapes and their attributes**

Geometry is the study of space and shape. It provides a way to describe, interpret, and imagine the world (Clements 1999). In mathematics, we refer to geometric shapes (square, triangle, circle, rectangle). While children may also encounter and explore other shapes (heart, flower), the focus here is on two- and three-dimensional geometric shapes.

For young children, shape knowledge develops through a combination of visual and tactile exploration, which begins in infancy. During the preschool years, the emphasis shifts to using language to describe shapes and their attributes. Over time, this helps children recognize, name, and compare shapes, as well as combine (compose) and separate (decompose) shapes. They also begin to explore transformations of shapes (flip, turn, rotate) and may develop an intuitive understanding of symmetry. (Note that children need adult-initiated experiences to accurately label and describe transformations and symmetry.)

It is important to provide children with multiple examples of shapes and their attributes in different contexts and using various materials. For example, offer a variety of triangles, not just equilateral triangles. Turn a square and ask if it is still a square—and why. Show both examples and nonexamples of shapes, encouraging children to identify the nonexamples and explain what makes them different. For all children, but especially multilingual learners, many of these terms may be completely new. Providing only one example can limit their understanding of the concept, so exposing them to a variety of examples is crucial for building a strong foundation.

Teaching strategies. Language is important in all areas of mathematics but especially so in geometry. The following are some helpful strategies that teachers can use to help children develop more precise language as they explore attributes of two- and three-dimensional shapes:

> Introduce both two- and three-dimensional shapes, giving children opportunities to explore them. Include both regular and irregular shapes. Engage children in drawing and tracing the shapes. Provide models (drawings, molds, scale models) and tools children can use to trace or copy them. Visual and physical shapes help young children grasp the essential attributes of each.

> Encourage children to sort shapes, and provide reasons for their groupings. Invite them to describe why objects are *not* alike.

> Provide accurate information to children to help them describe "their shape explanations as right as possible" (Early Math Collaborative, Erikson Institute 2014, 161). Young children get excited about seeing shapes in their environment, and they tend to overgeneralize. For example, a child might point to their sandwich cut into triangles and name it as a triangle. However, the corners of the bread are round. You could respond by saying, "It does look like a triangle. It has three sides. But what do you notice about the corners? They're round. But it *reminds* us of a triangle, doesn't it?"

> Suggest to children that they combine (compose) and take apart (decompose) shapes to create new shapes, such as combining two triangles to make a square or rectangle and vice versa. Engage them in discussions about these transformations.

> As three children explore different shapes, Miss Mei-Ling asks how many triangles they need to make a square. The children discover they can use two triangles to make a square and combine squares to make other shapes. Miss Mei-Ling then asks them to see if they can make a square with two different triangles, and the children discover they cannot. "The sides don't line up!" says Amir.

> Provide materials that have symmetry that is vertical (meaning the left/right halves are identical) or horizontal (meaning the top/bottom halves are identical)—for example, doll clothes, a teeter-totter, a toy airplane, and a leaf with a center axis. For contrast, provide similar but asymmetric materials—for example, a glove, slide (from the side), toy crane (from the side), and an irregularly shaped leaf. Engage children in discussing how the two sides (or top and bottom) of objects are the same (symmetrical) or different (asymmetrical).

> For multilingual learners in particular, point to objects and use gestures; short, clear sentences; and rich oral descriptions.

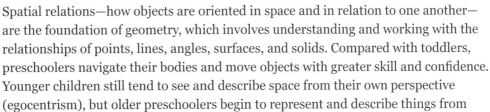

Spatial relations—how objects are oriented in space and in relation to one another—are the foundation of geometry, which involves understanding and working with the relationships of points, lines, angles, surfaces, and solids. Compared with toddlers, preschoolers navigate their bodies and move objects with greater skill and confidence. Younger children still tend to see and describe space from their own perspective (egocentrism), but older preschoolers begin to represent and describe things from another person's point of view (perspective taking). Children are also increasingly able to visualize and mentally manipulate spatial relationships and describe relationships between objects and places with more precision (Early Math Collaborative, Erikson Institute 2014).

Teaching strategies. Because mathematics is the search for relationships, early instruction should focus on physical experiences through which children construct understandings about space. Teachers do this primarily by providing materials and giving children ample time to explore them, as described in these strategies:

> Create different types of space in the classroom and outdoor area—small spaces for children to maneuver into and around; large open areas where children can move about freely; and spaces for children to crawl over and under, in and out, up and down, and around and through. Talk with children about their relationships with objects and one another. Provide a space and means for children with developmental delays or disabilities to have this same discovery and participate with other children while experiencing the space.

> Create an obstacle course for children to explore. Invite them to create their own courses and explain to others how to move through it, using directional and positional vocabulary.

> Provide materials, time, and ample space for children to build with construction toys. Notice and occasionally comment on the dimension and position concepts the children use: "Yes, I see you made a driver's seat *up front* and made a steering wheel to fit *on top of* the dashboard. I wonder where you will put a spot for Dhalia's wheelchair to fit?"

> Read books that emphasize direction and orientation, such as *Rosie's Walk,* by Pat Hutchins.

> Look for mobile apps that allow children to move and transform shapes. Manipulating shapes on a screen allows children to do what their hands may not yet have the dexterity to perform, and it is especially valuable for those with limited motor control or difficulties with eye-hand coordination.

ADULT-GUIDED experiences are especially important for learnings such as:

| Geometry and Spatial Sense | Creating, naming, and transforming shapes |

The ability to accurately name, describe, and compare shape, size (scale), and volume is important for children to acquire during the preschool years. Many teachers emphasize shape naming but miss opportunities to go beyond this skill to develop children's deeper understanding by describing attributes, comparing, and transforming. With appropriate experiences and input, children are more likely to learn to transform shapes and be able to describe the transformation (for example, "I'm making this bridge longer by adding more blocks at the end and holding it up in the middle"). They can also create and label symmetry in their two- and three-dimensional creations. Language is critical with all these activities; as vocabulary expands, so does geometric understanding.

Teaching strategies. Building on preschoolers' explorations of shapes, explicitly focus the children's attention on features and what the shapes will do (for example, "Which of these shapes can roll?"), and provide words for these characteristics. Provide opportunities for children to identify shapes in various transformations, including reflections and rotations and (de) compositions. For example, try these strategies:

> Comment on and ask children about differences in the size and scale of things that interest them, such as their own bodies, food portions, or rocks. Encourage them to alter two- and three-dimensional materials and comment on the transformations.

> Identify and label shapes and their characteristics throughout the children's environment. Go on a shape hunt in the classroom or neighborhood (for example, a "triangle search"). Use increasingly sophisticated vocabulary words; for example, say, "On our walk, let's look for all the square signs" or "You used cubes and rectangular blocks to build your dollhouse." Identify shape names in children's home languages as well as English. (Showing children the connections between words in different languages, such as *triangle* and *triángulo* and *cube* and *cubo,* is an effective teaching strategy for multilingual learners. These are called *cognates*.)

> Use accurate definitions of shapes. For example, a rectangle is defined by having four sides and four right angles, not "two long sides and two short sides." Avoid common mistakes. For example, a square *is* a rectangle. (Many adults tell children a square is not a rectangle!) It is a special kind of rectangle because all the sides are the same length. A diamond is not a geometric shape, although some commercial posters use that incorrect labeling. (Instead, use the word *rhombus* with children.) Note that young children need many opportunities to explore a variety of shapes, in different arrangements and orientations, and talk about them before they can fully grasp their definitions. However, they will not need to unlearn incorrect definitions later if you accurately expose them to mathematical ideas at an early age.

> Encourage the exploration of shapes beyond conventional ones such as circles, squares, and (equilateral) triangles. Young children enjoy hearing and learning names such as *cylinder* and *trapezoid*. Even if they do not fully grasp the meaning and characteristics, they become attuned to the variety of spatial phenomena in the world. Also important is giving children diverse examples of triangles and other shapes, not just the equilateral triangle that is the only example offered in many classrooms.

> Use real shapes when focusing on attributes. Be cautious when showing pictures of 3-d shapes, which are actually in 2-d form and can be confusing for young children. Look for shapes that may feature prominently in various cultures (for example, those used as design motifs in clothing, banners, or symbols). Encourage children to build structures like those in storybooks and information books. Refer to the books and talk about how the children are re-creating or modifying the structures or both.

Geometry and Spatial Sense | **Articulating position, location, direction, and distance**

With appropriate adult guidance, preschoolers can use position and direction words and follow orientation directions. They also can move beyond their egocentric perceptions to predict another's perspective. For example, with experience they can give appropriate directions or instructions to another person.

Teaching strategies. Young children need you to supply vocabulary for position, location, direction, and distance concepts, of course. But they still master such ideas through a combination of concrete experience and mental imagery, so provide many opportunities for them to represent these concepts in two- and three-dimensional ways. Consider the following suggestions:

> Make comments and ask questions that focus on location and direction, such as "You attached the sides by putting a long piece of string between the two shorter ones" or "Where will your road turn when it reaches the wall?" Comment on location in children's drawings using position words: "What's poking out behind the curtain?"

> Engage children with making and interpreting maps—for finding a hidden object, for example. Children can draw diagrams of the classroom, their rooms at home, and other familiar places. Simple drawing apps on a tablet can be used for this purpose, especially for children whose motor or coordination abilities are limited.

> Create occasions for children to give directions—for example, when helping each other or leading during large group. This requires them to use position and direction words, such as "Hold the top, and push down hard into the dough."

> Use movement to focus on spatial concepts. Provide objects that children can throw safely, such as beanbags and foam balls, and talk with children about distance. Use simple movement directions for games and dances at large group time. Invent variations to games and dances (for example, the "eensy, weensy spider" might crawl "down" into a cave or wriggle "through" a tunnel). Engage the children in making up their own variations. Adapt this activity for children with physical disabilities or sensory needs; they should have opportunities both to participate and to lead.

Measurement

"Measurement is any process that produces a quantitative description of an attribute, such as length, circumference, weight, temperature, volume, or number" (Early Math Collaborative, Erikson Institute, n.d.). In the preschool years, learning about measurement focuses on three big ideas (Early Math Collaborative, Erikson Institute 2014):

> **Many different attributes can be measured, even when measuring a single object.** For example, one could measure a teddy bear's length, height, width, and weight.

> **All measurement involves a "fair" comparison.** This includes aligning or equalizing beginning points, most often with direct comparisons between two objects. For example, two children stand back-to-back to determine who is taller or shorter.

> **Quantifying a measurement helps us describe and compare more precisely.** For example, children might use unit blocks to measure their height, count the blocks, and report, "I am six unit blocks tall."

Young children base their observations on perception, not standard units. Therefore, nonstandard measurement is the focus during the preschool years. Although standard measurement tools are often available for exploration (ruler, thermometer, yardstick, scale), educators do not expect children to be able to use them accurately until they are older. The goal for preschoolers is to use a nonstandard unit of measurement (Unifix cubes, blocks, paper clips, links) to determine an object's size, weight, or volume.

Of the key knowledge and skills in the area of measurement, child-guided experiences seem integral for the following:

> Comparing (seriating), or estimating without counting or measuring

Adult-guided experiences seem integral for the following:

> Counting or measuring to quantify differences

CHILD-GUIDED experiences are especially important for learnings such as:

| Measurement | Comparing (seriating), or estimating without counting or measuring |

Young children are able to grasp the basic concept of one thing being bigger, longer, heavier, and the like, relative to another. Making comparisons is the beginning of measurement. According to NCTM's (2000) standards, preschoolers should be engaged in comparing length, capacity, weight, area, volume, time, and temperature.

At first, children may make *general* quantitative comparisons by matching or ordering things ("My cup holds more water than yours") rather than *specific* comparisons that use counting or measuring ("I have two more oranges than you"). To estimate, they may use their various senses, such as eyeballing (visual), lifting (kinesthetic), or listening (auditory). They may compare length by aligning several twigs at the bottom and seeing how much they stick out at the top or listen to instruments to compare their loudness.

Teaching strategies. You can draw on children's interest in comparing to focus their attention on quantitative differences. Try these strategies:

> Encourage children to move at different rates throughout the day and comment on relative speed. Make transitions fun by asking children to proceed to another area or activity as slow as a snail or as fast as a rocket. Invite children to make their body as tall as they can or as short as they can or to wave the streamer up high or down low.

> Call children's attention to graduated changes in nature. Comment on seasonal fluctuations in temperature (for example, "It feels colder now than it did when we went to the pumpkin patch. We're wearing heavier jackets"). Plant a garden, and ask children how long they think it will take before the seeds germinate or the vegetables are ready to be eaten.

ADULT-GUIDED experiences are especially important for learnings such as:

| Measurement | Counting or measuring to quantify differences |

Preschoolers use nonstandard units, such as how many steps it takes to cross the schoolyard in each direction or the number of song verses that are sung in the time that it takes to clean up different areas of the room. Older preschoolers and kindergarten children may be able to understand the idea of standard units, and with well-conceived learning experiences, they can begin to determine differences in quantity by systematic measurement. They may use their knowledge of numbers to make comparisons. With your assistance, they can acquire the understanding that it is useful to employ conventional units and measuring devices.

Teaching strategies. There are many opportunities throughout the day for children to measure, such as while building something or resolving a dispute. However, preschoolers usually don't think to measure or quantify things to solve these problems. Actively encourage children to use measurement with strategies such as the following:

> Provide nonstandard measuring materials, such as string, plastic chains, or paper towel tubes for length; sand timers for duration; and bucket balances and unmarked bags of clay or sand for weight. Encourage children to use them to answer questions or solve problems. When children ask measurement-related questions ("Which one is heavier?") or have disputes ("I am too taller by a whole, big lot!"), ask them which of these materials might help them arrive at an answer or a solution.

> Pose measurement challenges that children will be motivated to solve (for example, "I wonder how many cups of sand it will take to fill all twelve muffin tins?"). For comparisons, you might ask questions like "Did the cup or the jar hold more?"

> When resolving social conflicts with children, ask how they could use measurement to guarantee a fair solution—for example, "How can we make sure everyone gets to use the tablet for the same amount of time?"

> Use visual models to help children understand and quantify differences. For example, make a daily routine chart where the length of each part in inches is proportional to its duration in minutes. Such representations are helpful for multilingual learners and children with developmental delays or disabilities who may be adjusting to the program's routine.

> Create opportunities for group construction projects, such as laying out a garden, making a bed for each doll within a defined space, or re-creating a supermarket after a class field trip. These often lead to situations where children have different opinions and need to measure to find out who is right or what solution will work. Sometimes you will need to suggest this method of resolving the difference of opinion.

> Informally use standard measurement terms, such as inches, pounds, or degrees (for example, "My puppy gained five pounds since the last time I took him to the vet").

Patterns, Functions, and Algebra

In the preschool years, learning about patterns, functions, and algebra focuses on two elements. The first, identifying patterns, involves recognizing and copying patterns and determining the core unit of a repeating pattern. This includes visual, auditory, and movement patterns. The second element, describing change, is about using language to describe the state or status of something before and after a transformation, as in, "When I was a baby, I couldn't drink out of a cup" or "When we raised the ramp a little higher, my car went all the way to the bookshelf."

Of the key knowledge and skills in the area of patterns, functions, and algebra, child-guided experiences seem to help children with the following:

> Recognizing, copying, and creating simple patterns

> Recognizing naturally occurring change

Adult-guided experiences may be especially significant for the following:

> Identifying and extending complex patterns

> Controlling change

CHILD-GUIDED experiences are especially important for learnings such as:

| Patterns, Functions, and Algebra | Recognizing, copying, and creating simple patterns |

For young children, this area encompasses an awareness of patterns in the environment (visual, auditory, temporal, movement). Rittle-Johnson et al. explain that many children are able to succeed on a more sophisticated pattern activity than they are frequently encouraged to do at home or at school (2015). Preschoolers can develop the ability to copy or create simple patterns with two elements, such as *abab* or *aabb* (for example, alternating slices of apple-pear-apple-pear on a plate; a movement sequence that goes jump-jump-clap-clap-jump-jump-clap-clap). Even before they know the word *pattern*, children notice recurring designs or routines in their lives, whether it be the polka dots on their clothing, the stripes on a kitten's back, or the order of each day's activities.

Teaching strategies. Simple observations and questions can lead children to notice and create regularity and repetition in the objects and events in their environment. You can help children discern common patterns and series with the following strategies:

> Ask children to do or make things that involve series and patterns, such as using drawing or sculpting materials to represent their families from the smallest to the biggest members. Other materials that lend themselves to pattern making include string and beads in different colors and shapes, blocks of varying sizes, and pegs and boards.

> Acknowledge the patterns children spontaneously create in art and construction projects by using math language to describe what you observe. For example, name a child's pattern aloud: "I see you made a pattern with blue and red. It goes blue, red, blue, red, blue, red" (Rittle-Johnson, Fyfe, & Hofer 2022). Music provides many opportunities for calling attention to patterns: "You beat out two loud, one soft, two loud, and one soft beat with the rhythm sticks." The verbal repetition, together with the visual representation, is especially useful for multilingual learners exploring new vocabulary words. As children become more comfortable with patterns, you can ask questions about their patterning and encourage them to make observations (Rittle-Johnson et al. 2022).

| Patterns, Functions, and Algebra | Recognizing naturally occurring change |

Noticing and describing changes includes identifying what natural variables are causal. For example, children see changes in their own bodies (such as getting taller) or the growth of a flower. Although they are often unable to identify the causal factor accurately, young children do make guesses, both right and wrong, about the changes they see (for example, "I'm 5 today. That means I'm taller" or "The flower grew up because the wind blew on it from the bottom").

Teaching strategies. The most important strategy you can follow in this area is to acknowledge children's awareness of changes in their environment and initiate situations in which children can create, observe, and investigate change. For example, comment on children's experiments with color mixing at the easel. Repeating and extending children's comments about the changes they observe lets them know that you are listening to them. Calling their attention to change and showing that you are interested in their reactions and explanations is also a form of acknowledgment. Consider the following strategies:

> Repeat children's comments to acknowledge their spontaneous seriation. For example, when Zahra said, "These giants are the hungriest because they have the biggest teeth," Mrs. Allen said, "So the giants with the biggest teeth will be able to eat a lot more food than the giants with small- and medium-size teeth."

> Extend children's comments. For example, Asher was washing his hands at the sink when Ms. Janine turned on the water in the next sink full blast. Asher said, "Mine is running slow." Ms. Janine turned down her water and said, "I made mine slow*er* like yours."

> Call children's attention to cycles in nature with concrete examples. Point out the seasonal variations in trees or the changing thickness of children's jackets from fall (lightweight) to winter (heavy) to spring (back to lightweight).

ADULT-GUIDED experiences are especially important for learnings such as:

| Patterns, Functions, and Algebra | Identifying and extending complex patterns |

With experience and adult input, children can learn to work with more advanced pattern types. For example, older preschoolers and kindergartners are able to analyze, replicate, and extend the core unit of a complex repeating pattern with three or more elements (*abcabc*; 1-22-3-1-22-3), provided they see or hear it several times (Clements 2004; Clements & Sarama 2020). They can also begin to recognize what are called "growing" patterns—that is, patterns in which successive elements differ (rather than repeat) but still proceed according to an underlying principle, such as counting by 1s or 2s (2-4-6). The same principles apply to patterns in nature. Younger children may notice past and present seasons; older preschoolers are ready to grasp the cycling of four seasons in a year.

Teaching strategies. You can play an active role in helping young children identify and create multipart repeating and growing patterns and sequences using strategies such as the following:

> Comment on the patterns children create, identifying repeating units. For example, Leah showed a painting of "two rainbows" to Ms. Oksana. It was actually two sequences or patterns of color that were exactly the same. Ms. Oksana pointed to each and commented that one rainbow had green, red, purple, and yellow, and so did the other.

> Introduce children to the books and catalogs with complex patterns used by ceramic tilers, landscape designers (brick and paver patterns), and fiber artists (weaving, quilting, needlepoint, basketry). Engage children in describing the patterns and finding corresponding examples in their own environment that contain one or more comparable repeated elements, such as the walkway to the school or a knitted woolen hat.

> Call children's attention to complex patterns and sequences in their environment, such as markings on plants and animals or arts and crafts in their community. Collect things with complex patterns on a nature walk, and have children copy and extend the patterns (or create their own comparable ones) at small group or art time.

> Provide mobile apps or computer programs that allow children to recognize and create series and patterns.

> Sing songs with repeating patterns (where verses and chorus alternate) or growing patterns (countdown songs such as "I Know an Old Lady Who Swallowed a Fly"). Comment on the patterns, and encourage children to identify them.

> Use movement to focus on patterns, including traditional dances with simple repeating steps. Older preschoolers can sequence three movements. If children can master these, encourage them to be leaders and suggest three-step sequences.

Younger children spontaneously notice changes in themselves and their environment. Older preschoolers not only observe but can also begin to articulate the reasons for such changes. Moreover, they can deliberately manipulate variables to produce a desired effect. For example, they may alter the choice of materials and their arrangement to better represent something in a collage or alter the length and angle of a ramp to affect the speed of a toy car.

Teaching strategies. Promote awareness of and curiosity about change by fostering a spirit of inquiry. Children will begin to pose the kinds of questions that scientists use when they want to know about the properties of materials and how they operate, and then predict and estimate or measure the results to satisfy their curiosity. Children are eager to manipulate variables and see the outcomes. Here are some strategies to encourage their explorations:

› Highlight when change occurs as children play with materials, such as a box and rocks ("The box used to be filled with rocks; now it's empty"), when working with clay ("That piece of clay was round and chunky, but you pounded and rolled it, and now it's flat and thin"), or while reading books ("The puppy used to be in the basket. Now he's in the bathtub!").

› Make "I wonder what would happen if . . ." statements (for example, "I wonder what would happen if you made this end of the ramp higher").

› Ask "Suppose you wanted to . . ." questions (for example, "Suppose you wanted to make the car go slower. How do you think you could do that?").

› Encourage older preschoolers to anticipate the consequences of their proposed solutions to social problem-solving situations. If they foresee difficulties, have them consider how to change all or part of the solution to avoid them.

Data Analysis

Data analysis is all about asking questions and finding answers. Data is gathered and then organized in a way that the information can be used to answer the question. In the preschool years, learning about data analysis focuses on three elements: collecting and categorizing data (for example, the favorite foods of children in the class); diagramming, graphing, or otherwise recording and displaying the data (for example, an object graph, pictograph, bar graph, or tally chart with marks); and asking questions, deciding what data is needed, and then interpreting the data gathered to answer the questions (for example, what to have for snack).

Of the key knowledge and skills in the area of data analysis, child-guided experiences may be particularly important for the following:

> Making collections and sorting/classifying by quantitative attributes

Adult-guided experiences may be especially significant for the following:

> Representing gathered information
> Interpreting and applying information

CHILD-GUIDED experiences are especially important for learnings such as:

| Data Analysis | Making collections and sorting/classifying by quantitative attributes |

Children love to collect and sort things. Sorting involves noticing, describing, and comparing the attributes of things (animals, people, objects) and events. Young children can classify according to one attribute (for example, shape) and when they are a bit older by two attributes (such as shape and size). Children also typically classify objects or phenomena according to temperature, loudness, speed, duration, and weight.

Teaching strategies. Because children are natural collectors, they will eagerly initiate and respond to suggestions in this area of mathematics. By showing interest in their collecting and arranging, and by asking skillful questions that focus on the measurable attributes of the materials children gather, you can extend child-guided explorations. Consider using the following:

> Encourage children to make collections of items in the classroom, natural objects gathered on field trips, and various objects they bring from home. Provide containers (bowls, boxes, baskets) for them to sort the items. Ask them to explain and describe their collections, especially attributes related to characteristics that can be measured.

> Have children explain why things do *not* fit into the categories they have created. For example, pick up a feather and ask, "Would this feather fit there?" while gesturing to a pile of metal objects.

> Provide opportunities for children to experiment with materials whose attributes involve all the senses, such as shape, texture, size, color, pitch, loudness, taste, and aroma. Although some of these attributes are not directly measurable, children can still compare them in quantitative terms, such as whether one piece of fabric is smoother than another swatch of material. This is an excellent activity for children with developmental delays or disabilities, but also be sensitive to individual children's sensory overload. Provide textures that children with developmental delays or disabilities are familiar with, such as the fabric of their favorite raincoat.

> Acknowledge and repeat children's attribute labels, including invented ones ("This fruit feels *squishier* on my tongue"). Use common words to build children's vocabulary ("You used a lot more *blue* in the top part of your painting than on the bottom part"), and introduce new language to expand their descriptive language ("This cloth feels *silkier*").

ADULT-GUIDED experiences are especially important for learnings such as:

Data Analysis ⟩ **Representing gathered information**

Representing information for purposes of data analysis means documenting categories and quantities with numbers, diagrams, charts, graphs, counters (for example, one button for each occurrence), and other symbols. These activities involve knowledge of key mathematics concepts.

Teaching strategies. Children are naturally curious about their environment, but their investigations tend to be limited in scope and haphazard in procedure. Adult intervention can make children's explorations and conclusions more systematic and meaningful. The following strategies help children use mathematics to answer questions that interest them:

> Provide materials children can use to record and represent data, such as clipboards, graph paper, pencils, and simple mobile apps.

> Pose questions with answers that require children to gather and analyze data, such as "How many bags of gerbil food do we need to feed Pinky for one month?" Focus on things of particular interest to children, such as their bodies (height, age, hair color), animals and nature (types of pets), the dimensions of things they build, and what they and their friends like and dislike (foods, favorite story characters). For example, chart the ingredients children like best in trail mix, and use the data to make snacks in proportion to their tastes.

> Be alert to situations that lend themselves to documentation, such as construction projects that involve multiples of materials. For example, if children build a train, help them chart the number of cars or units in the track. If the cars have different sizes, create rows or columns and encourage children to record the number of each.

Data Analysis > **Interpreting and applying information**

This component of data analysis refers to making and testing predictions, drawing conclusions, and using the results of an investigation to establish or clarify facts, make plans, or solve problems.

Teaching strategies. Without adult intervention, children's mathematical inquiries often end with just collecting information. They may need help to analyze the data to draw conclusions. Children's learning is less likely to end there if teachers encourage them to apply it to related topics and to solving problems. Try strategies such as these:

> Encourage children to test out their hypotheses to resolve differences when they arise. For example, if children debate who in the group runs the fastest, help them select a beginning and endpoint for a racecourse, record and enter their running times with a stopwatch, and discuss the results to reach a conclusion.

> Make simple summaries, and comment on the data the children have collected or displayed (for example, "So in our class we have two children who are 5 years old, eight who are 4, and six who are 3").

> When analyzing the data displayed on a graph with young children, begin by reading the question posed and then asking the children an open-ended question ("What do you notice about our data?," "What is the data telling us?," or "What do you think the answer to our question is?"). Then, based on the children's responses, ask more close-ended questions ("Which one has more?," "Which one has less?"). This encourages the children to think critically and make sense of the information collected.

> Encourage children to predict the outcome of something, record their predictions, and then compare the predictions with the results. For example, have each child guess how far a toy car will travel using a ramp and then compare how use of force affects how far the car travels. They can record their estimates and the outcomes, then discuss which estimates were most accurate and why. You might have the children use a digital app to document and record and even take videos of their experiments. Encourage children to discuss patterns they find in the data.

• • •

This chapter demonstrates that young children are eager to enter the world of mathematics. If adults create an atmosphere that encourages investigation and engages children in reflection using English, their home languages, and accommodations and adaptations for children with developmental delays or disabilities, they will experience the pleasures of math in their daily lives. In addition, as NAEYC and NCTM (2010) explain, "positive experiences with using mathematics to solve problems [will] help children to develop dispositions such as curiosity, imagination, flexibility, inventiveness, and persistence that contribute to their future success in and out of school" (4).

For Further Consideration

1. Why do some early childhood educators underestimate young children's mathematical abilities? What does this underestimation say about how practitioners define this subject area and their self-perceived knowledge and skills?

2. Would you describe yourself as someone who is comfortable with math or as someone with "math anxiety"? How does, or how will, your attitude toward math affect how you engage children with this subject? What changes can you make if needed?

3. Do gender differences in mathematics (favoring the involvement of boys) seem to emerge in the preschool years? If your answer is no, what lessons can educators learn from early childhood practice to sustain girls' interest in this subject and prevent the emergence of a gender gap in later years? If your answer is yes, how can educators alter their practices to instill and fortify lasting interest in this subject by girls?

4. How can (and should) teachers take advantage of emerging technologies to enhance early learning in mathematics? Is there such a thing as harmful technology, or do the (dis)advantages lie only in its application?

Learning Objectives

1. To expand understanding of early childhood science as an engaging, essential element in young children's learning and development

2. To identify ways to enrich the classroom environment, culture, and curriculum and instruction to foster inquiry and learning in physical, life, and earth and space science

3. To evaluate current science instruction and plan to broaden strategies for supporting children's science inquiry and learning

CHAPTER 8

Science

Cindy Hoisington

As part of their study on living things, Ms. Amina's class is digging holes in their small outdoor nature space to plant seedlings they sprouted in the classroom from a variety of seeds. They have been observing, describing, and comparing the different parts of the seedlings and talking about how each part helps the seedlings live and grow (structure and function). Liam suddenly shouts, "A worm! I found a worm!" and all the children gather around to see it. Ms. Amina holds the worm on her palm and invites the children to look at it closely and touch it gently. The children make lots of observations such as "Look how long it is!" and "It's stretching on your hand!" Ms. Amina asks, "Do you think we can figure out what part is the head and what part is the tail?" and "Where do you think it lives?"

• • •

Tyler, 4, and Uri, 3, are attempting to build castles in the sand table using small cups, but the dry sand is not staying in place. Tyler asks Mrs. Charles for some water "so we can make the sand stick together," and she suggests they use the plant spray bottle. When Uri starts to spray water into a cup full of sand, Tyler says, "We have to be careful and use just a little water or the sand will get muddy. When I made mudpies with my sister, I got mud all over my shirt." Uri goes to the water table, brings back a tablespoon, and hands it to Tyler. They take turns spraying the water onto the tablespoon and then dripping it into the bucket.

• • •

Five-year-old Amelia is building in the block area. She points to show Ms. Danielle that she is using wooden cylinder blocks at the bottom of her tower and round foam blocks at the top. When Ms. Danielle asks why she chose those blocks, Amelia points to the wood blocks and says, "These ones are heavy so I can make my tower strong and big." She points to the foam ones and says, "And these are light, so they don't make my tower fall down." Her 4-year-old friend Petra says, "Let's wear hard hats like real builders do! Then we can make our towers really big."

Young children are novice scientists from birth, curious and driven to explore, understand, and make sense of the world around them. Like the children in the vignettes above, their exploration evolves based on their developmental level and prior experiences, such as investigating worms, using water to make sand "stick," and building strong block towers. With many opportunities to engage in *doing* science, children's understanding of concepts related to living things, matter and forces, and Earth's materials and processes grows increasingly sophisticated.

In preschool, the process of doing science is often called *inquiry*. Inquiry skills include the following:

> Wondering about phenomena (organisms, objects, materials, and events)

> Raising questions about phenomena; exploring and investigating

> Making careful observations using all senses and simple tools

> Collecting, representing, and recording data in a variety of ways

> Organizing data using charts, tables, and graphs

> Analyzing data and looking for relationships and patterns

> Generating ideas, explanations, and conclusions based on evidence

> Discussing and comparing ideas and listening to others' perspectives (Worth & Grollman 2003, 18)

Unlike the linear scientific method, inquiry is a vibrant, dynamic, and social process that almost always inspires more questions. Although young children are not systematic in their use of inquiry, they are very capable of engaging in higher-level thinking, including generating ideas, explanations, and conclusions based on evidence from their own experiences. Inquiry incorporates skills across developmental domains (physical, cognitive, linguistic, social, and emotional) that can be intentionally supported during children's science experiences.

The science domains—physical, life, and earth and space science—each provide opportunities for supporting not only young children's inquiry but also their foundational understanding of the core science ideas they will continue to investigate throughout the K-12 grades.

1. Physical science is the study of the nonliving world, including matter, forces, energy, and waves. Young children can explore the physical characteristics of objects and materials and what happens when they are pushed or pulled, mixed, heated, or cooled. They can explore sound and light, including shadows and reflections.

2. Life science is the study of living things including their structures, behaviors, growth and development, life cycles, diversity, and habitats. Young children can explore the characteristics, growth, needs, homes, and life cycles of plants and animals (including humans) and how they meet their needs in different environments.

3. Earth and space science incorporate studies of Earth's materials and processes, weather and climate, and Earth's place in the solar system. Young children can explore rocks, sand, soil, water, and landscapes; investigate weather and its effects; and observe the sky, sun, moon, and stars.

A Framework for K–12 Science Education (National Research Council [NRC] 2012) paved the way for the K–12 Next Generation Science Standards (NGSS; NRC 2013) and prioritized the importance of students doing science in order to learn it. It delineated eight science and engineering practices: asking questions (science) and defining problems (engineering), developing and using models, planning and carrying out investigations, analyzing and interpreting data, using mathematics and computational thinking, constructing explanations (science) and designing solutions (engineering), engaging in argument from evidence, and obtaining, evaluating, and communicating information. The practices describe the inquiry process in terms of the distinct activities scientists and engineers engage in as they do their work. Though the practices may sound complex for preschool, young children can engage with them at developmentally appropriate levels (see, for example, Hoisington 2024 for more information).

Making shaker instruments incorporates learning about the way physical properties of objects inside a container influence the types of sounds the instrument will make.

The framework also identified disciplinary core ideas in physical, life, and earth and space science as well as crosscutting concepts (such as cause and effect, structure and function, and patterns) that children begin to develop an understanding of long before they enter kindergarten.

The teacher's role in fostering children's science inquiry and learning is vital. Intentional teachers plan environments, experiences, and interactions that spark curiosity and exploration and promote critical thinking, collaboration, communication, and creativity (Whitebread & Neale 2020). They closely observe and document what children are doing, noticing, and talking about to inform their planning. They emphasize "science experiences" rather than "science activities" to distinguish meaningful, ongoing explorations from one-shot activities that may be exciting and "fun" but don't leverage children's capacities as young scientists.

Strategies for engaging children in inquiry, supporting their emerging understanding of core ideas and crosscutting concepts, and promoting their positive science identities and habits of mind (such as curiosity, persistence, and flexible thinking) appear in "Fitting the Learning Experience to the Learning Objective" later in this chapter, where they are considered separately as child-guided and adult-guided experiences. As for other areas of learning, this is not a rigid division.

Equity in Science

Many children, including girls, children of color, those with developmental delays or disabilities, multilingual learners, and those from low-resource communities, face systemic barriers to science and STEM (science, technology, engineering, and mathematics) experiences in the early years. This can limit their future education and workforce opportunities (AERA 2016). It not only affects individuals but also reduces diversity in the STEM workforce, which thrives on varied experiences and perspectives for innovation (NCSES 2023). Given these educational inequities, it is important to create early STEM environments that work for and support all children.

Intentional teachers foster inclusive classroom cultures of inquiry where all children's experiences, abilities, and ideas are valued. They explicitly connect the science children are learning in school to their lived experiences; use books and digital resources to extend children's inquiry; and engage male and female STEM role models who reflect children's cultures, languages, abilities, and interests.

Intentional teachers apply principles of Universal Design for Learning and create multiple entry points for children's active participation in inquiry. This includes, for example, introducing topics of study with visuals, drawing out individual children's prior thinking on the topic ("What animals do you think we might find outdoors?"), and offering a variety of ways for children to collect and represent data (such as using oral language and drawing to describe the animals they find).

Young Children's Development in Science

"Doing science" aligns with all the NAEYC principles of child development (NAEYC 2020), particularly principles 3, 5, and 6.

Principle 3: *Play promotes joyful learning that fosters self-regulation, language, cognitive and social competencies as well as content knowledge across disciplines. Play is essential for all children, birth through age 8* (NAEYC 2020, 9). Play and science inquiry are interconnected, as materials such as blocks, balls, manipulatives, sand, and water naturally lend themselves to science exploration and problem solving. This engages children's physical, intellectual, social, and emotional attention (Hoisington, n.d.). For example, Tyler's and Uri's play at the sand table evolves into a science and engineering exploration by introducing the challenge of making the sand "stick" and compelling them to experiment by adding water to figure out a solution. This exploration also connects them to key physical science concepts regarding characteristics of matter and how the properties of specific materials may change when mixed and introduces measurement as they add water to sand incrementally.

Principle 5: *Children are active learners from birth, constantly taking in and organizing information to create meaning through relationships, their interactions with their environment, and their overall experiences* (NAEYC, 2020). Just like scientists, young children seek relationships and patterns, making sense of the world and how it works based on evidence from their own experiences. In the earlier vignette, Amelia and Petra demonstrate different levels of reasoning when building with blocks. Amelia, a more experienced builder, recognizes a relationship between the weights of the building materials and structure stability. Petra, having observed workers at a construction site, attributes stability to wearing hard hats. Both of these ideas are important milestones in their reasoning that will evolve through further experiences and interactions with their teacher and peers (NAEYC 2020).

Principle 6: *Children's motivation to learn is increased when their learning environment fosters their sense of belonging, purpose, and agency. Curricula and teaching methods build on each child's assets by connecting their experiences in the school or learning environment to their home and community settings* (NAEYC 2020, 11). Children are motivated to engage in inquiry when they investigate questions and problems that are meaningful to them and when they encounter interesting phenomena to explore at school, at home, and in their community. For example, in one of the opening vignettes, when children in Ms. B's class discovered a worm in the outdoor space, she supported the children's agency by encouraging their interest. Ms. B also broadened the original focus of the learning experience by inviting the children to observe, describe, and think about the worm's characteristics and habitat, thereby extending the exploration of structure and function to include both plants and animals.

The early years and the types of science experiences young children have are instrumental in fostering positive attitudes toward science, beliefs in its usefulness to their own lives, and positive self-identities as capable science doers, thinkers, and learners (Pattison & Ramos Montañez 2022). Positive and engaging early experiences with science can ignite children's passions for specific topics of study that last into adulthood (Funk & Hefferon 2016).

Teaching and Learning in Science

All science teaching in the early childhood curriculum should build on children's innate curiosity and desire to explore their surroundings (Jirout 2022). Children need many opportunities to explore independently and with peers and to experience guided inquiry with the teacher's facilitation. They rely on adults to provide a "fascination-rich" environment, to support their explorations in a variety of ways, and to facilitate their reflection and sense making.

Multiple Pathways to Science Inquiry and Learning

The vignettes earlier in the chapter illustrate how children naturally engage with the science and engineering practices when questions, problems, or discoveries arise during play. Teachers can support this inquiry by helping children articulate their questions; try new ways to investigate phenomena; observe, collect, and record data; share and reflect on experiences; and generate ideas based on evidence from their observations.

You can support science inquiry and learning in various ways:

> Through single, stand-alone activities, such as sinking and floating, tracing shadows outdoors, or pumpkin carving. These adult-guided experiences aim to teach discrete information (such as that items sink or float in water, people's shadows change from morning to afternoon, and a pumpkin contains many seeds). A drawback of such activities is that they often focus on facts rather than big ideas, sometimes even promoting children's misconceptions (such as that items sink or float based on their weight or that only the sun creates shadows). Inquiry is limited to making and evaluating predictions as right or wrong. You can increase the inquiry potential of these activities by identifying a big idea for further exploration (for example, a shadow is created when an object blocks the path of the light); introducing an exploration message (for example, "We can explore our own shadows indoors and outdoors"); and extending the experience to include collecting, representing, and analyzing data (for example, "How is your shadow similar to and different from you?") and making claims based on evidence (for example, "My shadow is the same shape as me, but it has no eyes, no nose, and no mouth").

> Through informational texts or storybooks focused on science concepts, such as *Who Sank the Boat?* by Pamela Allen; *Me and My Shadow* by Arthur Dorros, or *From Seed to Pumpkin* by Wendy Pfeffer. Preferably, these are extensions of children's own explorations. Books in science can best serve as references or resources to prompt new exploration ideas, observe authentic images of phenomena, illustrate new perspectives, and reinforce vocabulary.

> In response to a question, problem, or unexpected event that arises during play. This could lead to independent inquiry, or teachers can leverage these moments to guide children's exploration. The sidebar "A Problem Launches Inquiry: Why Aren't the Clothes All Dry?" more fully describes this pathway.

> By implementing a "topics of study" approach that promotes cycles of inquiry around related big ideas in physical, life, or earth and space science. Well-chosen topics are anchored in a big idea, maximize hands-on and minds-on inquiry, and can be explored and discussed over time and across settings.

The Role of Children's Preconceptions in Science

Children's beginning explanations about how and why things happen are generally not scientifically correct (for example, hard hats make towers stronger; worms like bedtime stories; plants are not living; the sun goes around the earth; all round things float; heavy balls roll faster than light ones). This is to be expected because children have a limited range of experiences to draw on. However, such preconceptions are important milestones in children's efforts to make sense of the world and how it works, because they represent opportunities for reflection and provide launching pads for further inquiry.

Early childhood educators don't have to be science experts to be excellent science teachers. Teaching science in preschool does require a willingness to build your own knowledge and skills, so consider accessing science resources to do that. Engage in your own science inquiry on a topic before introducing it to children. Resist the urge to provide oversimplified scientific explanations, and don't hesitate to say, "I don't know. I wonder how we can figure that out together."

Science Topics That Excite and Engage Young Children

The domains of physical, life, and earth and space science each present opportunities for exploring a wide range of everyday phenomena that children find fascinating and that many adults take for granted. For example, water draws the attention of young children and can be explored from different perspectives: as a liquid and how it moves and flows (physical science), as a survival need for all living things (life science), or as a material in Earth's ponds, lakes, and oceans (earth and space science).

A Problem Launches Inquiry: Why Aren't the Clothes All Dry?

As you read the following vignette, look for how an exploration emerges from children's play, how they engage with the science and engineering practices, and how their interactions with the teacher support their thinking and ongoing investigation.

1. **A problem arises during the children's play that is unexpected.**

   The children in Mrs. Takanishi's preschool class wash all the doll clothes in the morning and hang them outside to dry. When they go outside in the afternoon to bring the doll clothes in, they discover that some are dry, some are still damp, and several are nearly as wet as they were when the children hung them up in the morning!

   "Now I can't put the blue shirt on Sam [a doll]," says Manuel, disappointed.

   "You can use the red one," says Ivan to Manuel. "It's dry."

   Manuel accepts the red shirt from Ivan but eyes the blue shirt longingly.

2. **The children identify a relationship between the sun and the dry clothes.**

   Mrs. Takanishi knows that her preschoolers won't reach a scientific explanation, but she sees a good opportunity to support their inquiry in relation to properties of matter (the colors and structures of the different fabrics) and energy (the sun warms the earth's surface). She asks, "Do you have any ideas about why some doll clothes are dry, some are a little wet, and some are still very wet?"

   The children share their thinking with comments such as "Maybe because the blue shirt is bigger and it takes longer to dry," "The yellow dress is even bigger than the blue shirt, and it's dry already," and "Maybe yellow clothes dry faster than blue clothes?"

   "Mmm," says Mrs. Takanishi. "The yellow dress and the red shirt are both dry, and they are next to each other on the clothesline. I wonder if that matters."

   Ivan says, "Hey, I can see the shadows of the red shirt and the yellow dress on the ground!"

   "I know!" exclaims Soledad. I can only see my shadow really good on sunny days! The sun made the clothes dry!" There is a chorus of agreement.

3. **The children explore further and collect data that does not "fit" with their first explanation.**

Mrs. Takanishi acknowledges the children's thinking and raises a question. "So you're thinking some clothes are dry because they're in the sun and some clothes are wet because they're in the shade. Okay. Does that mean you're predicting that all the clothes in the sun will be dry?"

"Yes!" says Manuel. "We'll show you! Me and Jenna can feel the ones in the sun. Ivan and Soledad, you feel the ones in the shade!"

The children divide into two groups and call out their observations. They soon make another discovery. A couple of items in the sun are still wet and a couple in the shade are dry.

"So, some clothes in the sun are still a little wet, and some clothes in the shade are dry," says Mrs. Takanishi to confirm their observations.

4. **The children generate ideas to explain new evidence and make a plan to continue their exploration the next day.**

"Did you move them?" Ivan asks Mrs. Takanishi.

"No," she answers, laughing. "I was inside the classroom with you all morning. What other ideas do you have?"

The children offer explanations, including "White clothes dry faster than purple clothes" and "At the beach my bathing suit dried quick, but my towel took longer because it's like a blanket." Charlotte remembers an activity the class did with sponges and water and suggests that maybe they hadn't "squeezed all the water out of the wet clothes."

Back in the classroom, Mrs. Takanishi lists all the ideas on chart paper and helps the children make a plan to investigate further.

They decide that the next day they will wash two identical shirts and hang one in the sun and one in the shade. Mrs. Takanishi suggests that tomorrow they also look at the clothes in the sun that took longer to dry and see if they are similar in any ways.

Manuel takes the dry red shirt inside. "I sure hope it fits Sam," he says.

Adding materials that extend children's exploration of how water looks, moves, and flows supports their learning about water as a liquid.

Children's Inquiry and Learning in Physical Science

Physical science inquiry is especially rich with opportunities for direct, hands-on exploration, and children can immediately observe the effects of their actions on objects and materials. Early childhood programs, with block areas, water and sand tables, manipulative toys, musical instruments, art areas, and outdoor areas, are well-suited for physical science explorations at any time of year. Children engage with physical science as they, for example, design and build block structures; discover different shades of red when mixing colors at the easel; create a system to move water in the water table using basters and clear tubing; and notice vibrations as they create and use instruments to make sound. Children may ask or wonder about questions such as "Which blocks will make the tallest tower?," "How can I make an even darker red?," "How hard do I have to push this ball to get it up the ramp without falling off at the top?," "Which of these tools will squirt water the farthest?," or "How does changing the container change the sound the pebbles make?"

Children's Inquiry and Learning in Life Science

Life science inquiry is primarily observational, and from a preschooler's perspective, plants and animals take a long time to grow and change. Life science explorations also involve ethical considerations that don't apply in physical science. Inquiry outdoors is influenced by geographical location, climate, and weather.

As members of the living world, young children are fascinated by their own growth and development and by the characteristics and behaviors of other living things, especially animals. Children engage with life science concepts as they, for example, investigate and categorize seeds, measure their own growth over time, observe a tree in the playground over the course of the year, create temporary indoor habitats for insects and other small creatures, nurture plants in a school garden to maturity, and compare how they are similar to and different from other family members. Children's wonderings about the living world may include "How do plants eat?," "How can trees be alive?," "How do seeds know what plant to grow into?," "Are worms baby snakes?," "Do bugs have teeth?," "Why do dogs chase cats?," and "Where did the dinosaurs go?"

Children's Inquiry and Learning in Earth and Space Science

Earth and space science incorporate elements of both physical and life science and are especially enjoyable to young children, who love being outdoors and exploring nature in all weather conditions. Children engage with earth and space concepts when, for example, they play with and investigate their shadows; compare different types of soil, sand, and rocks; collect data about the weather using rain gauges and windsocks; engage in reduce, reuse, and recycle activities; and explore and enrich outdoor habitats that provide homes for plants and animals. Extended weather charting routines across the year engage children in observing the sun, clouds, wind, temperature, and precipitation, as well as using and creating measurement tools that deepen their inquiry and learning about weather. Children's questions and wonderings related to earth and space science may include "Why do puddles form in some places but not others?," "Why doesn't it ever snow where we live?," "Where does my shadow go when it's cloudy?," and even "Are the shaking trees making the wind blow?"

Drawing the ramps they built supports children's abilities to create scientific representations and their literacy and fine motor skills.

Integrating Science with Other Learning

Science is a perfect vehicle for integrated teaching and learning. Doing science supports underlying cognitive skills, such as executive function (the "air traffic control center" of the brain; see Chapter 3), that are critical to developing more easily observed academic school-readiness skills—for example, knowledge of letters and print (Center on the Developing Child, n.d.). Science promotes language and literacy development and learning as children share their observations, ideas, and explanations with others through talking, drawing, and writing (Duke 2019). As they engage in inquiry, children use mathematics and computational thinking as they count, measure, organize, and analyze their data and as they use vocabulary to describe size, shape, length, and weight. Representing their science-related actions and ideas through painting, creating models, and dramatic play engages children in the arts. Science also supports the broad skill sets so important in an increasingly science- and technology-oriented world and workforce: critical thinking (evidence-based thinking) and problem solving, collaboration, communication, and creativity and innovation (Center for Childhood Creativity 2017).

Materials That Promote Inquiry and Exploration

Provide materials that promote scientific inquiry throughout the classroom and the outdoor play space, beyond a designated science area or center. Consider these suggestions:

Art center: Paint pumps, craft sticks, plastic spoons, brushes, ink pad and stamps, stapler, hole punch, scissors, plastic molds, tape, glue, string, yarn, ribbon, large-eyed tapestry needles, buttons, beads, pipe cleaners, rolling pin, wire or canvas mesh, fabric scraps, straws, paper clips

Dramatic play center: Cooking utensils (wooden spoon, spatula, ladle, whisk, tongs, funnel, scoop, garlic press, measuring cups and spoons, timer, potholders, bag clips, food mill, rolling pin, cookie cutter, colander), cleaning equipment (broom, dustpan, vacuum cleaner, buckets, sponges, rubber gloves, clothespins), medical equipment (stethoscope, blood pressure cuff, slings, canes, crutches, syringes, gauze pads, adhesive tape), dress-up clothes with various types of fasteners (zippers, buttons, hook-and-loop tape, snaps), keys, telephone, toaster, stove, mailbox

Block center: Wood blocks, cardboard blocks, foam units, wood chips and shims, ruler, yardstick, measuring tape, cartons and boxes, large elastic bands, foam padding, tape

Woodworking center: Screwdrivers, hammers, pliers, clamps, hand drills, levels, dowels, fasteners, and other hardware (nails, screws, nuts, bolts, washers)

Sand table: Pails and shovels, plastic containers of different shapes and sizes, muffin tins, mesh strainers

Water table: Turkey basters, dish soap, bubble wands, funnels, clear plastic tubing and connectors, squirt and spray bottles, pipettes

Outdoor play space: Sand and water table equipment, rope, wagon, sawhorses, dump truck, wheelbarrow, gardening tools (spade, hoe, rake, gardening gloves, kneeling pads, watering can, hose), balls, hand pump (to inflate balls), construction materials (wood scraps of different sizes and shapes), containers for collecting things

Connecting Teaching to Children's Lives

By Melany Spiehs

During morning center time Skylar, age 4, and Luna, age 5, play in the classroom loft. Skylar dangles a long piece of yarn over the side, and Miguel, age 3, reaches up from below to get it. Curious, Ms. Ellison moves closer to the action, watching and listening.

Luna: You can't play up here, Miguel. We already have three friends in the loft.

Miguel: I know that. I just want to give you something I made in art center.

Skylar: Tie it to our string, and we can pull it up.

Miguel struggles with the yarn for a few minutes trying to attach his craft stick creation. Eventually he decides to wrap the yarn around his art piece, and the girls start to pull it up using the top rail of the loft as leverage. The artwork makes it halfway up but breaks free of the yarn before the girls can grab it.

Ms. Ellison realizes the students are engineering a pulley system and asks guiding questions.

Ms. Ellison: What is it you are working on here? I wonder how we could get Miguel's artwork up to you without it falling back down? Is there something we could attach to the yarn?

Skylar: I think we need a bucket. My dad uses a bucket to carry nails up to the roof at work.

Luna: We could get a bucket from the sand table!

Ms. Ellison: Who wants to try tying the knot?

Luna: I do! (*Ties the string to the bucket with some help from Ms. Ellison.*)

Miguel: (*Puts his art in the bucket and smiles as his friends pull the bucket to the top of the loft.*)

Luna: Cool, Miguel! I like your art.

Miguel: It's for you.

Luna: Thank you. Will you put it in my cubby? I'm going to lower it back down in the bucket.

The other children observe and ask to try the simple machine. Over the next several weeks the class explores pulley systems. Ms. Ellison refreshes her knowledge of simple machines, and the class learns about the parts of a pulley, how pulleys work, and how people use them in everyday life to open window blinds or ride in an elevator. The class creates small pulley systems in the block center and large pulley systems in their outdoor classroom over tree branches. The children are amazed at how much weight they can lift using a pulley system!

In this vignette, the children exhibit collaborative problem-solving skills as they engineer a simple machine to solve a problem that arises during their play. Using her funds of knowledge, Skylar references a time she saw her father using a bucket in his work. The cooperative nature of this experience honors a community value of working together to accomplish a goal. Ms. Ellison provides support by asking questions that help children reflect on and revise their original plans. The children explore engineering naturally, and Ms. Ellison provides vocabulary, materials, and experiences that extend the physical science and engineering embedded in their play. Ms. Ellison integrates mathematics into this experience by discussing measurement concepts like weight and height. Ms. Ellison's inquisitive approach and attentiveness to the children's ideas facilitate both their critical thinking and problem solving.

Fitting the Learning Experience to the Learning Objective

Engaging young children in the three domains of science—physical, life, and earth and space—is essential for their holistic development and for building an understanding of the world around them. Explorations in all the domains support children's inquiry, their positive science identities, and their scientific habits of mind. Teachers maximize children's inquiry and thinking through both child-guided and adult-guided experiences.

Exploring Physical Science

Of the key knowledge and skills in the area of physical science, child-guided experiences seem particularly important for the following:

> Exploring objects and materials

> Identifying and solving problems that arise in play

Adult-guided experiences seem to be especially significant for the following:

> Expressing investigation questions using language

> Making reasoned predictions

> Generating claims, explanations, and solutions

CHILD-GUIDED experiences are especially important for learnings such as:

Children need uninterrupted time to gain familiarity with new objects and materials and how they can be used, so they benefit from multiple chances to play, build, and create with a variety of items. These child-guided experiences create equity among children who have had varying levels of experience with the materials and pave the way for more focused investigations as children begin to raise questions about what, how, and why different objects and materials behave as they do.

Teaching strategies. Help children extend their investigations with strategies like these:

> Add new objects and materials to the learning areas or rotate objects across areas that prompt children to explore in new ways. For example, add tree blocks (blocks made of actual branches) or plastic cups to the building center that don't stack as easily as unit blocks; colored transparent building tiles to a shadow center for observing colored shadows; basters, clear tubing, and funnels to the water table to explore water flow; or sponges instead of paintbrushes at the easel to expand children's experience with tools.

> Be responsive to children's ideas and suggestions for using classroom materials. For example, encourage them to try out their idea for using tape to secure their block structures or paint to embellish their playdough creations.

> Adapt science materials and experiences as needed to support children with developmental delays or disabilities. For example, provide one or two new items at a time so they can become familiar before being introduced to more. Periodically partner children with developmental delays or disabilities with peers to explore materials together, especially if a child does not have one-on-one adult support.

Exploring force and motion motivates children to design and build structures that will make objects move using a variety of materials.

Young children's inquiry is stimulated when problems or discrepant events (that is, things they didn't expect) arise, such as a ball repeatedly skipping off a ramp or a different color appearing than what they anticipated in a color-mixing activity.

Teaching strategies. Use strategies such as these to support children's problem solving:

❭ Avoid the temptation to jump in and explain or solve children's problems for them. Instead, ask questions that help them observe more closely (for example, "Where exactly is the ball jumping off the ramp? What do you notice about where those two boards come together?") or make suggestions (for example, "What have you tried already?" or "Have you tried putting the boards closer together?").

❭ Remind children of a prior experience in which they had a similar problem and how they solved it (for example, "Remember last time when you got light pink, but you wanted dark pink? What did you do to make the pink darker that time?").

❭ Encourage children to ask each other for help. Try making a list with suggestions for peers children can go to when different problems arise (such as "When you can't reach something up high, go to Johanna" or "When you need help mixing paints, ask Michael"). Ensure every child in the classroom is included as an "expert."

ADULT-GUIDED experiences are especially important for learnings such as:

Exploring Physical Science ❭ **Expressing investigation questions using language**

Although young children wonder about everything, they often need support to articulate their questions. Because cognition and language go hand in hand, supporting children to verbalize their questions also supports their thinking.

Teaching strategies. Try the following strategies to help children articulate their questions:

❭ Play alongside children and model asking questions out loud. For example, you might build alongside them in the block area and say, "I wonder how I could make a doorway in my barn." Model collaboration by asking to join children's play or inviting them to join yours.

❭ Join children's play as a guide on the side rather than a sage on the stage, or pair children who have complementary skills. Be attentive to what children are doing and noticing, and try interpreting their questions from their interactions with materials ("It looks like you're wondering how to change the shape of that shadow").

Asking children to make predictions is a typical strategy in preschool science, and physical science is a great context for predicting since children can immediately test and observe the results of their actions.

Teaching strategies. Encourage children to articulate their ideas and reasoning with these strategies:

> Ask children to give reasons for their predictions by asking, for example, "What makes you think so?" This helps children think more deeply about evidence and their own thinking and helps you understand their reasoning process to provide appropriate follow-up. For example, if a child predicts that a plastic ball will float in water, it's helpful to know if they think that because they once saw a beach ball float or because their mother once told them, "Don't throw that ball in the water because it will float away."

> Ask children to compare their predictions to what actually happened without referring to their predictions as right or wrong. For example, ask, "How is what happened similar to/different from what we predicted?" (It's often helpful to have a record of their predictions and their reasons for them!) This supports children to think flexibly and feel confident about sharing their ideas without worrying about whether or not they are giving the "right" answer.

> Visual aids such as charts with picture cues or images that illustrate potential results provide another level of support for all children to make, test, and reflect on their reasoned predictions.

This child is investigating how objects move on a ramp as the teacher records his observations, which supports his understanding of how data can be used.

Children come to school with many ideas about how the world works, including preconceptions such as a rolling ball stops because it runs out of energy (*just like I do when I exercise*) or that objects float or sink due to weight (*because my dad floats, but I sink without my floatie*). Uncovering and addressing preconceptions through hands-on and minds-on inquiry is critical; otherwise, children are likely to hold on to their preconceptions into their future school years (Kambouri 2011).

Teaching strategies. Try these strategies to encourage children to explain their ideas, using evidence from their explorations:

> Be on the lookout for your own misconceptions so you don't inadvertently communicate them to children, and avoid simplifying abstract concepts to explain what you and children observe. For instance, the scientific explanation for why objects sink or float (relative densities of water and objects) is generally beyond what preschool children can grasp. Focus instead on helping children investigate observable characteristics and behaviors of objects, then generate ideas about which properties seem to influence sinking and floating. This will lay the groundwork for children's later understanding of density.

> Avoid the temptation to correct children's preconceptions in the moment. Instead, acknowledge their ideas, draw out their reasons for them, and use their preconceptions as launching pads for ongoing explorations. For example, to address the typical misconception that all plastic things float, plan an exploration that includes wiffle balls, toy boats, spoons, and other plastic objects that sink when they fill with water.

Exploring Life Science

Living things, especially animals, are fascinating to young children and can be explored in urban, suburban, and rural environments. Familiarize yourself with your outdoor space, address any potential hazards, and establish a clear protocol for children's handling of living things (such as ask the teacher before touching any plants or animals). When you model curiosity and a sense of wonder about observing insects and other small creatures, children are likely to follow suit.

Of the key knowledge and skills in the area of life science, child-guided experiences seem particularly important for the following:

> Making close observations and noticing details

> Learning about their own growth and development

> Researching and role-playing community helpers who care for living things

Adult-guided experiences seem to be especially significant for the following:

> Learning and using vocabulary about living things

> Representing observations of living things

CHILD-GUIDED experiences are especially important for learnings such as:

Exploring Life Science > **Making close observations and noticing details**

The ability to observe accurately is essential in science. Young children observe the world with all their senses, and over time and with practice they become more aware of details. For example, a child's observations about leaves might progress from "The leaf is green and big" to "The leaf looks like a hand, it has lines on it, and it smells like a lemon."

Teaching strategies. Try these strategies to promote children's detailed observations:

> Provide observation tools such as hand lenses and demonstrate how to use them correctly. For example, a hand lens is meant to be held near the eye while bringing the living thing up to the hand lens, not held at a distance close to the living thing.

> Model looking closely at living things and commenting on details, such as "Let me get a closer look at that!" and "Look! I can see spots on it!"

> Respond to children's observations of living things with enthusiasm and interest. Be sure to follow up and draw the attention of other children. This affirms the importance of observing and appreciating the living world.

Exploring Life Science > **Learning about their own growth and development**

Children are especially interested in their own growth and the new skills and abilities they are developing. This creates a natural intersection for connecting them to the wider world of living things.

Teaching strategies. Provide opportunities for children to investigate themselves as living things:

> Supply nonstandard and standard measuring tools, such as toy cars, Unifix cubes, and measuring tapes, so children can measure and record their own and one another's heights. Discuss how and why they seem to get different results when they use different units of measurement.

> Encourage families to collect photos or other artifacts of their children as babies and copy them to share. Use them to prompt conversations with the children about how they are growing and how their skills, needs, and preferences are changing.

> Emphasize that everyone is similar in some ways and unique in some ways, but together they all make a community. For example, everyone eats, communicates, plays, and learns, but they may eat different foods, speak different languages, play different kinds of games, and learn in different ways.

Exploring Life Science | **Researching and role-playing community helpers who care for living things**

Children naturally engage in dramatic play of all types and especially enjoy playing the roles of workers they observe in their families and communities. They also enjoy meeting people who have interesting jobs and learning about how and why they do those jobs.

Teaching strategies. Expand children's life science explorations using these strategies:

> Invite a community helper or family member who has a job, career, or hobby related to studying or caring for living things to visit the classroom. Invite them to bring some tools or artifacts they use to share with children and talk about their jobs and how their interests developed. When possible, choose individuals in nonstereotypical roles and who represent the diversity found in your community.

> Help children set up a veterinarian's office, zoo space, park ranger's office, farm, or garden center in the dramatic play center. Collect children's ideas about what materials are needed or can be adapted for the area. Join in the play and help children gradually add materials to support more complex dramatic play.

ADULT-GUIDED experiences are especially important for learnings such as:

Exploring Life Science | **Learning and using vocabulary about living things**

Make sure children are learning words and the concepts the words represent simultaneously. Introduce new and challenging words children can use in everyday conversations as well as more scientific vocabulary.

Teaching strategies. Introduce and use a variety of words to promote children's language and thinking:

> Have conversations about words and their meanings and draw out children's prior knowledge of a word before providing the definition. Acknowledge and discuss words children invent, such as *squinchy* or *flippery*.

> Plan, introduce, and use challenging words to name and describe living things and their parts as children are ready (such as *striated, lobed, antennae,* and *segments*). Obtain and provide translations of target words in children's home languages.

> Label children's living things drawings with their permission and invite children to use new words. Ask open-ended questions such as "How shall we label this part of your plant?" and scaffold by offering choices ("Shall I write 'fruit' or 'root'?").

> Use books about living things to introduce or reinforce the meanings of new words. Point out target words in text and support children's understanding of them across contexts (such as by reading about and then creating a worm *habitat*).

> Introduce new vocabulary using real artifacts or images; for action words, use whole body movement and gestures. For example, have children use their bodies to represent animal movements such as stretch, burrow, creep, or leap.

Exploring Life Science ⟩ **Representing observations of living things**

Symbolic communication (like drawing, writing, demonstrating, building, and role playing) helps preschoolers focus on details and begin to think more abstractly as they re-create their observations using different media. Representing their observations supports early literacy skills as children add letters and numbers to label or describe their drawings. Observational drawing may be new for many children and requires time and encouragement.

Teaching strategies. Try these strategies to support children's representations:

> Have children draw the plants and animals they observe indoors and outdoors. Encourage them to notice and represent details, using hand lenses for a closer look. As they progress through a topic of study, their representations become more detailed, and you can help them label the animal's or plant's parts.

> Provide materials like paint, pastels, clay, and playdough for children to make three-dimensional models of the animals and plants they observe.

> Ask children to imitate plants and animals in action, like trees blowing in the wind, a seed sprouting, or a worm burrowing in the dirt.

Exploring Earth and Space Science

Experiences in the outdoors benefit children's overall health and well-being and develop the sense of connection to nature they need to become environmental caretakers (Louv 2010). Take children outdoors as much as possible, adhering to your school or program's guidelines for being out in different types of weather. If the outdoors is not a viable option at your setting, set up an observation post at a window and maximize the use of books, online resources, and materials brought in from the outside. Model a positive attitude toward all kinds of weather and avoid labeling weather as "good" or "bad."

Of the key knowledge and skills in the area of earth and space science, child-guided experiences seem particularly important for the following:

> Sorting and categorizing Earth's materials

Adult-guided experiences seem to be especially significant for the following:

> Measuring the components of weather using tools

> Observing change over time

CHILD-GUIDED experiences are especially important for learnings such as:

| Exploring Earth and Space Science | Sorting and categorizing Earth's materials |

Children are natural collectors. They naturally compare, sort, and categorize items by their characteristics during their play (Langer et al. 2003). First, they separate objects that share an attribute (such as all the red leaves). Then, they begin to sort objects into groups and use the words *same* and *different*. Next, they categorize according to different attributes—for example, by color and then by shape. Natural objects are especially interesting and challenging for children to sort because their colors, shapes, and sizes are not as distinctly different as those of buttons or beads, and this encourages children to notice more detailed similarities and differences.

Teaching strategies. Encourage children to sort and categorize Earth's materials using these strategies:

> Make a general rule that only items on the ground may be collected and nothing may be pulled off trees or other plants.

> Prepare a simple observation kit with clipboards, paper, and pencil and accustom children to observing natural items outdoors in their natural settings.

Snail Topic of Study: Learning and Sharing Scientific Knowledge and Ideas

The following vignette is an example of how effective teaching blends child-guided and adult-guided experiences. Although the children's questions and interests guide the learning, Ms. Faith facilitates their inquiry and anchors it in big ideas about living things by designing experiences that balance child- and teacher-initiated investigations. The children become fully immersed in the following science and engineering practices as they investigate garden snails and develop a beginning understanding of core ideas in life science.

Asking questions (science) and defining problems (engineering)

The children in Ms. Faith's class find a garden snail on a wall in the playground and wonder what it is, if it's alive, what it eats, if it has a family, and why it lives in the wall. Some children wonder if it will bite them, and others say snails are bad for plants. Ms. Faith realizes that garden snails will be an excellent topic of study (they exhibit many interesting characteristics and behaviors, and at her program's geographic location the snails are safe for children to handle). She does some research on snails, identifies a relevant core idea that is responsive to children's interests (that all living things have structures that help them meet their needs in a particular environment), begins to plan some inquiry-based experiences, and identifies target vocabulary. Because several of the children speak Hmong, Ms. Faith learns a few key Hmong words related to snails and shares these words alongside the English words with the whole class.

Developing and using models

With support from Ms. Faith, the children continue to observe snails outdoors and make notes about their environment. They research what snails need and find out that snails like certain types of plants and a moist environment. With this knowledge, they create a snail habitat indoors using a plastic tank and some dirt, rocks, plants, and other things they found outside where the snails were. They also watch a video on how to handle snails gently and safely.

Planning and carrying out investigations

The children observe the snails every day on a transparent tray using hand lenses. They draw pictures of the snail from the top and bottom and begin to notice details such as their antennae and their feet. They wonder how snails can walk with one foot! With Ms. Faith's support, the children notice and describe how the snails use their parts to move about, eat, and explore their environment. They investigate how snails respond to different levels of light and whether they prefer iceberg or romaine lettuce.

Analyzing and interpreting data

The children record their indoor and outdoor observations through drawing and emergent writing in journals. For Max, who has a physical disability that makes fine motor skills challenging, Ms. Faith provides cutouts of the snail's body parts to assemble. When the children share and compare their data, they decide that their indoor snails don't like light, prefer romaine lettuce, like to pile on top of one another, and need to be sprayed with water every day.

Using mathematics and computational thinking

The children use mathematical vocabulary to describe the shapes, sizes, and patterns on individual snail shells. They have a snail race and measure and compare the lengths of the "snail trails" the snails make on chart paper. Ms. Faith helps them create a graph showing how far each snail moved and which one "won" the race.

Constructing explanations (for science) and designing solutions (for engineering)

The children continue to collect data about the snails' outdoor home and construct explanations about why the grassy stone wall is a good habitat for snails. They postulate that the snails like shade and wet dirt and that they need the rocks and leaves to hide in so birds won't eat them. Inside, they continue their investigations about how snails move and are surprised to learn that each snail's foot is like a giant muscle. Some of the younger children say, "The snails could go faster if they had more feet!"

Engaging in argument from evidence

When disagreements arise among the children about what to feed the snails, Ms. Faith facilitates a discussion. Although everyone knows the snails like plants and lettuce, some think the snails would enjoy pizza (Ms. Faith, having had prior experience, knows that the snails would not eat it and thus would come to no harm). This leads to another investigation and more opportunities to collect, organize, and analyze data.

Obtaining, evaluating, and communicating information

Ms. Faith and the children do research with books and online to learn more about snails and how best to care for them indoors. During the last week of the study, they create a mural of their drawings of snails and their habitat to share with their families. Because the children continue to show interest, Ms. Faith decides to support snail explorations beyond the four weeks she originally planned, incorporating increasingly focused investigations that are responsive to children's emerging questions.

This vignette illustrates how a balance of child-guided and adult-guided experiences can sustain children's interest, deepen their knowledge, and support inquiry-based learning. The snail topic of study enabled the children to develop expertise about snails, but their deep-dive experiences went beyond snails. Children engaged in all of the science and engineering practices; developed their scientific habits of mind and their science identities; and were introduced to essential big ideas related to the characteristics, needs, life cycles, and habitats of living things as well as the crosscutting concepts of structures and function and patterns.

> When children collect natural items, encourage them to sort the items in different ways. For example, they might sort rocks by color, shape, size, and texture and sequence them from smallest to largest. As an alternative, bring in mixed natural objects like bean seeds for children to sort and classify.

> Draw children's attention to the characteristics of soil and sand in different parts of the outdoor area. If possible, provide different types of purchased or donated soil and sand for children to use in the sand table.

Learning to classify based on increasingly specific characteristics begins with sorting into groups. This child is separating flowers from rocks and sorting the flowers by type.

ADULT-GUIDED experiences are especially important for learnings such as:

| Exploring Earth and Space Science | Measuring the components of weather using tools |

Different components of weather, including sun, clouds, temperature, and precipitation, offer many opportunities to make predictions and observations, record and represent data, and obtain information from weather apps or websites (Ashbrook 2016). They also offer an excellent context to extend children's concept of measurement to include creating and using tools to measure the components of weather.

Teaching strategies. Try these strategies for helping children measure the weather:

> Create windsocks with children to measure wind speed and direction using crepe paper strips, construction paper, and string. Specific instructions can be found online. Hang them outdoors, preferably in a location that can be seen from a window.

> Create rain gauges to measure rainfall using empty, clean two-liter bottles. Cut one bottle in half, then place the top upside down inside the other half. Further instructions can be found on a number of websites. Place the bottles outside in a protected location before a predicted rainstorm.

> Create "cloud viewers" using paper towel tubes. Tape two tubes together binocular style and have children observe and describe clouds on different weather days.

> Draw children's attention to the weather's effects on the environment and the living things that inhabit it, including themselves. Ask questions such as "How are we dressing differently now that the weather is getting colder?" or "Have we found any insects in the playground lately? I wonder why not."

Preschoolers are growing more aware of how time plays a role in the natural and physical world (Van Scoy & Fairchild 1993). Earth and space science explorations help children notice how landscapes change over shorter and longer periods of time.

Teaching strategies. Draw children's attention to change over time with these strategies:

> Help children notice changes that occur over a short period of time. For example, draw their attention to how water collects in different areas of the playground after a rainstorm. "Where do you see the biggest puddles? Why do you think the puddles on the pavement are bigger than the ones on the grass?"

> Point out changes in the landscape caused by humans, such as trash in the parking lot or the appearance of birds at a birdfeeder. Draw out children's ideas about ways to support positive impacts and put them into action by, for example, having a fundraiser to buy a trash barrel for the parking lot and adding another birdfeeder.

> Draw children's attention to evidence of longer-term changes and prompt their thinking about causes. For example, notice out loud how worn down the path to the playground is getting or how the fence by the street is rusting. Ask questions that prompt children's observations and thinking about what might be causing these changes.

Obtaining, Evaluating, and Communicating Science Information

One of the science and engineering practices, obtaining, evaluating, and communicating information, refers to the process of collecting and comparing data from various sources and sharing what was learned with others.

Of the key knowledge and skills in the area of obtaining, evaluating, and communicating information, child-guided experiences seem to be especially significant for the following:

> Obtaining data from direct exploration and sharing observations and ideas with peers

Adult-guided experiences seem to be especially significant for learning such as the following:

> Developing confidence in participating in science talks

> Learning and using new vocabulary

> Collecting, recording, organizing, and analyzing data

> Using books as sources of science information to extend and enrich inquiry

CHILD-GUIDED experiences are especially important for learnings such as:

| Obtaining, Evaluating, and Communicating Science Information | Obtaining data from direct exploration and sharing observations and ideas with peers |

As emphasized throughout this chapter, children's direct experiences, observations, and their developing ideas are central to their science inquiry.

Teaching strategy. Try this strategy for centering children's direct explorations and facilitating peer-to-peer conversations:

> Use a consistent teaching framework that includes these components: eliciting children's combined knowledge, thinking, and questions on a topic; providing ample time for collaborative explorations of phenomena; and facilitating peer-to-peer conversations that provide opportunities for children to share and compare their observations and evolving ideas.

If available, a digital device can make images available to the full group and support group conversations about children's work.

ADULT-GUIDED experiences are especially important for learnings such as:

| Obtaining, Evaluating, and Communicating Science Information | Developing confidence in participating in science talks |

Concepts and the language we use to name and talk about them are intimately connected. Participating in science talks supports children's beginning understanding of science concepts and their scientific thinking as well as their language and literacy, speaking and listening, and cognitive skills (Romeo et al. 2018).

Teaching strategies. Using individualized approaches and promoting positive interactions during science experiences and discussions help to ensure that all children develop confidence in communicating their science experiences, observations, and ideas. When you facilitate science talks, you also give children a clear message that their science experiences, observations, and ideas are important. Try these strategies for maximizing children's participation in science talks:

> Use props and visuals to draw out children's prior knowledge and current thinking. For example, before a weather exploration, pass around an outdoor thermometer, a windsock, or a pair of binoculars and ask children if and where they've seen the tool before and what

they think it's used for. After an outdoor shadows exploration, show images in a book such as *Shadows and Reflections* by Tana Hoban and ask children how the shadow images in the book compare to the shadows they observed outdoors.

> Use questions that center on what children are doing and observing rather than ones that suggest correct scientific answers. Questions such as "What are you trying to do?," "How did you do that?," and "What will you try next?" support children's inquiry and encourage them to talk.

> Ask children why they *think* something occurred. For example, ask "Why *do you think* the shadow changed shape when you moved the flashlight?" rather than "Why did the shadow change shape when you moved the flashlight?"

> Explain less and listen more. Support children's reflection by asking questions such as "What happened when you tried to knock down the cup with the wiffle ball? What happened when you used the tennis ball?"

> Scaffold language to support multilingual learners and children with language disabilities in talking about what they did or noticed. Although close-ended questions have a bad reputation in early childhood, they can be used to promote inquiry while reducing language load. For example, during a ramps exploration, try asking "Did your ball go this way or that way?" instead of "Which way did the ball go?" Use hand motions to indicate directions, or break down questions by asking, for example, "Which ball knocked down the cup? Was it the heavy ball or the light ball?" (Hoisington, Mercer Young, & Winokur 2021). Alternatively, consider having the child show what they did and what happened while you provide the language.

> Be aware of potential biases and misconceptions about children's language abilities—such as those arising from the "30-million word gap" study discussed in Chapter 6—which may lead to undervaluing the linguistic strengths of children who speak a language or dialect that is not General American English (Golinkoff et al. 2018; Lee-James & Wallen 2024). Recognize and build on each child's communication strengths to facilitate inclusive science talks that reflect the experiences of all children.

Obtaining, Evaluating, and Communicating Science Information **Learning and using new vocabulary**

Science provides an excellent context for vocabulary learning, especially when explorations are extended over time. Children can learn science terms such as *predict, observe, evidence,* and *claim,* but science also offers many opportunities to teach cognitively challenging everyday words to describe objects and organisms, what they are doing, and how they are doing it. Language and cognitive skills are mutually reinforcing. When children have lots of words to talk about what they are doing and observing, they also have words to *think* about their experiences. Children need to hear multiple repetitions of a word in different contexts and have many opportunities to use it in order to make it their own.

Teaching strategies. Support learning and using new vocabulary using these strategies:

> Introduce and teach the basic vocabulary children need to share what they are doing and observing. For example, as children explore balls and ramps, provide words to name different balls and their actions, such as *roll, stop, fast,* and *slow.* As an inquiry progresses, introduce more complex and abstract vocabulary. In a study of light and shadows, these might include words such as *lighter, darker, transparent,* and *reflection.*

> Introduce related words and make connections to words children already know. For example, you might introduce the words *smooth* and *textured* or *rigid* and *squishy* together, describing *textured* as bumpy and *rigid* as hard.

> Talk about and play with words. Many words, such as *drop,* have multiple meanings. When you introduce *drop* in relation to a water exploration, for example, talk about children's current understanding of what it means (e.g., to drop something). Invite children to experiment with new words and make up words that sound like water dripping or flowing.

> Use new words repetitively in different situations and settings. For example, on Day 1: "I see you are brushing the frost off your boots!" Day 2: "I scraped frost off my windshield this morning." Day 3: "There is frost on the grass outside. Come and look! I wonder if there will be frost on the slide on the playground."

> Use pointing, facial expressions, gestures, and body language as visual cues to word meanings.

> Josie and Mei-lin, who is a multilingual learner, are putting shells and rocks on the balance. Josie gets paper and markers and says to Ms. Rebekah, "We're gonna draw a picture with six shells here (pointing to one side), a line down the middle, and two rocks here (pointing to the other side). Right, Mei-lin?"
>
> Ms. Rebekah comments, "You are going to draw a picture of how you got the shells and rocks to *balance*," as she moves her hands up and down and then brings them side by side.
>
> Mei-lin smiles and responds by imitating Ms. Rebekah's movements. When they finish their drawings, Ms. Rebekah walks with them over to the balance and holds their pictures next to it. She says, "You both drew pictures to show how you made the shells and rocks *balance*!" using the same hand movements she used before.

Obtaining, Evaluating, and Communicating Science Information > **Collecting, recording, organizing, and analyzing data**

Recording, compiling, and organizing data are critical activities in science because they enable scientists (and children doing science) to analyze and make claims based on multiple sources of evidence. Listening to and considering the observations and evidence of others also supports children's critical thinking and collaboration skills. Science is a perfect context for introducing children to different ways of organizing data on charts, tables, graphs, and Venn diagrams.

Teaching strategies. Use the following strategies to support recording and organizing data:

> Provide drawing and writing tools with clipboards in the learning areas. Encourage children to collect data, for example, about investigations they are doing related to matter and forces, living things, or light and shadow by representing their observations or recording quantitative data. For example, suggest they draw the shadows they make or record how many times one ball rolls farther than another off the same incline.

> Transcribe children's descriptions of their recorded data or representations and support emergent writing. Ask probing questions such as "Can you tell me more about this part of the shadow you drew?" or "Is this the number that shows how many times that ball rolled farther?"

> Introduce children to different ways of organizing data. Use charts to list the group's descriptions (such as what we noticed about squirrels outside) or ideas (such as what we think makes shadows). Tables work well for charting characteristics of individual objects or organisms. For example, list the name of each ball with its picture in one column and children's descriptions of its properties in the other. Graphs work well for organizing quantitative data such as the number of different kinds of plants children found in different parts of the outdoor area or how far different balls rolled off the same incline. Venn diagrams are good for comparing phenomena that are similar in some ways and different in others.

Obtaining, Evaluating, and Communicating Science Information > **Using books as sources of information to extend and enrich inquiry**

Informational text, storybooks, and mixed-genre books (a fictional story that incorporates authentic science content) can all be used for multiple purposes in science.

Teaching strategies. Introduce children to different purposes for using books with these strategies:

> Use informational texts to do research on a current topic of study (for example, *Great Pets: An Extraordinary Guide to Usual and Unusual Family Pets* by Sara Stein, 2003) or compelling questions that arise and cannot be answered through direct investigation, such as "What kinds of animals live in Australia?"

> Use books to inspire children's explorations. For example, use *13 Buildings Children Should Know* by Angela and Annette Roeder or *Dreaming Up* by Christy Hale to inspire building activities and engage children in thinking about how the designs of buildings relate to their functions (for example, "Why do houses have doors and windows?").

> Introduce stories that center children's cultures in their exploration. For example, *El viejo y su puerta (The Old Man and His Door)* by Gary Soto tells the story of an older Mexican gentleman who discovers multiple ways to use a door he carries on his back to help his neighbors, including as a ramp. It also includes a delightful language mix-up in Spanish between the words la puerta (door) and el puerco (pig).

> Use books with detailed and authentic scientific photos and images as prompts for discussion, even if the text is aimed at older readers, such as *A Drop of Water* by Walter Wick. You don't always have to read the text to enjoy and learn from a book!

> Use mixed-genre books such as *Oscar and the Moth: A Book About Light and Dark; Oscar and the Frog: A Book About Growing;* and *Oscar and the Cricket: A Book About Moving and Rolling* (all in English and Spanish and available on YouTube) by Geoff Waring. These books enable children to identify with a character who is exploring the same questions they are.

> Use narratives with science themes to help children evaluate the information in a book for scientific accuracy. *The Very Hungry Caterpillar, The Grouchy Ladybug,* and *The Very Busy Spider* by Eric Carle are very useful for this purpose and can all be found as read-alouds on YouTube.

> Look for books that feature men and women scientists and STEM professionals who represent a variety of ages, abilities, ethnicities, cultures, languages, and backgrounds, such as *Scientist, Scientist, Who Do You See?* by Chris Ferrie, and *Ada Twist, Scientist* and *Iggy Peck, Architect* (both available in English and Spanish) by Andrea Beaty.

> Start a library of wordless children's books focused on science topics, or make paper or digital copies, that families can borrow. Check out *The Snowman* by Raymond Briggs, *Have You Seen My Duckling?* by Nancy Tafuri, *Flashlight* by Lizi Boyd, *A Ball for Daisy* by Chris Raschka, *Wave* by Suzy Lee, and *Chalk* by Bill Thomson. Wordless books are invaluable for supporting science conversations, particularly between children and adults in families for whom English is not their home language.

Learning About Technology (Including Traditional and Digital Tools)

From the moment they are born, children are surrounded by technology, including basic everyday tools for eating and self-care (such as forks, spoons, and toothbrushes) and more complex household tools (such as dishwashers and microwaves). Preschoolers are particularly fascinated by tools adults use at home and how they work (such as manual and electric household and fix-it tools). Young children are also growing up surrounded by digital technologies (such as smartphones, tablets, apps, and games) and represent the next generation of digital natives—people who were born into a digital world, are comfortable and confident inhabitants of it, and are fluent with using digital technologies in all areas of life. Current conversations even include the use of artificial intelligence in early childhood education (Kazi 2021).

In early learning programs, children are introduced to many traditional and digital tools, including tools for making art, for building, for writing, for playing games, and for doing science, such as hand lenses, bug boxes, tape measures, balances, and cameras on smartphones or tablets to capture observations and creations. As they acquire competence with a particular tool, they think about how that tool can help them accomplish a goal (such as measuring the growth of a plant) or solve a problem (such as identifying a suitable container for an outdoor animal). A primary goal of using digital devices and tools with young children is to familiarize them with their various uses in learning and problem solving, and supporting their digital literacy skills from an early age (Donohue 2017; Donohue & Schomburg 2017).

Of the key knowledge and skills in the area of technology, child-guided experiences seem particularly important for the following:

> Using and investigating traditional tools

> Gaining familiarity with digital devices and resources

Adult-guided experiences seem to be especially significant for the following:

> Using digital tools for communicating and collaborating

> Extending and expanding real-world science explorations

CHILD-GUIDED experiences are especially important for learnings such as:

| Learning About Technology | Using and investigating traditional tools |

Using everyday tools as well as science tools for observing, measuring, and recording data offers children many opportunities to investigate how a tool's structure (how it is made) relates to its function (how it is used), an important crosscutting concept in science.

Teaching strategies. Support children's use of traditional, nondigital tools using these strategies:

> Talk with children about the familiar tools they use every day and how their structures make them useful for different purposes. For example, "What foods are good to eat with spoons? Why do you think so? What about forks?" and "Who has sneakers with laces? Velcro? Zippers? Elastic? What purpose do they all serve?"

> Encourage children to use the same tool for different purposes. For example, children might use masking tape to hang up drawings of their structures or to tape pieces of cardboard together to make a ramp.

> Create opportunities for children to use multiple tools for representation. For example, they can use playdough, sticks, pebbles, toothpicks, or other items to make models of the living things they find outdoors.

Computer literacy is increasingly essential in today's world. NAEYC and Fred Rogers Center explain, "Effective uses of technology and media are active, hands-on, engaging, and empowering; give the child control; provide adaptive scaffolds to ease the accomplishment of tasks; and are used as one of many options to support children's learning" (2012, 6). Becoming comfortable and confident about using laptops, tablets, smartphones, and navigating digital programs, apps, games, and other resources takes time and practice. Used thoughtfully and with intention, digital devices and media can "expand children's access to new content and new skills" (NAEYC 2020, 13), especially for preschoolers with limited access at home.

Teaching strategies. Try some of these strategies for supporting children's independent use of digital technology:

> Choose digital apps and games that are open-ended and promote discovery. High-quality educational games pose a problem, ask children to solve it, and provide feedback. Programs that pose problems with "correct" answers can be productive if the feedback prompts children to try different solutions. If the program does not do this, then an adult working alongside the children can.

> Introduce new devices, programs, or apps to a few children at a time and support them to try it out. Then make them available throughout the day.

> Promote social interaction by planning partner or small group activities that encourage peer mentoring.

> Choose child-friendly hardware, such as oversized keyboards, colored keyboard keys, touchscreens, and assistive technologies—such as a switch—that may be provided by a child's therapist.

ADULT-GUIDED experiences are especially important for learning such as:

| Learning About Technology | Using digital tools for communicating and collaborating |

Digital technologies can and should be used collaboratively. Children often prefer working with a friend to working alone when using digital devices. Adults play a critical role in mediating children's exposure to and use of devices in early learning and leveraging their use to support communication and collaboration:

> Just because children may feel comfortable with technology does not mean that they will be independent with it without any instruction or scaffolding. In the same way that children gain emergent knowledge of reading from interactive reading experiences, watching others read and write, and receiving instruction, young children learn emergent digital literacy skills by watching and using technologies with others. (Fantozzi 2022, 11)

Teaching strategies. Try out these strategies for supporting collaboration and communication with technology (Fantozzi 2022):

> Talk about ways to use a device, such as a tablet, together. As a group, set guidelines for collaborating, such as remembering that each partner has a voice about selecting the characters and setting as they are working on a virtual puppet show.

> Encourage children to describe how they are using a device or program, share any challenges they are having, and build on each other's ideas as they use it to create. Refer children to each other when they are interested in trying something new or get stuck ("I've seen Clara add drawings and voice-over to her photos; ask her if she will show you how she does it").

| Learning About Technology | Extending and expanding real-world science explorations |

Technology is especially important to science; tools are both products of science and serve to push science forward. Digital devices, resources, and media, along with traditional science tools, can play a valuable role in early science education when used in conjunction with children's direct physical, life, and earth and space science explorations. Consider that children cannot experience some essential characteristics such as weight, texture, or density through digital experiences, and digital animations seldom represent the details of real objects, materials, and organisms. In addition, depending on the exploration and the device, moving and manipulating objects on a digital device (such as changing the incline of a ramp) may require more or less fine motor and eye-hand coordination skills than the direct experience, which may challenge or support children with fine motor delays or disabilities.

Teaching strategies. Try some of these strategies for integrating technology with inquiry:

> Take smartphone or tablet videos of children's explorations using the slow motion function to help children more closely observe how their building topples or which ball makes it to the bottom of a ramp first.

> Do research with children online about physical science concepts (for example, "Can feathers and bricks really hit the ground at the same time?" and "What animals live in South America?").

> Showcase the diversity in the STEM workforce, jobs, and careers, with special attention to STEM workers who represent the ethnicities and cultures of children.

> Provide access to YouTube videos related to science concepts or phenomena children are exploring, such as *CBeebies: Minibeast Adventures with Jess—Snail Adventure* on YouTube. Be sure to preview for ads and queue up videos to bypass them.

> Look for vetted media resources such as Let's Be Scientists/Everyday Learning (PBS 2025), PEEP and the Big Wide World (WGBH Educational Foundation 2025), and PBS Play and Learn Science (Christensen et al. 2019).

● ● ●

Science learning and literacy has become essential for navigating the demands of an increasingly science- and technology-oriented world and for pursuing training and careers in a rapidly changing workforce. Introducing children to foundational science concepts and intentionally facilitating opportunities for them to engage in rich, authentic science inquiry is more important now than ever. Fortunately, young children and science are a natural fit. And when children's playful science inquiry and learning are supported and facilitated by invested, nurturing adults, these early experiences can have lifelong impacts on children's science learning, self-efficacy, and interests and on the development of skills across the domains. A broad set of skills considered essential to life and work now and in the future—including critical thinking and problem solving, collaboration, communication, and creativity—are supported by the types of science experiences and interactions described in this chapter.

For Further Consideration

1. Some early childhood educators still view science as a subject only appropriate for older students. What might you say to convince them that science is developmentally appropriate for young children and belongs in preschool? What examples might you use from your own program, or one you have observed, as evidence?

2. What do you think about or feel when you hear the word "science"? How do you think your attitudes toward science developed? What kinds of science inquiry and learning experiences did you engage in as a young child? What experiences and people were most influential in how you think and feel about science now? Consider how you will ensure that you support positive science attitudes and self-identities for all the children you work with or will work with.

3. There is evidence to suggest that persistent stereotypes about what science is and who scientists are continue to influence adults' perceptions about which children are more likely to succeed in science and related fields. This implicit bias is likely to influence how adults interact with different children when it comes to science. What advice would you give to a program or school leader who wants to address adults' STEM biases at their setting?

4. What are some ways you currently use digital technologies with children? How might you consider using them to support children's learning in physical, life, and earth and space science?

CHAPTER 9

Social Studies

Crystal N. Wise, Betül Demiray Sandıraz, and Anne-Lise Halvorsen

The preschoolers in Ms. Sharif's class take a walk around the block at outside time. They pass the bodega, a fish store, the pharmacy, a produce stand, and a used clothing store. In front of the produce stand, Adam waves to Mr. and Mrs. Torricelli, the owners, who are piling fruit on the carts.

"They live upstairs from me!" Adam announces.

Concetta points to the fruit and says, "Manzanas and plátanos," and Ms. Sharif replies, "Yes, apples and bananas."

"Look! Mr. Franks," pipes up Adeela. "He's painting the wall next to his grocery store."

"He's painting it the color we voted for," says Rajeev.

The children continue talking about the neighborhood places they visit with their families and the people who work there (for example, "the man at the shoe store," "the money lady [cashier] at the corner store," "the popcorn guy at the movies") and what they notice about how the community is being cared for (how clean the sidewalks and streets are, whether trash and recycle bins are available).

Learning Objectives

1. To identify and describe the social systems and social concepts that are key to a quality social studies curriculum

2. To explain how socialization in and beyond the early childhood setting influences young children's development in social studies

3. To examine personal strengths and biases that may support or undermine a nurturing and respectful learning environment for all children

4. To describe general and specific strategies and practices for teaching and learning in social studies

Later that day, at large group time, Rajeev offers, "Ms. Sharif, I saw a lot of trash on the ground by the fish store."

Ms. Sharif asks, "Did anyone else see what Rajeev saw?" A few heads nod, and there are choruses of "Yeah!" and "Me too!" Ms. Sharif leads the children in a discussion about what they noticed on their walk and possible ways to address it.

Many young children experience a rich community of interaction among family, neighbors, and other members who are integrally involved in everyday life together in children's homes and neighborhoods. For some children, the early childhood setting offers their first experience of a community outside their homes. As children learn to get along, make friends, and participate in decision making, they are engaging in social studies learning. The social studies curriculum can also expand children's horizons beyond the school into the neighborhood and the wider world.

The National Council for the Social Studies (NCSS), the national organization in the United States for social studies education, defines social studies as "the study of individuals, communities, systems, and their interactions across time and place that prepares students for local, national, and global civic life" (NCSS 2023). Social studies is both a broad and deep subject area that draws on knowledge, skills, and values from a range of disciplines and topics, all with the aim of helping children develop knowledge and dispositions needed to be active and engaged participants in public life who can make reasoned decisions for the public good (NCSS 2010).

Social studies learning can be categorized into two components with 10 themes: social systems (individual development and identity; time, continuity, and change; people, places, and environments; culture; individuals, groups, and institutions; power, authority and governance) and social concepts (production, distribution, and consumption; science technology and society; global connections; civic ideals and practices). These components and their themes guide a quality social studies curriculum for pre-K through grade 12. Early childhood teachers integrate the themes into children's learning experiences over time in ways that are appropriate to children's developmental levels, build on their previous knowledge and understanding, and reflect their cultures. As Mindes (2015) notes,

> In the preschool years, intentional teaching of the social studies focuses on exploration of self, family, center or school, transportation, current events, and everyday activities. To plan these themes in a rich way, teachers incorporate the sociocultural context of the places where they teach. Thus, a center or school with children from diverse cultural backgrounds incorporates activities that reflect the children's lives. (16)

Although social studies learning is related to social and emotional development (see Chapter 4), these content areas are increasingly differentiated in the early childhood curriculum. Social studies learning helps children connect to the larger society around them as they become aware of the practices, times, places, and values that both associate them with and distinguish them from others. Social and emotional learning underlies this growing awareness—for example, children need to form a unique self-identity before they identify where they fit in a group. However, social studies leads children down a wider and more divergent set of paths as they gain knowledge of

Social studies education is guided by several resources, the most central of which are the *National Curriculum Standards for Social Studies* (NCSS 2010) and *The College, Career, and Civic Life (C3) Framework for Social Studies State Standards: Guidance for Enhancing the Rigor of K–12 Civics, Economics, Geography and History* (Swan et al. 2013). Other sources such as the *Roadmap to Educating for American Democracy* (Educating for American Democracy 2024) and the *Social Justice Standards* (Learning for Justice 2014) provide excellent guidance. Each of these resources includes standards for K-12 education that can be modified for preschool learners. In addition, some goals in the social and emotional development domain of the *Interactive Head Start Early Learning Outcomes Framework: Ages Birth to Five* (Head Start Early Childhood Learning & Knowledge Center, n.d.) are relevant to early childhood social studies education.

themselves and their immediate community. In social studies learning, young children begin to gain an understanding of the principles and practices that guide the institutions of the society in which they live.

Intentional teachers play a crucial role in laying the foundation for this understanding. Knowledgeable about age-appropriate social studies content and pedagogical approaches that align with children's developmental needs, interests, and abilities, teachers create a classroom environment that promotes active exploration, inquiry, and hands-on learning experiences in social studies. Opportunities to engage in meaningful and authentic experiences, such as field trips (real life and virtual), guest speakers, community visits, and interactive discussions, help children connect classroom learning to the world beyond school. Teachers also incorporate a variety of resources, materials, and manipulatives, such as books, photographs, artifacts, and maps, to support children's exploration and understanding of social studies concepts. By creating a rich and stimulating learning environment, teachers support children's curiosity and the critical thinking and problem-solving skills that are the foundation for their participation in formal school settings and eventually the larger society.

Strategies for teaching and learning in the two components of social studies—social systems and social concepts—appear in "Fitting the Learning Experience to the Learning Objective" later in this chapter, where they are considered as child-guided and adult-guided experiences.

Young Children's Development in Social Studies

From the moment of birth, children are attuned to their social world. Preschoolers are already quite adept at observing and interpreting the behavior of others with respect to themselves. They are socialized by adults, other children, books, toys and other learning materials, and the media. The increased presence of technology, digital games, and media in children's lives exposes children to people and places far away from their worlds. On the one hand, these socializing influences can help children better understand themselves and promote positive identity development (for example, Curenton et al. 2022); on the other hand, they can reinforce stereotypes and limit how children perceive themselves and their abilities (for example, Golden & Jacoby 2018) as well as how they perceive others.

The ways educators and the larger school community welcome and treat children and families, especially with regard to their social identities such as race and ethnicity, contribute to the ways children come to view themselves and others. Rather than make assumptions and generalizations based on children's group identities, intentional teachers get to know each child and family for who they are as individuals. Although people with the same group identity may share qualities, there are also large variations within groups; as such, children's group identities are recognized and valued but not used as the basis for assumptions about what children are interested in, how they will behave, what practices are important in their families, and so forth.

The early childhood setting is critical for helping children develop the knowledge and skills they will need to live in a complex and increasingly diverse society. Beginning with their interactions with the individuals in their families, neighborhoods, and early learning settings, young children establish a foundation that will enable them to branch out to encounter new people and settings when they are older and participating as adults in the world. For example, preschoolers learn about human diversity—language and culture, living environments and relationships, abilities and needs, beliefs and practices—by interacting with a wide range of adults and peers. They take on different roles during dramatic play, solve problems collaboratively, read stories and informational books about interesting people and situations, explore the art of many cultures, go on field trips in their communities, virtually explore the broader world, and care for the indoor and outdoor learning environment as participants in their communities and stewards of their world. These types of skills and understandings are evident in the following vignettes:

> Since Anna is absent when it is her turn to pass out the napkins at snack time, the preschoolers decide that Marcus, who is next on the list, should do it that day. However, they agree that as soon as Anna comes back, it will be her turn, even if another name is next on the list by then.

● ● ●

> During morning meeting, Sophia, who has a visual impairment, tells how she asked her classmates to push their chairs in after snack time. She knows that a tidy room is helpful to everyone, but a clear path is also something she needs to navigate the room (Dorsey et al. 2024, 53).

● ● ●

When the children go for walks around the neighborhood, they are often greeted warmly by the older adults living in a nursing home near the school. The children know many of the adults by name and refer to them as their "grandfriends." During large group time, the children decide to make valentines for them.

● ● ●

During community walks where the children are empowered to observe and think about their community's needs and how they can make a difference, they notice that not having sidewalks makes it difficult for them to get to certain places. As the group discusses getting more sidewalks for people to get around, one child asks, "How do we make that happen?" (Wise et al. 2024, 27)

Children also develop an understanding of and skills in democracy by finding ways to address issues that are important to them, learning to make their voices heard, actively listening to other perspectives, and taking collective action. Children learn that democracy in the early childhood classroom involves what is in the common good for the group. Feeling valued and having a sense of belonging, learning from a variety of perspectives, exploring and respecting ways people are similar and different, and having information that challenges and counters stereotypes all help to foster a sense of caring and justice in the classroom community (Marsh et al. 2020).

The development of social studies knowledge and skills parallels early learning in other areas. It progresses from the simple to the complex, shifts from a self-focus to taking the perspectives of others, and involves learning about social systems (such as how communities operate) and specific social concepts (in history, geography, and so on; Seefeldt, Castle, & Falconer 2013). Two cognitive components are especially important to social studies learning in the preschool years. One is the child's growing awareness of social norms and customs (at home, at school, and, through media exposure, to the wider culture), also known as socialization. This socialization also includes moral development—how children reason about what is right and what is wrong (Paley 2000). The other cognitive component is using classification skills. Preschoolers are increasingly adept at identifying things that are the same and things that are different. They also begin to realize that two or more things can be similar in some ways and dissimilar in others. These cognitive and social understandings help children engage with social studies in ways that are meaningful to them, connect them with others, and promote equity and diversity. When children are able to appreciate similarities and differences and see that each person is valued by the adults in their learning community, they are better able to connect with and understand people and ideas that are different from their own.

Teaching and Learning in Social Studies

Two general strategies are helpful in enabling young children to acquire an understanding of social studies and apply this learning in their daily experiences: starting with concrete experiences and moving to general principles, and helping children grow from self-awareness to more awareness of others.

Building from Concrete Experiences to General Principles

Because preschoolers can form mental representations, they can apply their concrete knowledge of the here and now to the there and then (Villotti & Berson 2019). This means they can picture situations they have not (yet) experienced themselves, such as real people living in times and places they have never seen or imaginary creatures doing things they have never done. Young children use concrete signs, such as clothing, facial features, furniture, plants, and transportation, as clues about the "when and where" of the situation depicted. They also draw on their own experiences—for example, visiting a relative's home where things appear and are done differently from how their family lives—to understand the general idea that things can change with time and place.

Interactions with a variety of people also help children become aware of the principles that shape and explain human relationships. For example, as they talk with others about their home lives, preschoolers learn that families have different living arrangements, languages, jobs, celebrations, religious beliefs, evening routines, and food and music preferences. With adult support, they begin to form mental categories within which to classify this information. Thoughtful, well-timed adult comments can help children create these structures for appreciating similarities and differences (for example, "Xavier's dad is a teacher, un maestro, and Malcolm's mom paints houses, un pintor de casas. People have different jobs"). Discussing differences in ways that are respectful and positive reinforces the notion that different does not mean less than ("Yes, Jessamyn has a prosthetic leg to help her walk. People move in different ways; some people use a prosthesis, some use a wheelchair, and some have another type of mobility aid—a tool or piece of equipment that helps them get around").

Moving from Self-Awareness to Awareness of Others

An important principle of social studies is that personal actions can affect others, beginning with the people one knows personally and extending to other people and systems around the world. This knowledge motivates people to act responsibly. So, for example, when adults share appropriate classroom decisions with children, the children learn that their choices and actions matter. They can see the results themselves. This model of shared control helps preschoolers feel empowered and spurs them to take further responsibility.

Intentional teachers lead by example, demonstrating kindness and empathy toward all children and adults and honoring their strengths and contributions to the learning community. They ensure that their perspective on a child's choice or action is not based on a preference for their own cultural practices or any assumptions springing from implicit bias. They take note of children and families' cultural practices, including what is considered appropriate in the homes of children from cultural backgrounds different from their own, as they plan experiences for children. They are aware of the nonverbal and verbal messages children receive, both in the classroom and in the wider society, and are mindful of how these messages shape how children view who is important and who is not. When you create a supportive and inclusive community where everyone feels valued and respected, children learn that everyone has unique needs and strengths and that it's essential to understand, accept, and value others just as they are.

It is especially important to focus on the positive outcomes of children's behavior. Too often, adults call attention to the negative effects of unsocial actions (for example, "You took all the purple markers and crayons. Now there are no purple ones left for others to use"). However, if teachers want children to feel empowered, they need to acknowledge children's capacity for bringing about positive changes. You can do this by commenting when children assist others ("Isabel, that was helpful when you explained to the other children at the table that Alberto wanted a muffin when he called it a 'magdalena'"), recognizing collaborative problem solving ("You found a way to use the dump truck together"), and acknowledging voluntary attempts to help in the classroom ("You wiped up the water so no one would slip"). The simple gratification of knowing they have acted in socially responsible ways encourages children to do more of the same.

Connecting Teaching to Children's Lives

After a windstorm breaks small branches off the trees surrounding their preschool, several 4- and 5-year-old boys begin building a "clubhouse" by dragging branches and bunches of leaves to a corner in the playground fence. When Valeria (4 years old) starts dragging a branch to join them, the boys shout, "No girls allowed! No girls allowed!"

Mrs. Simons checks in with Valeria about her feelings. She considers encouraging the boys to welcome Valeria into their play but hesitates. She decides to address the underlying ideas, especially that girls can't or shouldn't engage in play that emphasizes physical strength or that "real boys" don't include girls in their play.

To find out what the boys are thinking, Mrs. Simons asks, "Why do you think no girls are allowed?" She listens carefully to the boys' responses: "Girls can't move the big branches," "And they can't build high!," "We're going to be superheroes! Girls can't be heroes," and, finally, "We don't like girls."

Mrs. Simons realizes that if she does not address this situation, it will reinforce the stereotype that boys don't have to pay attention to others' feelings. Seeing an opportunity to expand their thinking, Mrs. Simons suggests testing the boys' claims. She says, "Well, let's find out if girls can move the big branches and build high or not."

Since many of the children are now gathering around, she invites everyone to join in the challenge. "What do you think is going to happen?" she asks. With much laughter the children run and gather branches. Some girls are faster than some boys, and some boys are faster than some girls. Everyone is able to add branches to the clubhouse, which is suddenly much higher!

Bringing the children back together, Mrs. Simons says, "It looks like both girls and boys can lift big branches and build high. Thinking that boys are better at these things than girls is a stereotype."

Several children repeat the word *stereotype*. (Preschoolers love big words!) Mrs. Simons clarifies: "Stereotypes are unfair. In our school we want everyone to be treated fairly. What can we do so that we can be sure that we play together fairly?"

The next steps are suggested by the children. One suggestion is a sign that says "Everyone can play here."

"How about," says one of the boys who began this episode, "if we want to play alone, we just say, 'You can have a turn in a few minutes'?"

Knowing that one interaction is never enough to help children think in new ways, Mrs. Simons plans and carries out further activities. She adds books to the classroom library that feature strong, fast female athletes and firefighters. At large group time, she reads books in which girls and boys play together in big muscle games. She invites a female carpenter to help the children build with real tools, and she begins a curriculum on being a hero, about all the ways boys and girls can be powerful helpers.

Mrs. Simons begins with a child-initiated teachable moment and follows up with teacher-initiated activities. In addition, she later discusses her plans and reasoning with her colleagues at their next staff meeting. Together they consider the frequency of gendered exclusionary play in the program and agree to take the important step of identifying how (explicitly and implicitly) they may be supporting a binary view of gender in their classrooms. For example, how often do they call out "boys and girls" rather than "children"? Do they ask "strong boys" to help move furniture and big blocks? Do they comment on girls' clothing or hair instead of asking about their interests and accomplishments? Do they support boys' tender, sharing, inclusive behaviors or mainly comment on their noisy, power-focused play? The teachers agree to observe each other as well as the children and see what changes they can make to avoid the damage that gender stereotypes can have on children's sense of themselves and others.

Adapted, with permission, from J.O. Edwards, "How to Get Started with Anti-Bias Education in Your Classroom and Program," *Exchange* (January/February 2017): 78–79.

Children are not immune to the stereotypes and biases that pervade society. Intentional teachers are steadfast, proactive, and nurturing in addressing harmful words or actions toward others and guiding children to be conscious of ideas and behaviors that exclude or demean others. As illustrated in the vignette, it is critical to build children's awareness and challenge stereotypes and biases through courageous conversations, shared readings, explorations, and play. Another part of this important work is collaborating with colleagues to reflect on the presence and absence of explicit and implicit bias in the early childhood setting and consistently reevaluate and generate responses to unjust practices and situations.

Fitting the Learning Experience to the Learning Objective

The terms *social studies, socialization,* and *society* all come from the Latin root word *socius,* which means companion, partner, sharing, fellowship, or union (*American Heritage Dictionary of the English Language* n.d.). Therefore, any effective practices (described in Chapter 2) that bring children and adults together to work and play for the common good of the group can promote social studies learning. For example, a shared daily routine creates a sense of community, cleaning up as a group distributes the responsibility for maintaining equipment and materials so everyone can use them, and greeting children in the languages spoken by their families helps all children feel as if they are part of the classroom community. The goal of such experiences is to help children act and think beyond their own self-interests to consider the principles that govern and affect the world around them.

As mentioned previously, social studies learning in early childhood provides opportunities for children to engage with real-world issues and experience through two components: social systems and social concepts (NCSS 2019). Social systems are the norms, values, and procedures that affect human relationships in our day-to-day lives. For preschoolers, they include valuing diversity of people and cultures, becoming aware of the people and places in their community, understanding the need for groups to have rules, and beginning to participate in the democratic process. Preschoolers also begin to develop a foundation for engaging with social justice concepts. Although young children are often thought of as focused primarily on themselves and defining fairness as everyone getting the same, they can define fairness as equity. That is, with adult support and opportunities to practice, children can act from an equity stance by giving up resources, prioritizing others' needs, and advocating for others (Lee et al. 2022). In the past, topics included under this component were typically subsumed under social skills, a topic discussed in Chapter 4. However, as researchers and educators discovered that early experiences in this area form the foundation for later citizenship, these topics were defined, expanded, and moved to the emerging curriculum domain of social studies.

The second component is social concepts. Its subject matter is what is traditionally thought of as social studies—the standard disciplines taught later in school. In the context of the early learning setting, children experience and explore real-life events, scenarios, or problems from the classroom, their communities, and the larger society through books, play-based and inquiry activities, explicit instruction, and discussion (NCSS 2019). Through these experiences children learn disciplinary thinking and practices reflected within the social studies disciplines. These include economics, which for preschoolers involves thinking about decision making and understanding resources and exchanges. History at this age focuses on the sequence of events, as young children are increasingly able to recall the past and anticipate the future, as well as learning about people in the past who have made a difference. Preschool geography is about locations and their relationship to one another. Preschoolers are also interested in the lives of people from other parts of the world, provided these are made concrete and connected to their own lives (such as customs related to food, housing, games children enjoy, and family relationships). Ecology includes the study of the ways that humans interact with and affect the natural environment— not how the natural and physical world operates (which is covered under science; see Chapter 8). Although mastering these disciplines within social studies is not the goal for preschoolers, meaningful early experiences can have a positive impact on the rest of their lives.

Rich learning experiences in early childhood social studies rely on engagement in both child-guided and adult-guided experiences around social systems and social concepts. As with every domain in this book, grouping concepts and skills as child-guided versus adult-guided experiences is not rigid. Careful attention to children's emerging abilities will help you decide which approach works best for each child at a given time.

Social Systems

Children naturally observe human diversity and roles within families and communities, but they rely on adults to help them understand, respect, and celebrate these differences. Likewise, adults play a crucial role in guiding children to understand the reasons behind rules and agreements, fostering their ability to participate in decision making and respect the democratic processes within the early learning community. Of the key knowledge, skills, and dispositions within the social systems component, child-guided experiences seem particularly important for the following:

> Valuing diversity

> Learning about people and places in the community

Adult-guided experiences seem to be especially significant for the following:

> Understanding rules in the context of a group

> Creating and participating in democracy

CHILD-GUIDED experiences are especially important for learnings such as:

| Social Systems | Valuing diversity |

Diversity among humans takes many forms, including gender, race, ethnicity, ability, age, religion, family structure, and ideas. Valuing diversity means accepting, appreciating, and celebrating the differences between others and oneself as normal and positive. It means treating people as individuals and not as stereotypes.

Children are keen observers of similarities and differences in the people and world around them. They ask questions about observations that interest, confuse, or trouble them— sometimes making adults uncomfortable. They may make inaccurate or even hurtful statements that indicate they are trying to figure things out based on their limited understanding. Through observing and participating in day-to-day relationships and interactions, they learn the values and social norms of their settings, including how bias, discrimination, and inequities are enacted, sustained, internalized, and challenged. Preschoolers are old enough to have encountered, enacted, and possibly internalized harmful attitudes and behaviors from the cultures that surround them, both those aimed at them and those aimed at others (see, for example Iruka et al. 2022 and Waxman 2021). However, when children's social and cultural identities are affirmed, and when they have experiences with people who are different from them, are supported to make sense of the differences, and have their questions answered honestly and accurately, children can learn to accept that differences exist and that they can be respectful and kind to everyone.

Young children are also keenly interested in issues of fairness, and with support they can learn to recognize injustice (unfairness) toward others, develop language to describe it, and develop the capacity to act against prejudice and discrimination (Derman-Sparks & Edwards, with Goins 2020; NAEYC 2019a).

It is important to create a nurturing and safe environment for children to grapple with differences and injustices. To help children grow in these areas, engage in consistent self-reflection of your own identities, beliefs, and experiences with diversity and how they influence your teaching practices. Consider whether shifts in your thinking and practices are needed to better promote justice and equity in your work with children and families.

Teaching strategies. Implement the following strategies on an ongoing basis to thoughtfully foster children's positive identity development and their understanding of diverse ways of interacting with each other and the world:

> Model respect for others by the way you listen to and accept children's ideas and feelings. Let children see you treat everyone equitably and fairly, including children, families, coworkers, and community members.

> Prioritize the development of warm, supportive teacher-child relationships with each child. Consider how each child experiences sustained emotional support with each adult in the classroom, with specific attention to how children from historically marginalized groups experience care and connection from adults in the classroom (Goldberg & Iruka 2023).

> Avoid judgmental comparisons. Instead comment on specific attributes and accomplishments without labeling one as better than the other. For example, if you say to Jillian, "I like red hair," Nicole may infer there is something wrong with her brown hair. A better observation would be "Jillian has short, red hair, and Nicole has her brown hair in braids."

> Be careful not to stereotype cultures and to emphasize that not all people who belong to a particular cultural group share beliefs and practices; there is diversity *within* groups and cultures. For example, among the girls in the class, there are some who like to play with dolls and some who do not; among children who have Mexican ancestry, some may speak Spanish and some may not.

> Remember that diversity is also reflected in the things people create and value. Hang reproductions of artwork in diverse media and representing different cultures at eye level throughout the room. Explore a variety of styles of music and dance, being sure to include the many styles that children's families enjoy. Go to places and events in the community that highlight local diversity, such as different kinds of shops, festivals, concerts.

> Invite families to share their family traditions, foods, and celebratory occasions with all the children.

> Anticipate questions children might have and answer them simply and honestly. For example, a child might say, "My parents said boys can't wear pink." You can help the child understand the inaccuracy and potential hurt of such a statement without disparaging them by asking a question such as "Does anyone have a different idea?" Thoughtfully explore this topic with the children; if a child doesn't point this out, note that many boys (and men) do wear pink. You might follow up by reading a book about gender and gender roles.

- In the dramatic play area, include work clothes and tools used in different types of jobs as well as equipment used by people with various ability levels, such as crutches and magnifiers. The latter are most meaningful when children have had opportunities to meet, interact with, and ask questions of people who use that equipment. Provide a range of clothing representing the cultures and activities of the children and their families (and others that may be unfamiliar to the children), including everyday styles. Find out from families what is meaningful for them and discuss how to avoid appropriation and offensiveness.

- Put empty food containers and the cooking utensils used to prepare a diverse range of foods in the dramatic play area. Be sure to include labels that represent the multiple languages spoken by children at home and at school.

- Feature books, magazines, and catalogs with illustrations and photographs of people performing nonstereotypical jobs, families of varying structures, and people of different ages and appearances.

> When teaching about or celebrating holidays and traditions, focus on the ways the children's families and the community choose to celebrate specific occasions. Make clear that children can enjoy and value learning about each other's holidays while also honoring their own families' beliefs and traditions (Derman-Sparks & Edwards, with Goins 2020). Teach and engage children in discussions to appreciate the similarities and differences.

Social Systems   **Learning about people and places in the community**

The first roles preschoolers become aware of are those played by the people in their families. At first, they are concerned about the roles that affect them directly, such as who cooks their meals, provides comfort when they feel hurt or upset, or reads to them at bedtime. When they feel secure about having their basic needs met, young children next begin to pay attention to the roles family members perform outside the home, such as their jobs or the volunteer work they do. As their world expands, preschoolers also take an interest in the services performed by people outside the family, such as doctors, firefighters, police officers, teachers, bus drivers, zookeepers, performing artists, and barbers and hair stylists. These roles often appear in their dramatic play experiences.

Teaching strategies. Materials and experiences inside and outside the classroom can support children's interest in learning about people and places in the community. Here are some ideas:

> Build on children's initial interest in the relationships within their own families. Provide materials for dramatic play (dress-up clothes, housewares, shop and garden tools, office equipment). Talk about what family members do at home (for example, "Sean's daddy made dinner last night" or "Mattie did the laundry with her mom. She helped sort los calcetines, the socks") and the roles they play outside the home (for example, "Charlotte's grandmother sings in the choir at their church").

> Make a class book with photos of children's families performing different roles (planting a garden, taking the bus to the library).

> Invite family members to come to the classroom and share their roles, especially if they can bring related materials for the children to use themselves (such as subway passes, wrenches, tuning forks, spools of thread, and empty cartons clearly labeled with their former contents).

> Include children's literature that represents diverse families and family roles. Be sure books do not perpetuate stereotyped narratives about families (McCormick & West 2022).

> Take field trips and invite visitors to the classroom so children can expand their awareness of people and roles in their community. On neighborhood walks, point out people at work—for example, people who are driving delivery trucks or repairing roads. Visit various places of work, especially those that often show up in children's dramatic play, such as the fire station or supermarket. Bring back materials (grocery bags, receipt pads) children can incorporate into their play scenarios.

› Use community walks as a way to learn about the history of the neighborhood where the school is located (Rodríguez & Swalwell 2022). Get support from guides who can offer diverse perspectives about the rich history of the community. Focus on the collective efforts of community members and their roles in creating and sustaining the neighborhood. Investigate the naming of significant places and streets, accessibility, and architecture of the neighborhood (Rodríguez & Swalwell 2022).

ADULT-GUIDED experiences are especially important for learnings such as:

Social Systems **Understanding rules in the context of a group**

Creating, following, and refining rules (agreements or norms for how to act or what to do) is a fundamental part of functioning in a community. Just as licensed programs must follow health and safety rules, programs and teachers have rules that children must follow, such as how many children can be in a play space, how to use the bathroom, and how children should treat others. Children may create rules for games they invent. Sometimes the group establishes policies for preserving quiet areas or respecting block structures built by others.

It is important for children to learn that rules are not designed simply for the sake of having rules; they are designed to protect people, to ensure that people are treated justly, and to protect property and the environment. But rules are not always created or enforced equitably. Groups may decide to revise or change rules if they are not effective or are unjust. Understand, however, that some children and families will have different values and preferences around questioning rules, especially if it involves questioning a teacher.

Encourage children to engage in collective decision making about classroom rules and whether they need to be revised. Setting rules also can be a way to deal with interpersonal conflicts, especially if they affect groups of children or the whole class. Have the children act out the rules, and use photos of the rules to serve as nonverbal reminders. This can be especially helpful for some children with developmental delays or disabilities and for multilingual learners.

Self-Reflecting on Rules

Rules reflect the perspectives and cultures of the rule makers. Consider your own perspective on classroom rules (Rodríguez & Swalwell 2022). What agreements or rules do you generally have in your classroom? Why do you have these agreements or rules? Do they benefit some children and not others? Do they tend to support extrinsic motivation rather than children's intrinsic motivation? Are there some agreements or rules broken frequently? If so, why and by whom?

To promote equitable treatment for all children, involve children and, when beneficial, other stakeholders in rulemaking. Revisit rules as needed with children; engage in ongoing, intentional opportunities to explore; and consider your own implicit biases as part of preservice and ongoing in-service training (Gilliam et al. 2016).

Teaching strategies. Young children need explicit information and guidance from teachers to understand, establish, and follow rules governing classroom behavior. They also need help sorting out when rules may be fluid (for example, when players agree to change the rules midgame) and when they must remain fixed (for example, when they deal with health or safety). Competence in respecting and making rules begins in childhood and continues to develop into adolescence and early adulthood. You can lay the foundation for this development by carrying out practices such as the following:

> Make children aware of basic health and safety rules that have everyday meaning to them. Be concrete and positive, offering simple explanations ("Soap and water get rid of the germs, so they don't make us sick"). After discussing a few simple rules with children, write them out in short words and pictures, and post them at children's eye level.

> Realize that some children with developmental delays or disabilities may become overwhelmed by feelings related to rules. Be sure to demonstrate the important rules and provide plenty of patient reminders and opportunities for practice.

> Talk with families to better understand the cultural practices and rules children are expected to follow at home. Consider ways you can integrate these into the development of classroom expectations (Gilliam et al. 2016).

> During small group time or a class meeting, describe a problem that affects everyone and invite children to suggest one or more rules to solve it. Avoid making assumptions about the problem by seeking to understand how each child perceives the problem and the solution. Typical examples include children running through the block area and knocking things down or cleanup taking so long that it shortens outside time. Encourage children to discuss the pros and cons of each suggestion from their own perspectives. Write down and post the rules they decide to try, and refer to them when appropriate. Revisit the rules as a group in a few days to see whether or not they are working.

> Establish guidelines and procedures with the children for carrying out responsibilities in the classroom, such as cleaning up, passing out snacks or meals, and deciding who will do which jobs. When children decide the guidelines, they are more likely to take ownership of them and hold classmates accountable for following them.

> Use positive approaches to redirect children's behavior when rules are violated. Avoid practices like the use of behavior charts or other strategies that publicly embarrass children and erode their feelings of belonging in the classroom. Focus on practices that include proactive relationship building with each child, such as spending time with each child *outside* of conflict situations, holding calm and supportive individual discussions about behavior, and listening carefully to children's perspectives (Gartrell 2023; Jung & Smith 2018).

Making Up Guidelines to Govern Play

When children's play becomes too rough or dangerous, thus endangering their physical or emotional safety, adults need to step in to set limits. However, children can often be involved in creating guidelines to ensure their own comfort or safety (see also Gartrell 2023), as illustrated in the following example.

> After Steven, age 4, goes to a wrestling match, he gets several classmates in his preschool interested in playing "wrestling" during choice time. They use an area rug as their mat, push up their sleeves, and enjoy the rough-and-tumble play. The game goes on for several weeks, becoming progressively elaborate; for example, they give themselves wrestlers' names and develop a scoring system.
>
> In the second week, however, a few children voice that the play is too rough. Ms. Yahel knows that several children enjoy it and that it promotes learning in many areas, so at the beginning of choice time one day when the wrestlers are setting up their game, she voices her concern: "What guidelines can we make so that no one will get hurt?" She writes down their ideas—14 in all—and posts them on the wall above the mat. The rules include no hitting or pinching or head butts; only boys can play (dropped when a few girls protest); the referee has to be able to count to 10 (to know when to declare a match over); and you can't wrestle unless you have a wrestler name.
>
> The children refer to the guidelines in subsequent weeks as their interest in wrestling continues. If a guideline is not followed, the other children—rather than Ms. Yahel—are always quick to point out the infraction. Ms. Yahel explains to the families what the group has decided and assures them that the rules in place both help the children stay safe and enjoy the play.

Democracy in the early childhood classroom means that there are conditions of equality and respect for the individual. For young children, democracy is learning that everyone has a voice, even those who do not share the opinions of the majority. Democracy entails compromise and negotiation. An individual may not get their way, but they have the satisfaction of being heard, and decisions can be reviewed and revised if needed.

Children develop a sense of democracy from their experiences with rulemaking and social problem solving. Quality early interactions and play situations in home and early learning settings can support the development of the skills necessary (such as socioemotional and cognitive abilities, helping others, working in groups, and respecting others) for democratic participation (Adair et al. 2017; Kemple 2017). Race and socioeconomic status are important factors related to what children learn and experience in this process (Lo 2019). Children as young as 4 and 5 years old observe and learn whose voices matter and whose behaviors are seen as good. In turn, they decide to engage or disengage in civic spaces based on the match or mismatch between their identities and expectations from them (Hauver 2019).

To ensure that democratic approaches are inclusive of each child's personal and cultural identities and practices, it is essential to engage in reflection that goes deeper than your own perspective and experience. Consider democracy through the lens of each child:

> How do the families approach social problem solving, including compromise and negotiation?

> How might approaches to democracy differ for children depending on their personal, cultural, and community contexts?

Teaching strategies. Participating in a democratic society and in a democratic classroom requires similar skills. Young children are not ready for abstract civics lessons, but fostering the development of skills in appropriate, concrete ways prepares them to become responsible and productive citizens. To bring about this understanding in ways that make sense to children, teachers can use strategies such as these:

> Help children develop perspective-taking and turn-taking skills. Remind children to listen before they add their ideas to the discussion. Ask them to repeat what they hear and verify it with the speaker. Role playing helps them adopt the behavior and viewpoint of another. Because preschoolers are developing skills in taking turns, use a tool to help so they will not have to fight for a turn to speak and be heard. For example, you can use a timer or a talking stick. Such tools are especially effective for encouraging children who tend to be reserved or quiet to participate in group processes.

> Comment when you see children working collectively. Observe aloud how much more can be accomplished as a team than as one or two individuals. For example, note that when children work together, they can offer different perspectives, and those different perspectives can lead to a better solution to a problem than just one perspective.

> When children are engaging in hurtful behaviors toward another child—name calling, teasing, excluding—gently but firmly intervene to support the targeted child and help everyone learn better ways of interacting (Derman-Sparks & Edwards, with Goins 2020). Teach children skills that help them stand up for themselves and others when, for example, someone is being shamed or excluded (Payne et al. 2020a).

> When conflict among children arises, provide all parties with an opportunity to share their perspectives (see the "Engaging in Conflict Resolution" section on pages 86–88 in Chapter 4). Likewise, be sensitive to children who may be reluctant or unable to speak up in social problem-solving situations and provide safe and comfortable ways for them to become involved in generating and carrying out solutions. (See "Helping All Children Participate in Classroom Democracy" on page 254.)

> Use everyday problems and social interactions that occur in and outside of the classroom to create and participate in democracy. Have classroom discussions about what children observed or experienced in their classroom, school, neighborhood, and so on that felt unfair (Payne 2020). Use these as starting points for thinking about steps to take action for making a change. For instance, after identifying a problem that affects the classroom community, determine who to communicate with to solve the problem (Swalwell & Payne 2019). These activities can help children see the beauty and power of their communities (Wise et al. 2024). Ensure safe spaces and trusting relationships for all children to participate.

> Introduce other ideas and vocabulary words that are at the core of democratic principles and actions. For example, ask children to indicate their preferences (for instance, for a color or food) by a show of hands. Count and record the results on chart paper, using the appropriate vocabulary words such as *more/greater* and *less/fewer*. Use other terms that apply to social processes, such as *is/is not, same/different, all/some, other/else, before/after, now/later,* and *when/where/with whom*. Help children develop an overall sense of the patterns in human interaction and the principles governing behavior.

> Expand conversations children may initiate about their families' voting at election time. Keep your explanation of the voting process simple, such as "People who can vote get to say who they think will do the job best or what decision a community should make. Whoever is picked by the most people wins the job, and whatever decision is picked by the most people is the decision the community will follow." Be sure to avoid expressing evaluative comments about candidates or issues—keep the focus on the process of voting.

Helping All Children Participate in Classroom Democracy

A central goal of social studies education is helping children develop skills for citizenship, including collaborating, listening, considering others' perspectives, reconsidering their own perspectives, negotiating, and resolving conflicts. Social studies education overlaps with social and emotional development and social justice education. Here are some ways teachers can draw on these three areas to develop children's skills for participating in a democracy.

Skills for citizenship need to be explicitly modeled, taught, and retaught. Developing these skills is not a linear process. With one step forward there can often be two steps backward, but children require repeated opportunities to practice these skills, including problem solving and collaborating (for example, Payne et al. 2020b). Some children seem to instinctively know how to get along with others, but most need scaffolding and support. Although your instinct may be to temporarily separate children who are overly aggressive with others, recognize and take advantage of opportunities to help these children learn how to solve social problems in a more democratic fashion. To do this, learn what is behind the challenging behavior. It is serving a purpose—to express fear or mistrust, to compensate for an inability to communicate wants and needs, or to overcome emotions children have not been taught how to manage. Children need reassurance that their needs will be met and their rights respected. Help them to understand that their goals can be achieved with nonthreatening, nonaggressive behaviors.

Coach children in appropriate social behavior and call their attention to its positive consequences. For example, Fox and Lentini (2006) describe how a teacher used coaching to help a child who typically muscled his way into a play situation. During a visit to a

Social Concepts

Some social concepts, such as economics and history, emerge from children's own experiences, such as observing exchanges of goods and services or recalling past events from photos. However, understanding concepts in disciplines like geography and ecology typically requires adult guidance to help children become aware of their surroundings and how their actions affect the environment. Of the key knowledge, skills, and dispositions under social concepts, child-guided experiences seem particularly important for the following:

> Understanding simple economics—resources and exchanges

> Understanding history—connecting the past, present, and future

Adult-guided experiences seem to be especially significant for the following:

> Understanding geography

> Appreciating ecology

hands-on museum, the teacher saw the child approaching two others who were playing in the magnet station. Anticipating a conflict, she knelt beside him, acknowledged his desire to play, and reviewed the steps the class used to solve social problems. The child then approached the magnet station and asked his peers if he could play too. One peer moved over to make room on the bench, while the other gave him a magnet. The child looked to his teacher, who gave him a wink and a smile. A few minutes later, when the teacher checked back, the three children were using the magnets together and sharing observations about which materials did (and did not) stick.

Children who are targeted by aggressive behavior may also need encouragement to defend their rights by voicing their needs and feelings or expressing themselves in acceptable ways. This is particularly true of children who are timid or reluctant to speak up in social problem-solving situations. They may lack the words or may be concerned they will be overridden by their more outgoing or outspoken peers. Begin by validating these children's feelings and reassuring them—with gestures and facial expressions as well as words—that you will wait patiently while they express their feelings and will see that their needs are met. Be sensitive to their body language and help them identify their emotions (always checking that you are interpreting them correctly). Ask them to suggest solutions, give them ample time to respond, and repeat what they say so that others involved in the situation can listen to and hear their perspective. After they and the other child(ren) agree on a solution and put it into action, check back soon and periodically thereafter to make sure that the less assertive child's wishes are being respected. Provide unobtrusive encouragement (such as smiles, nods, and descriptive comments, such as "I see the sand timer has almost run out. I wonder whose turn it will be next").

For more on solving social problems with children, see Chapter 4. For additional strategies to help children with behaviors that may create challenges in the classroom, see Gartrell (2023) and Kaiser and Rasminsky (2021).

CHILD-GUIDED experiences are especially important for social concepts learnings such as:

| Social Concepts | Understanding simple economics—resources and exchanges |

Economics education focuses on helping children understand how individuals, businesses, and organizations make decisions about how to use their resources (Swan et al. 2013). Although this area of study can seem abstract, young children actually know many things about this area. They understand what resources are used to cook food; they observe garbage collection, park maintenance, and health care. Moreover, they are constantly making decisions about how to spend their time and energy, and they can recognize opportunity costs of their decision making (for example, "If I play with blocks during free play time, I won't have time to visit the sensory table"). Observing the roles of family members and others in the community, they develop basic ideas about reciprocity, including the exchange of money (Moore et al. 2023). They know that money, or its equivalent, comes in various forms (paper and coins, plastic cards, electronic funds/mobile pay systems, checks), and preschoolers have opinions about how money should be spent. At this age, they are more likely to judge an item's worth by its importance to themselves rather than by its actual market value.

Teaching strategies. Adult guidance can help children begin to think critically about the role of businesses and services within their community and their role as civic agents. Try the following strategies:

> Provide materials and props so that children can incorporate money and the exchange of goods and services into their dramatic play. Build on typical family experiences, such as going to the grocery store, paying the doctor or babysitter, or purchasing new shoes. Children enjoy using play money in these scenarios, but they also like to make their own. Provide strips of paper, rocks, beads, and other small items to use as pretend money.

> As you partner with children in their play, make comments and pose occasional questions to help them consider simple economic principles, such as limited resources, how goods and services are produced, and the relationship between work and money. For example, you might ask at the children's grocery store, "How do I make a decision about what to buy if I don't have enough money for everything I want?," "How much do I have to pay you to decorate the cake?," or "How much more will it cost if I order the large salad instead of the small one?"

> Extend children's learning about goods and services by taking regular trips to a nearby grocery store or market if possible (Adams 2015). Point out the products (such as bananas and rice) that are available in the store. Engage children in a discussion of how they and their families use the products, noting similarities and differences in how they use the products. The products can also become a source of inquiry. Encourage children to ask questions they have, such as "Where did the bananas come from?" or "How did the milk get to our store?" Also, help children consider how the lack of access to certain products might affect someone or their family and ways they might help.

> When you read books that include stories with people buying and selling things, briefly engage children in discussing the transactions. Older children might enjoy pondering "What if" questions. For example, if you know that all of the children's families buy groceries at local stores, you might ask the children, "What if there were no stores to buy our food? Where would we get the food we need to eat?"

Connecting the past, present, and future helps young children better understand the experiences of the human story across time. Thinking about time in this way engages children in understanding both continuity and change as well as the reasons behind change. Since this type of thinking is challenging for young children, start by associating events in their daily lives to periods of time. Older preschoolers understand that time moves forward, and they can look backward and understand that the past and present can affect the future (for example, they can wear the jacket they were given yesterday to school today). A growing vocabulary (words such as *before* and *after*, *first* and *last*, *then* and *next*) enables preschoolers to understand and talk about time (Thornton & Vukelich 1988).

Teaching strategies. With a consistent schedule, children become aware of the daily sequence of events in the program on their own. However, it helps if adults occasionally point out (or ask children to identify) "what we just did" or "what comes next." Materials and books also provide many opportunities to help children develop a sense of time. Try these strategies:

❯ Post out and discuss your program's daily schedule to help children become aware of events in the present, recent past, and immediate future. Use pictures, photos, cards, objects, and words to help children represent and sequence the parts of the day. Some programs begin the day with a message board that reminds children of the recent past and near future, such as a photo of a new material you introduced yesterday that children can play with today.

❯ Use and encourage children to use an expanding vocabulary of time and sequence words. Begin with terms such as *before* and *after*, *first* and *last*, *yesterday* and *tomorrow*; include their home-language equivalents for multilingual learners. Then introduce expressions such as *once upon a time, then and now, a long time ago,* and *when you grow up*. Hearing and using these words help children think about the passage of time.

❯ Provide concrete representations, such as books, artwork, and music, to make children aware of the distant past and far future. Invite families to share artifacts (or photographs of artifacts) from their family or community history along with the stories behind the artifacts as a way for children to discover what life was like in the past and to value the power of their families and communities (Kye 2024; Wise et al. 2024). Media images might similarly encourage them to think about futuristic settings where people have superpowers, travel in unusual vehicles, and use fantastic equipment to accomplish their goals. Young children may assume these already exist, but older preschoolers are beginning to understand that people have yet to invent them.

❯ Provide technologies from the past, such as telephones, kitchen utensils, or toys, and compare them to contemporary ones. (For technologies such as transportation, show the children photographs from various times in the past and from the present.) Invite children to talk about how these technologies have changed over time, and why they think these changes have occurred.

ADULT-GUIDED experiences are especially important for social concepts learnings such as:

Social Concepts 〉 **Understanding geography**

Geography is commonly associated with maps and mapmaking; however, it encompasses the richness of the world through both physical geography and human geography (Brillante & Mankiw 2015). Physical geography consists of the study of the natural environment, whereas human geography explores the interactions between humans and the environment. Understanding human geography requires a sense of place, which comes from feeling a sense of belonging (Brillante & Mankiw 2015). In the early childhood years, exploring the geography of immediate surroundings and local environments is beneficial for children to develop a sense of place (Fertig & Silverman 2007). Research shows that young children can engage with three areas of geography: reading simple maps (Giancola et al. 2023), identifying familiar locations and landmarks (Casey 2021), and recognizing prominent features in the landscape (Lowrie et al. 2022).

To make decisions about the most meaningful and relevant starting place for exploring geography learning, educators must understand the communities in which children live. Children who live in a rural area experience much different surroundings than do those living in an urban area. Some children live in neighborhoods where they do not have access to outdoor spaces or nature, either at home or in their early learning programs. Some children's homes are in areas where exploring the outdoor environments might be difficult or dangerous. Some children's families do not have homes; asking these children to share about their neighborhood environment can be problematic and harmful. Consider children's personal experiences when facilitating discussions about place.

Teaching strategies. Help preschoolers engage with geography by beginning with their daily experiences—where they go, what they do there—and then branching out to a wider range of places and features. The following strategies will make learning about geography interesting and appropriate for young children:

> Talk with children about the places in the community that are familiar to them and their families. These include their homes, the homes of friends and family members, schools, parks, libraries, stores, places of public transportation, office buildings, restaurants, and movie theaters. Take walks around the school building to find locations that are important and meaningful to the children, such as the front door, office, other children's classrooms, and the kitchen.

> Involve children in rearranging the location of centers and materials in the classroom to reinforce their sense of belonging. Include signs, prepared by children, that show the location of materials and how to use them. Ask families to share some family pictures to be used and displayed in the classroom (Brillante & Mankiw 2015).

> Draw simple maps or diagrams of the classroom, school, and neighborhood. Include obvious features such as doors and windows, the playground and parking lot, benches, bus stops, and stores. Talk about the maps with the children, emphasizing how the various places are related (for example, the direction and distance one must travel when getting from one place to another).

> Provide flags, stickers, or other symbols for children to use to mark places on the map. Older preschoolers may begin to draw their own simple maps (for example, a diagram of the classroom showing the different interest areas and some of the materials located in each of them).

> Display a map of the neighborhood near the block area and encourage children to use it to work together to re-create the neighborhood using blocks and other props such as cars, people, animals, and signs (Colker 2013).

> Use concrete representations, such as books, photos, artwork, songs, and puzzles, to connect children to places beyond their own experience. They are interested in learning about the food, clothing, houses, toys, and animals in locations other than where they themselves live. Preschoolers also enjoy looking at road and contour maps, globes, aerial photographs, and compasses if these are connected to their personal experiences. Discuss familiar landscapes (the hill behind the school, the river that winds through town) as you look at photos of other locations with similar features.

Social Concepts > **Appreciating ecology**

Children are immersed in their environment and have a relationship with it. Learning about human-environment interaction involves understanding one's role as caretaker of the planet. For young children, this begins with regular and enjoyable encounters with the natural world. As stated by the World Forum Nature Action Collaborative for Children in its Universal Principles for Connecting Children with Nature (NACC 2021):

We believe that regular connections with the natural world encourage children to develop

> Respect for local cultures and climates and for themselves as part of nature

> Feelings of unity, peace, and well-being as global citizens

Children's emotions, attitudes, and values about nature are formed early in life (Chawla 2021). They must develop a love for nature before they can think about the environment abstractly and become its guardians (Honig 2015; Sobel 2008). Therefore, to support young children's bonds with nature, provide opportunities to play in nature, take care of plants, and cultivate relationships with animals. Spending time in nature and having role models who care for nature are the biggest contributing factors to children becoming environmental stewards in adulthood (Giusti et al. 2018).

Teaching strategies. Try the following strategies to inspire young children to care about the environment and to make ecology a meaningful subject for them:

> Help children become aware of and appreciate nature. Except during days of extreme weather conditions, include time in your daily routine to go outside each day. Call attention to the feel of the sun and wind on children's faces and examine the plants and animals native to your area. Involve the children in projects such as planting a garden or making and hanging a simple bird feeder.

> Encourage children to take care of the indoor classroom and outdoor learning environment. For example, they can learn how to use materials in ways that avoid damage; help with simple repairs (like taping the torn corner of the snack chart or a book cover); strategize ways to reuse or repurpose materials; and plant, label, water, and weed the program's garden.

> Talk with families about the importance of children having outdoor time when possible. Although not all families are equally concerned about the environment, they can appreciate nature's benefits to their children's physical and mental health. If safety is an issue in the neighborhood, help parents form an advocacy group to encourage civic leaders to establish safe play zones or to network with one another to construct play yards on nonschool grounds.

● ● ●

When it comes to content areas in the early childhood curriculum, social studies is more recent and perhaps often overlooked, yet it is also the oldest area of study in general. The preschool classroom is a microcosm of the larger society. As concerns mount about the unraveling of civil behavior in the fabric of our social world, early childhood educators, in partnership with families, can help to lay the foundation for a future that guarantees that everyone has an opportunity to fulfill their human potential while working to improve the human condition of all people and respecting the rights of others and the sustainability of the planet.

For Further Consideration

1. What role can early childhood programs play in fostering children's appreciation and respect for diversity (race, ethnicity, religion, social class, and other social and cultural identities)?

2. As the US population becomes more culturally and linguistically diverse, the potential grows for differing social values and beliefs between home and school. How can early childhood professionals view families' cultures from an assets-based perspective and use their funds of knowledge in the program?

3. What rationales should be used for preschool classroom rules? How can adults respond when children suggest a rule that could endanger their health or safety or that of others or would be unjust for some members of the classroom?

4. Because of heavy advertising in the media and other influences, preschool children may become aware of economic disparities between their families. How can teachers handle comments (positive or negative) the children might make about differences in how families choose to spend their resources?

5. How might approaches to democracy differ for children depending on their personal, cultural, and community contexts?

6. Human-environment interaction is an important topic in geography and features prominently in the news at the time of this writing. How can early childhood educators make concerns about nature and the environment pertinent to young children?

CHAPTER 10

Creative Arts

Julia Luckenbill and Keely Benson

Four-year-old Celia maneuvers her wheelchair behind the puppet stage, adapted to accommodate her wheelchair. She puts the goat puppet on her right hand and the troll puppet on her left hand. Then she places the goat puppet hand on the edge of the stage. She tells the following story to her teacher, Mr. Ryan, and two other children, Lance and Valentina, sitting out front: "The biggest Billy Goat Gruff went trip, trip over the bridge. But then the troll jumped up again!" Celia makes the troll puppet lift until it is on the edge of the stage with the goat puppet.

"You have to say, 'Heh, heh, heh,'" says 5-year-old Lance. "That's how you know the troll is mean."

When Celia says, "Heh, heh, heh," Mr. Ryan imitates her and encourages the other children to do the same. Lance talks in his deepest "really mean troll" voice, while 3-year-old Valentina, whose English-language skills are just emerging, watches and listens at first. On the third repeat, however, she joins in, saying "heh" with a grin.

"I wonder how else you know it's a mean troll?" muses Mr. Ryan.

"He has a frowny face!" says Lance. "See!"

Celia looks at the frowning puppet, then thrusts it forward for everyone to see. Then she continues with her story. "The troll said, 'Who is going over my bridge?' 'It is I, the Biggest Billy Goat Gruff!' 'I'm going to eat you up!' 'No,

Learning Objectives

1. To examine concrete examples of effective teaching practices in visual arts, music, movement and dance, drama, and art appreciation with young children

2. To describe differences between adult-guided and child-guided arts exploration and distinguish appropriate situations for each

3. To identify ways to create an engaging environment and curriculum that support children's development in the creative arts

you aren't!" Celia pushes the two puppets together and then ducks the troll puppet under the stage, hiding him in her lap. "Then all the other goats came out and crossed the bridge to eat grass." Celia shakes the troll puppet off her hand and throws it backward over her head. Then she brings the goat puppet back up and bends her hand to make it bow. As she wheels herself back out front, Mr. Ryan leads the group in clapping.

"My turn," says Lance. He chooses the bear and a tan-colored felt person puppet. "There was a bear in a cage at the circus," his story starts as he lifts the bear puppet, "and the boy freed him and then the bear went 'grrr!' and it chased the boy"—Lance lifts the person puppet—"and he was scared, but then they were friends and went to McDonald's until the boy's daddy called him home to bed." When he finishes, Lance lays the puppets on the stage, gets a blanket from the nearby doll carriage, and covers them up.

"The daddy let the bear inside to sleep with the boy?" asks Mr. Ryan.

"Um, yeah," answers Lance. "The boy made the bear invisible so his daddy couldn't see it."

This time, Valentina is the first to clap. Mr. Ryan gestures toward the stage and asks if she would like a turn with the puppets. Valentina shakes her head, but she reaches out and picks up the bear puppet. Celia wheels back behind the stage and brings out the troll puppet, which she hands to Valentina. Sitting with the group rather than behind the stage, Valentina puts a puppet on each hand and tentatively waves them around.

"El gnomo, troll," Mr. Ryan says as he points to one, and "Oso, bear," he says as he points to the other.

Valentina says, "El gnomo, heh, heh," then tries the word *bear* in English.

"Grrr!" says Lance.

"Grrr!" say Celia and Mr. Ryan.

Valentina laughs. "Grrr!" she says quietly, then louder. "Bear, grrr!"

The story themes and interactions in this vignette illustrate the value of artistic learning for children's social, emotional, and intellectual development. Engaging in the arts does the following for young children:

> Opens up new avenues for them to express themselves and communicate with others

> Lets them share who they are and what they are thinking

> Supports them in building social interactions (Bernier et al. 2022)

> Builds connections between their inner and outer lives by linking family and community cultures with the school (Chappell & Cahnmann-Taylor 2013)

The arts are also valuable in promoting development in fine motor, language, critical thinking, creativity, and early math skills (Jantz 2022). For example, the work of Eisner (2004) applies critical thinking in the arts to educational practices across many disciplines. Müller and colleagues (2018) summarize research showing that arts teaching and learning can improve children's social and emotional skills. They conclude that the arts can be a critical link for children in developing the crucial thinking skills and motivation they need to be more successful in self-management and decision making and in social interactions. Access to a music curriculum in preschool has been shown to support children's growth in language and literacy, prosocial behavior, and large motor development (Barrett 2022). Improvisational games can strengthen social problem solving (O'Neill 2014). Consider the vignette with Mr. Ryan at the opening of this chapter: As the children acted out the story and explored dramatic elements, they developed language and social skills by respectfully taking turns as performers and audience.

Importantly, the creative arts—visual art, music, movement and dance, and drama, as well as appreciation of these art forms—are also intrinsically rewarding. That is, engaging with art is important for its own sake. The arts can be joyful and empowering for all children, providing a sense of wonder, competence, and agency when experienced in a judgment-free setting. Child-guided and adult-guided experiences in the arts can complement each other to create a nurturing, stimulating environment where children feel empowered and inspired.

Both self-expression and intellectual components in an arts curriculum for children are reflected in the Common Core State Standards for elementary-age children (NGA Center & CCSSO 2010) and National Core Arts Standards for pre-K–12 (National Coalition for Core Arts Standards 2014). These components are also reflected in guidance for recommended practices in preschool, such as those included in NAEYC's "Early Learning Program Accreditation Standards and Assessment Items" (2022b). You can learn more about current National Core Arts Standards for pre-K through 12th-grade classrooms at www.nationalartsstandards.org.

A quality approach to the creative arts in early childhood programs encompasses a range of activities that foster expression, exploration, and appreciation of various art forms. These can be organized into the following categories:

> **Visual art:** Visual art includes activities such as drawing, painting, sculpting, and collage making. Using a variety of materials such as crayons, markers, paints, clay, and found objects, children explore color, shape, texture, and form.

> **Music:** Music activities involve singing, listening, playing instruments, and moving to music. Children learn simple songs, rhymes, and chants, and they use age-appropriate musical instruments such as drums, xylophones, shakers, maracas, rain sticks, and steel drums to explore rhythm and melody.

> **Movement and dance:** Movement and dance activities involve exploring various movements, rhythms, and expressions through creative movement. Children engage in activities such as stretching, bending, jumping, and dancing to music, either individually or in groups.

> **Drama:** Drama as discussed in this chapter includes dramatic play, theater, storytelling, puppetry, and improvisation games. Many drama activities involve play scenarios in which children create and share characters, stories, and settings using props, costumes, and their own imagination.

> **Art appreciation:** Art appreciation involves introducing children to various forms of art and helping them develop an understanding and appreciation of a range of artistic expression across different art styles, techniques, and cultural traditions.

Intentional teachers play a crucial role in fostering children's creativity and artistic development through the incorporation of the creative arts into their curriculum. Early art education has long been overshadowed by a heavier emphasis on early math and literacy learning (Haslip & Gullo 2018; Sabol 2010). This emphasis limits children's development of key skills such as creativity, self-expression, and executive functioning. Limiting exploration of the creative arts is particularly inequitable for children in communities that lack resources and opportunities for art education outside the school day (Haslip et al. 2017). John Dewey (1934) believed that art experiences should be available not just to the talented few but to all children from an early age. He saw the arts as a great economic and social equalizer. This chapter is designed to help educators make this concept a possibility in today's early learning programs (Goldblatt 2006).

Strategies for development in and appreciation of creative arts appear in "Fitting the Learning Experience to the Learning Objective" later in this chapter, where they are considered separately as child-guided and adult-guided experiences.

Young Children's Development in Creative Arts

Developmental changes during the preschool years enable children to benefit in many ways from art experiences (Jantz 2022; PBS Kids, n.d.). As children's language skills develop, access to the arts provides new avenues for expression and communication. The ability to form mental images allows preschoolers to represent their experiences in different media. They can paint a picture of their family (visual art), make up a song about a puppy (music), stomp like a monster (movement), or act out a favorite story (dramatic play).

Although children's artistic skills develop noticeably in the early years, their growth is not clearly marked by beginnings and endings. Rather, much as adult artists do when they work with a new medium, young children tend to move back and forth between making representations that are accidental and intentional, simple and elaborate, and random and deliberate. In addition, they move between using unrelated elements and noticing and depicting relationships (Epstein 2012). This development is influenced both by motor and cognitive changes, in addition to sociocultural contexts, including peer and teacher involvement (Vygotsky 1978). Art appreciation also waxes and wanes, depending on children's cognitive and social experiences. Despite these fluctuations, theory and research can identify general progressions in art making. These relate to children's growing abilities in language, representation, and abstraction (see "General Developmental Progression in Making Art" on page 266). By understanding the developmental progression of artistic skills and abilities, intentional teachers can scaffold children's learning experiences. They can provide appropriate challenges and opportunities for growth and support children in reaching their full creative potential. The scaffolding that a teacher or peer provides to children can elevate their art making (Longobardi, Quaglia, & Iotti 2015).

General Developmental Progression in Making Art

- From accidental to intentional representation. Younger children accidentally create a form or movement and then decide it represents something. For example, they might pat clay into a rectangle and call it a car, or roll it on the floor and say it is a ball. This order is later reversed; children start with specific characteristics in materials or perform an action to match their mental image.

- From simple to elaborate models. Initially children hold one or two characteristics in mind when they draw, sing, move, or pretend. Later their representations become more detailed. For example, a younger child might pretend to be a baby by saying "waah! waah!" An older child might wriggle and make faces, crawl, suck on a bottle, or reach out to be picked up.

- From randomness to deliberation. When children are introduced to an artistic medium, they explore its possibilities without regard to the effects they create. As they gain more control over materials, tools, and fine motor skills, their actions become more deliberate. For example, after ranging all over the scale with their voices, children will later try to reproduce a specific pitch (note).

- From unrelated elements to relationships. Children become more aware of how marks, sounds, movements, and play themes relate to one another. For example, they make marks wherever their hand lands but later consider how marks or colors look next to one another. They combine movements into a sequence, or they let one play scenario lead logically to the next one.

Four general principles characterize the development of the creative arts in the early years:

> Representation emerges from young children's experiences. To form mental images and represent them using the arts, young children first need real, hands-on experiences with objects, people, and events. They then portray these concrete experiences by making drawings and models, copying and creating songs and movements, and inventing stories and pretend-play scenarios.

> Children's artistic representations develop together with their perceptual, cognitive, and social and emotional abilities. Representations begin simply and become more complex over time and with practice. Children gradually observe and portray more detail (perception), sequence and connect artistic elements (cognition), use art to express feelings and ideas (emotional growth), and involve others in their artistic endeavors (social development).

> Each child's representations are unique. Children use the arts to express themselves in ways that make sense to them. Their artistic creations and reactions reflect their individual interests, experiences, and personalities, as well as their home languages and cultures.

> Young children are capable of appreciating as well as making art. Young children's powers of observation and their finely tuned senses make them capable of appreciating and sharing ideas about the arts. Teachers can support these abilities by talking about those aspects of art

that interest the children, asking open-ended questions, introducing new vocabulary words, and talking about the process of creating—of experimenting without fear of failure (Wang, Benson, & Eggleston 2019).

Fostering Children's Artistic Identity

Children benefit from seeing themselves as artists and seeing people who look like them as artists. This representation helps build and celebrate each child's unique artistic voice, instilling a strong sense of joy, identity, and self-worth. When children see individuals who share their cultural background, ethnicity, or physical characteristics creating art, they are more likely to feel a sense of belonging and pride in their own creative abilities.

Seeing diverse artists and artwork broadens children's perspectives and helps inspire them to explore different artistic styles and techniques. As they understand and experience many ways to create and interpret art, they come to embrace their own unique artistic voice. This exposure can also help challenge stereotypes and promote inclusivity, fostering a more diverse and inclusive creative community.

Teaching and Learning in the Creative Arts

Although art educators agree that teaching and respecting art is vital to create a climate in which art learning can thrive, they differ on how to establish an artistic foundation in young children. Some believe that children's everyday lives provide them with inspiration and space to explore and create (Wang, Benson, & Eggleston 2019). Therefore, they support child-guided teaching strategies (Bresler 1993), which help children explore everyday experiences in depth—through discussion, small group activities, and field trips—because those experiences lead to elaborate creative arts expression.

Other theorists and practitioners advocate for direct, adult-guided teaching strategies that focus on specific attributes of things in the environment and the elements of art to improve visual and auditory discrimination. Highly directive approaches, however, such as teaching drawing by copying, are not effective with young children. Adult-guided art experiences do have value in how the adult stages the classroom environment for children's exploration and supports the development of both skills and concepts.

Art education, then, is best seen as both child guided and adult guided—a guided exploration approach (Bresler 1993; Wang, Benson, & Eggleston 2019). This approach involves teachers responding intentionally to children's skills, interests, and needs while balancing child choice and adult guidance (NAEYC 2020). The chapter discusses strategies for both types of experiences, valuing both children's and teachers' knowledge, experience, and sociocultural contexts.

Art or Craft?

It is important to note that developmentally appropriate adult-guided art activities are different from crafts. Usually an adult-led craft involves children following a series of directions to make an item or drawing that the adult has previsioned, such as a paper plate turkey at Thanksgiving. (For more examples, see "Process Versus Product Art" on page 270.)

An adult-guided project that is not a craft might include inviting all the children to try shading dark, light, and cross lines to learn the technique of coloring in a self-portrait. Or it might be guiding children at small group time to apply something to their own original work that they observed when studying a famous artist's image—for example, making a self-portrait of colorful lines similar to the style of Sandra Silberzweig. Here is another example:

> Mr. Wes offers a small group of children cookie cutters, clay tools, and a slab of clay. "Do you remember how we visited the bench at the food co-op and saw how clay artworks make up the design on the bench?" he asks. "I thought it might be interesting to make our own designs in clay. We will cut out the shapes of insects from the slab of clay. You can press any of the tools into your insect to make patterns and marks. See how the shell makes this kind of mark, but the stamp makes circles? You can decide what patterns your insect will have. When you are done, I will fire the clay, which means cooking it at an elevated temperature until it is hard like the clay on the bench."

General teaching strategies that acknowledge a blend of both approaches include the following:

> Provide open-ended art materials and tools. Include materials throughout the classroom to support art making, such as paints, crayons, canvas, clay, beeswax, blocks, natural materials, recycled paper and plastics, and tablet drawing programs (visual art); simple percussion instruments and other sound makers (music); scarves and streamers (movement); and dress-up clothes, props, and puppets (dramatic play).

> Establish a climate that supports creative risk taking. Creativity thrives when children know that expression is judgement free. If children feel that the teacher trusts and supports them, they explore beyond teacher-approved ways and are more willing to try new materials and forms of expression. They are also more apt to offer their opinion on what others create (art appreciation).

> Foster authenticity with children with disabilities. Ensure that art experiences are centered around the individual child—their strengths, abilities, and interests—which allows them to lead and express themselves fully. This approach is particularly important for children with disabilities, who may need more adult support and responsiveness to engage in a way that truly reflects their own perspectives and abilities. Letting children explore and experiment with little adult guidance is just as important for children with disabilities as for their peers, perhaps more.

> Create alongside children. On their own, children may use art materials in repetitive or stereotypical ways. However, adults can work and create alongside them, without being directive or creating artworks far beyond the skill level of the children. When this happens, children engage with the arts longer and are more likely to experiment with materials, tools, and ideas (Wang, Benson, & Eggleston 2019).

> Emphasize process over product. Allow time for experimentation, repetition, and reflection so that children can discover the properties of materials and practice using them. Cutting this process short or introducing too many materials at once may stunt their creativity (Wang, Benson, & Eggleston 2019). Resist pressure to highlight "polished" work and be ready to explain to families and school administrators why pressuring children to make a certain product a certain way is counterproductive to artistic development. (See "Process Versus Product Art" on page 270.)

> Encourage artistic collaboration. Creativity is often social. When children work together, their art increases in originality because they share and build on one another's ideas (Menzer 2015).

> Talk with children about the arts. Encourage children to describe and discuss the visual art, music, movement, or drama scenarios they invent. Use these conversations to increase their arts vocabulary. Ask them about their creations, and show genuine interest in their answers to your questions. Your words can invite deeper thinking.

> Incorporate art from the culture of children's families and communities and beyond. Intentionally include representative art from every medium in the everyday furnishings, materials, and activities in the classroom. Invite artists (including family members) to the program to share their work. If budget permits, take field trips where children can observe and experience art forms and content from many cultures. Explore art in books. Consider sharing links to short video clips and virtual field trips with the children's families for them to explore and discuss if they wish.

Process Versus Product Art

There is often confusion among teachers about what art really is. It is important to acknowledge the distinction between process-focused and product art, as the learning goals are drastically different.

Process-focused art emphasizes the creative journey rather than the end result. As children explore and experiment, working with materials over and over again, they learn about the properties of the materials and ways they can or cannot manipulate them. They gain mastery over their use. Freely exploring materials, tools, and approaches allows for individuality, creativity, imagination, personal expression, problem solving, and discovery. For example, during a process-oriented visual art experience, children might choose from a variety of natural materials like leaves or rocks to create a nonpermanent collection or display, arranging them and rearranging them several times. During a music and movement jam, children might move freely to diverse types of music, dancing or swaying, inspired by the music to move slow, fast, and so on, enjoying and expressing themselves through movement.

In contrast, product-focused art prioritizes the final product over the creative process. Usually there is one right way to use the materials, with specified steps, and the goal is often to make the outcome look as close to a teacher-created model as possible. Although it can help develop skills like following instructions, attending to detail, and using fine motor skills, this kind of close-ended project limits creative freedom and can make children frustrated if they feel their product does not measure up to the teacher's model. They may feel negative judgments on their work and lose interest or motivation, or they may come to depend on adults to tell them how to make art in the future so that everyone's creation is alike.

Product-oriented activities result in just that. A themed craft project might include affixing circle stickers to precut fish shapes and adding a googly eye at the head. A music and movement experience focused on a particular outcome may involve children learning and rehearsing a song for a musical performance, focusing on group collaboration for a cohesive and entertaining show.

Of course, open-ended art experiences, too, often result in a product, but each creation or artwork is different, reflecting that child's choices and imagination. Intentional teachers prioritize process art with preschoolers and use product-focused art experiences sparingly.

Both process-focused and product-focused art activities have their place in a preschool classroom and offer valuable learning experiences for young children. Be intentional about offering one type or the other by reflecting on what you want children to gain from the experience and providing opportunities that meet your objectives while still prioritizing exploration and child choice.

Connecting Teaching to Children's Lives

By Melany Spiehs

Mr. Oscar has been hearing children make negative comments about darker shades of skin in the dramatic play center with dolls, in the library center with books, and with each other throughout the day. To address this, he decides to explore the children's thoughts and misconceptions about skin color. He plans a large group science activity and introduces the word *melanin*, explaining that melanin protects skin from the sun, that some people have more melanin than others, and that because of this, they have darker skin.

Mr. Oscar invites the children to paint their self-portraits. The children excitedly look through the bottles of skin-colored paints. Some choose to mix one or more of the colors until they are satisfied that the color matches their skin.

Juana: Look at my melanin.

Maribel: See my melanin. I brown...like my dad.

Juana: My dad is brown, too. And my mom and my sister.

Maribel: My sister is brown like me. Her have melanin.

This vignette demonstrates the biases that young children may hold and one way that early childhood educators can respond after observing these biases. Teachers may respond in the moment by asking the child open-ended questions like "What did you mean by that?" or "Can you tell me more about that?" Teachers can then circle back to the issue later and fill in knowledge gaps or challenge biases with alternative narratives and experiences, like the one here, that will help children gain a different perspective.

Fitting the Learning Experience to the Learning Objective

Across the areas of the creative arts, children are most likely to explore materials, tools, and forms of expression on their own. They do not need prodding to squeeze clay, bang on a drum, bounce to music, pretend to be a character in a favorite book, or say whether they like a picture or song. However, children depend on adult guidance to advance their artistic development, including understanding the multiple possibilities of each artistic medium and moving into more complex forms of representation.

Visual Art

Visual art experiences provide opportunities for young children to express themselves by exploring colors, shapes, and textures through drawing, painting, and creating with varied materials, letting them bring their ideas to life with both freedom and a little guidance. Of the key knowledge and skills in visual art, child-guided experiences seem particularly important for the following:

> Exploring two- and three-dimensional art materials and tools

> Making simple representations from experience

Adult-guided experiences are especially significant for the following:

> Naming and becoming adept at using art materials, tools, vocabulary, and actions

> Making complex representations using imagination

CHILD-GUIDED experiences are especially important for learnings such as:

Visual Art ❯ **Exploring two- and three-dimensional art materials and tools**

Handling two-dimensional media requires having the manual dexterity to draw, paint, weave, and print with appropriate materials and tools. Manipulating three-dimensional media requires the manual dexterity and strength to mold, sculpt, or build with materials using one's hands or tools.

Teaching strategies. The primary role of teachers in encouraging young children to make visual art is to provide abundant and diverse materials, along with the time and space to explore them. Here are some suggestions:

> Set up a spacious, attractive, and permanent art area, which communicates to children that what happens there is important. Make sure there is ample room to work individually and collaboratively and to store easily accessible materials. Locate the art area near water, and have cleanup materials nearby. Try using vertical and horizontal workspaces (easels, walls, tables, pavement). There should be drying areas for finished work (clotheslines, flat surfaces, cubbies) and safe areas to protect unfinished work (including work-in-progress signs). Finally, look for display space at children's eye level.

> Provide a wide variety of tools and materials. Children need more than just the crayons, paints, playdough, and modeling clay typically provided in early childhood settings. Many inexpensive materials—recycled items, raw wool, carpet scraps, items gathered from nature—offer opportunities to create. Look for creative reusable resource centers or scrap stores in your local area or online, and ask families for specific items they may be able to contribute. For children with perceptual or physical disabilities, provide aids such as adaptive scissors, large paintbrushes and handgrips, and magnifying lenses. Providing hand-over-hand assistance is beneficial for some children. (For more information on adaptations for children with disabilities, see Extension Alliance for Better Child Care 2019.) Be careful not to overwhelm children with too many materials at once; rotate new materials into the art center gradually.

> Add sentence strips to your art center so you can write a title and the child's name as the artist.

> Provide easy access to materials so children can retrieve and use them independently and return unused supplies where they belong. If children are new to this independence, provide instructions and be patient as they learn to access materials, clean up, and put things away.

> Encourage in-depth exploration. Make comments and observations about what children are doing to foster their interest. Manipulate the art materials yourself, but do not make a model for them to copy. Let children work with their hands before introducing tools so they get a feel for each type of medium, its properties, and how their actions transform it.

Visual Art | **Making simple representations from experience**

This area of learning refers to young children representing familiar objects, people, places, and events through all forms of visual media. To do this, accept and take an interest in the child's initiatives. With appropriate support, children will gradually

Using Specific Feedback Versus Praise or Compliments

As Ms. Yeager approaches Mack painting at the easel, she is unsure of what to do or say about his painting, which contains a variety of colors and forms Ms. Yeager does not recognize. She usually tries to avoid praising children's efforts by saying vague things like "Your painting is beautiful. So colorful!" She could ask Mack questions about the colors and shapes she sees. Perhaps she should just ask if Mack wants to talk about it—or would it be better to wait for Mack to initiate a discussion?

Like Ms. Yeager, many teachers wonder how best to respond to children's art making. Although it is tempting to communicate interest in a child's art with phrases such as "Good job!" or "I like your pretty painting," such well-meaning compliments or statements of praise can discourage the child artist. They also contribute to children's reliance on adults' opinion or judgment of their efforts.

In contrast, offering specific comments and encouragement is an effective way to communicate positive feedback to young artists. For example, saying to a child "You used a new color of blue when you created the sky there. It looks like you mixed the blue and white very carefully" shows awareness of the process and lets the child judge the merit of their creation themselves. The teacher's encouragement and tone of voice communicate interest. Take time to slow down and observe, then comment thoughtfully on what the artist is doing while avoiding interrupting their process, and consider joining in the experience by imitating the artist and their method. The likely reward of encouragement is an authentic conversation about art and process.

elaborate on their art ideas. Remember that art can be a wonderful means of self-expression, which is especially helpful for multilingual learners, who face many obstacles to communication all day long.

Teaching strategies. Just being aware of children's experiences and interests will suggest numerous possibilities for the things they can represent in their visual art. You can build on and expand these possibilities using the following ideas:

> When children's experiences arise naturally in conversation, say, "I wonder if we could draw (or paint or construct) that at small group time?" Ask the children to suggest materials for representing the object or idea.

> Draw on imagery and experiences as subjects for visual representations. For example, take graphs of the objects that children play with and construct. Post them in the art area to inspire children to represent them in their artwork.

> Accept what children say when they announce they made something. If commenting, just mention the observable details. Be careful not to presume to know what is represented. Instead, listen closely and encourage them to describe the attributes they see in their creation, and be open to whatever they say they represented, if anything.

> Scaffold conversations by using open-ended sentence starters such as "Tell me more about . . ." or "I see you chose to use the color brown here." This language promotes discussion of their intentions, not your own.

> Keep a recording device handy to record what children say about their art; when a multilingual learner talks about their creation, use the recording later to ask a colleague, parent, or other person who speaks the child's language to translate what they said. Be sure to use those words in the home language if writing documentation for the piece.

ADULT-GUIDED experiences are especially important for learnings such as:

Visual Art	Naming and becoming adept at using visual art materials, tools, vocabulary, and actions

With teacher input, children develop the ability to differentiate and identify names and attributes of various materials, tools, and creative actions.

Teaching strategies. Supplying relevant terms while children are actively engaged in creating visual art makes the terms more meaningful. As children practice using materials and tools, they can control them better. Sometimes a child needs just a hint to get over a hurdle; other times they might need more instruction. Here are some suggestions:

> Provide the names of visual art materials, tools, vocabulary, and actions in context and when they are introduced to children (in English and in children's home languages when possible). Tie the names to concrete objects and actions as children experience them; for example, use the word *tint* to describe the result of a child mixing white paint with another color. Keep the statements simple and factual.

> Accept the language children use to describe tools, materials, and actions. Then add words to expand their vocabulary. For example, when a child says, "I mixed red and white," respond with, "Yes, I see you mixed red and white to create a tint."

> Ask children open-ended questions about materials, actions, and effects to encourage their use of visual art language. For example, ask, "What happened when you added a big squirt of red paint to your cup?" Or, if a child is comparing dry and wet balls of clay, wonder, "How do they feel? What happens when you try to roll them flat?" For children with emerging language or English skills, simply sitting beside them with a look of interest may encourage them to describe, with the words available to them, their artwork and how they created it.

> Make increasingly complex visual art materials, tools, and techniques available throughout the school year so that children have many opportunities to practice and refine their skills. For example, at the start of the year you might simply explore playdough with rollers and cookie cutters. Then throughout the year, introduce pizza cutters, knives, and scissors for the playdough.

> Provide guidance when you introduce children to more sophisticated art materials. Real watercolor paint sets provide more saturation. Narrow paintbrushes enable children to incorporate significantly more detail in their paintings.

> Do not change tools every day or two for the sake of novelty or variety. Leave artistic media out for a long time so children can experiment and become adept with them.

> Circle back to visual art materials that children used earlier in the year. Encourage them to apply new techniques to old, familiar materials, as in the following example:

The children in Ms. Grace's preschool class begin the year experimenting with paper with only their hands. They try tearing, twisting, crumbling, and rolling it. Next they use tools—scissors and hole punches. Finally they try glue and paint. Later in the year during small group time, Ms. Grace introduces the class to yarn and fabric. Again, the children work with their hands and then use tools such as scissors, crimpers, and large tapestry needles. Finally, they experiment with dyeing. Ms. Grace expands the learning, providing books with visual images of quilting and other fabric arts. After a few weeks, Ms. Grace brings out the paper again. Children are excited to see an "old friend," but now they apply the stitching and dyeing techniques they have used with fiber to paper. Some tear or cut strips and weave "paper tapestries." Others paint squares of paper and arrange them in "paper quilts."

Visual Art ❯ **Making complex representations using imagination**

When children make art, they often portray things that are not present or they have never experienced, including make-believe objects, people, and events. They also represent real things in fanciful ways. To inspire complex representations of children's perceptions across disciplines, teachers can incorporate materials and activities from domains such as literacy, mathematics, and science in the art center. As children grow, their visual art includes more details, such as facial features, architectural components, and natural elements. They strive for factual accuracy in size, spatial relations, and emotions.

Teaching strategies. Teachers can support this development by encouraging observant behavior and providing time and space for children to elaborate on their artwork without feeling rushed or confined. Try the following strategies:

> Read books, make up stories, and engage in other activities that inspire children to use their imaginations and represent their fantasies. Drama often involves the creation of artwork (props and scenery) to further children's role playing.

> Bring in reproductions of nonrepresentational or abstract artwork (for example, Jackson Pollock drip paintings, Joan Miró mobiles, Middle Eastern geometric patterns, Appalachian quilts, and Japanese ikat cloth). Encourage children to talk about what they see or feel in the imagery. Provide comparable materials and tools for them to create artwork of unreal or imaginary ideas, images, and events.

> Encourage the deliberate use of inspiration from other sources, including nature and artwork from children's home cultures. Provide materials and examples of artwork for children to observe and incorporate elements or techniques in their own work (similar to how adult visual artists use models for inspiration). The emphasis should not be on duplication of the model. Instead invite children to observe the attributes of the model and then respond to it in their own way. This technique can provide a helpful starting point, especially for some children with disabilities such as autism spectrum disorder. Even if they choose to replicate the art, the activity allows them to explore how art tools work, which can evolve into other representations later on.

> Encourage children to observe and describe things in detail and from multiple perspectives, even when they are not making visual art. Children's attention to such details may be reflected not only in their artwork but also in other content areas, such as when they analyze a problem with complex data from various viewpoints.

> Encourage children to share observations with one another as they make representations and to collaborate on visual art projects. Pair emerging English learners with children more fluent in English to provide the opportunity for them to find ways to communicate with each other.

Music

Music experiences provide opportunities for children to express themselves by exploring sounds, singing, and playing instruments. Children discover rhythm and melody through both playful exploration and gentle guidance. Of the key knowledge and skills in music, child-guided experiences seem particularly important for the following:

> Exploring sounds and the voice

> Playing simple musical instruments

Adult-guided experiences are especially significant for the following:

> Singing

> Understanding rhythmic and tonal qualities

CHILD-GUIDED experiences are especially important for learnings such as:

| Music | Exploring sounds and the voice |

Preschoolers connect sounds to their sources and begin to use sound as the basis for classification (such as loud and soft, fast and slow, thumping and tinkling). Young children also explore different qualities in their voices, including pitch, volume, and emotion.

Teaching strategies. Guide young children to become more aware of sounds in the environment, and encourage them to experiment with using their voice to create their own sounds. Some children may become overstimulated by sounds, so introduce sounds slowly and patiently based on children's auditory sensory needs. Try these strategies:

> Provide a variety of sound-making materials for children to explore, such as music players, timers, wind-up clocks, and gourds with dried seeds. Name and describe the sounds children hear with these materials, and encourage them to do the same.

> Imitate child-initiated sounds, and use your own voice in different ways, too. Experiment with your voice as you interact with children during play, transitions, and conversations.

> Read stories that provide opportunities for children to add sound effects and vocalizations, such as Mo Willems's *Don't Let the Pigeon Drive the Bus,* where the children can yell nooo! and imitate whispering, pleading, bus noises, and more.

| Music | Playing simple musical instruments |

Children enjoy playing instruments individually, in groups, and to accompany music. They focus more on the joy of creating musical sounds than on pitch or rhythm; teachers should follow that lead. Introduce simple instruments gradually to accommodate young children's manual dexterity and breath control, and model simple ways to use them.

Teaching strategies. Encourage young children to explore simple musical instruments and enjoy the sounds they produce with these suggestions:

> Fill containers (made of metal, wood, cardboard, or cloth) with beads, pebbles, sand, metal washers, or wood chips to make noisemakers. Be sure the lids are securely closed. Use these instruments at choice time, to signal transitions, and to play stop-and-start games at group time.

> Offer recordings of different musical instruments. Play selections that feature one instrument at a time so children can focus on the sound that each one makes. Provide pictures to accompany the recordings so children can see what the instruments look like.

> Use the sounds of instruments at transition times or give children choices about which instrument(s) to play. For example, say, "When you hear the drum, it's time to move to the rug for large group time," and then play two or three other instruments before playing the drum.

> When guiding children who are deaf or children with hearing impairments to engage with musical instruments, note that they will respond to music differently. Find ways to support these children; for example, place their hand on the guitar to feel the vibrations or have them take off their shoes to feel the vibrations of dancing music.

ADULT-GUIDED experiences are especially important for learnings such as:

Music › Singing

Singing abilities develop gradually. By age 3, children sing with lyrical quality, capturing the essential melody and/or rhythm of a familiar song. The tonal and rhythmic qualities of singing are well established by kindergarten age. Often songs are pitched too low for young voices; children find it difficult to sing an octave above what they hear until the fourth grade (Campbell & Scott-Kassner 2014 in Barrett et al. 2022, 394). When asking children to sing along, provide songs in their vocal range.

Teaching strategies. Singing is a universal pleasure shared by children and adults alike. The following strategies can help children develop their singing abilities:

> Sing with children at various times of the day. Young children enjoy singing many types of music, including sing-song nursery rhymes ("Rain, Rain, Go Away") and songs for special occasions ("Feliz Cumpleaños"). Be sure to include songs that represent the children's cultures (for example, "Soualle") and that include words in their home languages.

> Use songs to heighten children's attention and guide transitions (for example, chant or sing "Children wearing blue, it's your turn to walk to the bathroom and wash your hands"). This is a wonderful way to bring music into routines and cue adults, too!

> Make a point to model making up songs during free play, and invite children to try it. When adults loosen up and playfully sing, children do, too.

Music › Understanding rhythmic and tonal qualities

Music consists of both rhythmic qualities, like beat, rhythm, and tempo, and tonal qualities, such as melody and harmony (Pino 2023). Children typically understand rhythmic qualities before tonal qualities. Providing simple melodies with a limited number and range of pitches can help them grasp these concepts.

Teaching strategies. Help children gradually improve their understanding of the properties of music with the following strategies:

> Play a range of diverse music, including folk music from around the world; classical, jazz, merengue, marches, and waltzes; music from different cultures and traditions (for example, Indian raga, mariachi, and gospel and spirituals); and music with different types of instrumentation (for example, Native American flute, West African kora [harp], Australian didgeridoo).

> When you are exploring the elements of music, choose instrumental music. Children's brains attend to language first, which can distract them from processing other aspects of the music, such as tempo or instrumentation.

> If you observe that background music is preventing children or teachers from completing tasks, limit the music to intentionally chosen times when children do not need to focus on conversation, or only play music in select locations.

> Sing and play live music in which the rhythmic and tonal qualities vary. When possible, seek opportunities to experience live music from a range of cultures, whether this might be families who play music, local musicians, or field trips to music venues.

> Scaffold rhythmic chants and sound patterns using a serve-and-return strategy, and consider chants without words. Chants provide a fun structure to explore patterns and rhythm—for example, "Oh, John the Rabbit (Yes, ma'am), Got a mighty habit (Yes, ma'am)" by Elizabeth Mitchell (2010).

Movement and Dance

Creative movement and dance provide opportunities for children to express themselves by moving their bodies in fun and creative ways, exploring different actions and copying simple movements. Of the key knowledge and skills in movement and dance, child-guided experiences seem particularly important for the following:

> Moving the body in different ways

> Imitating simple movements

Adult-guided experiences are especially significant for the following:

> Imitating complex movements

CHILD-GUIDED experiences are especially important for learnings such as:

| Movement and Dance | Moving the body in different ways |

As young children gain greater motor control, they use their bodies in ways that are not merely functional. For example, they like to investigate how they can move from one point to another (by crawling, slithering, rolling, walking backward, hopping, and so on). Children delight in spontaneously testing the boundaries of what their bodies can do, a pleasure that supportive adults can share in.

Teaching strategies. To reinforce the joy that young children experience in moving their bodies, try the following ideas:

> Provide time and a range of spaces for children to move their bodies, both indoors and outdoors, using both locomotor and nonlocomotor movements. Offer simple equipment (such as low beams, steps and ladders, inner tubes, and Hula-Hoops) and provide several types of materials (such as scarves, streamers, and rhythm sticks) to encourage children to vary their creative movements.

> Offer simple challenges that inspire children to experiment with movement. Focusing on movement alone (that is, without music), ask children questions such as "How can we move to our cubbies without our toes touching the floor?" Then try adding music in a range of styles (fast, slow, smooth, and staccato), including the rhythms and moods of music from a variety of cultures. As children adapt their movements to the music, comment on the ways they do so ("Leah is sliding her walker back and forth in time to the gentle waltz music").

| Movement and Dance | Imitating simple movements |

Young children frequently copy the simple movements of people, animals, or mechanical devices. They may do this as part of a dramatic play scenario, in response to music, or simply for its own sake. Typical examples in preschool include galloping like a horse, driving a car, or spraying a hose back and forth to put out a fire. Imitating the simple movements of others can also be a form of social participation. For example, when children copy the actions of an adult or peer at large group time, movement becomes a way of saying, "I am part of the classroom community."

Teaching strategies. Encourage children's spontaneous inclination to imitate many types of movement with these strategies:

> Use songs and chants that already include movements (such as "If You're Happy and You Know It"), or create simple movement sequences for a song. For example, take a song with two parts (such as "We Are the Dinosaurs") and ask children to suggest a different movement for each part (march to the verse and pretend to eat or sleep to the chorus).

> Introduce simple movements at transitions and when beginning new activities (for example, "We're gonna stomp, stomp, stomp, stomp the sand away and brush, brush, brush, brush the sand away, and walk inside to circle time").

> Describe, and encourage children to describe, their creative use of movement throughout the day. For example, as a child is playing, you might say, "You're stepping slowly so the scarf doesn't fall off your head." This also helps children become more conscious of what they are doing and lets them be more deliberate in their actions.

ADULT-GUIDED experiences are especially important for learnings such as:

Movement and Dance ⟩ **Imitating complex movements**

Although children move their bodies in varied ways, the range of their movements can be limited. For example, while listening to music, 3-year-olds are likely to move in place (bending their knees or waving their arms), whereas 4- and 5-year-olds repeat a limited number of movement patterns (going up and down, side to side, or in a circle). However, if adults intentionally introduce more complex ideas—such as different body postures, actions, and hand gestures—children will try a wider range of movements in response to music and as a general mode of creative expression (Papazachariou-Christoforou 2022).

Teaching strategies. Expand the range of creative movements that young children imitate and create with these suggestions:

> Introduce and label new postures, movements, and gestures gradually throughout the day. Include movements every child can do. Once children have mastered a basic movement, demonstrate variations for them to try on their own. For example, alternate big steps and small steps; move your arms, legs, and entire body from various positions (for example, lying on your side).

> Encourage body awareness as children move within space; invite them to consider their own body movements as well as movements in relation to other people. For example, encourage students to stand in a circle and pretend to paint with different body parts, identifying those body parts as they go (Papazachariou-Christoforou 2022).

> Provide opportunities for children to embody their experiences and imagination using movement, expressing emotions like sad, mad, frightened, brave, friendly, shy, and silly ("How do you move when you feel happy?" or "Let's move to the snack table as though we're tired and sleepy").

Drama

Drama provides young children with opportunities to explore roles, emotions, and stories through imitation and imagination. Whether acting alone, with a peer, or in a group, children use gestures, sounds, and simple props to bring their ideas to life. Adult guidance helps deepen these experiences, supporting children as they create characters, build narratives, and collaborate with others.

The Magic of Make-Believe: Key Elements of Drama in Early Childhood

Drama experiences offer children the chance to express themselves by exploring new roles, re-creating real or imagined experiences, and collaborating with others to tell stories. Engaging in drama is essential for young children, as it nurtures their social, emotional, and cognitive development. Activities such as dramatic play, storytelling, puppetry, and improvisational games enrich children's lives by providing them a space to explore different perspectives and enhance their expressive abilities.

Adults play a supportive role in drama by joining and facilitating children's creative efforts, modeling flexibility and openness in imaginative play. This approach helps children develop essential skills, such as understanding narrative structure, interpreting emotions, and practicing empathy.

Core elements of drama in early childhood include the following:

- **Imitation and imagination:** Children use gestures, expressions, and sounds to represent familiar objects, people, and experiences.

- **Role playing:** Children explore new personas, often inspired by stories, real-life figures, or their own imaginations.

- **Storytelling and narrative building:** Drama provides a framework for children to re-create, adapt, and invent stories, enhancing their language and cognitive skills.

- **Improvisation:** Through games and interactions, children practice a technique known as "yes, and" (accepting others' ideas and building on them), active listening, and spontaneous storytelling.

- **Props and puppetry:** Props, costumes, and puppets help children express their ideas and represent their imaginative worlds.

- **Social collaboration:** Drama activities often involve peers, requiring children to negotiate roles, share ideas, and support each other's contributions.

Of the key knowledge and skills around drama, child-guided experiences seem particularly important for the following:

> Imitating sounds and actions and using simple props
> Pretending alone or with one other person

Adult-guided experiences are especially significant for the following:

> Imagining characters and events
> Pretending with two or more other people
> Exploring improvisational theater games and puppetry

CHILD-GUIDED experiences are especially important for learnings such as:

| Drama | Imitating sounds and actions and using simple props |

Young children use their bodies (gestures, facial expressions), copy sounds (human, animal, mechanical), and repeat words ("Go to sleep, baby") to represent the world they know. Engaging in imitative play with sounds, actions, and props builds children's foundational experiences in dramatic expression, fostering creativity, social, emotional, and language skills.

Teaching strategies. To encourage children to imitate sounds and actions and use simple props, try strategies like the following:

> Encourage spontaneous imitation throughout the day. Join children as they reproduce actions and sounds around them. For example, if a child flattens a piece of playdough and pretends to flip pizzas, improvise! Flatten some playdough too and mimic the same motions. Imitating a child's actions can create an action dialogue in which you and the child communicate with gestures instead of words.

> Provide simple props like blocks to build walls and household items to handle. Model their use, and consider creating additional props with students. Use Universal Design for Learning principles when setting up, such as selecting costumes with simple closures so that all children, including those with disabilities, can use them.

Very young children engage in dramatic play independently. For example, they may "drive" a block along the table. Parallel play (playing *alongside* others) typically begins around age 2, and social play (playing *with* others) emerges around age 3. In early preschool, however, social play usually involves making up a shared story with one other person. If a child has a disability that limits interaction, alternative methods can facilitate play. For example, a child with autism spectrum disorder may need guidance to accept suggestions during a pretend airplane flight. Teachers can ask about the child's preferred role (pilot), narrate their entry to the plane (It's time for the pilot to board"), and describe other actions to help include them ("Oh, I see Reese is wearing sunglasses to keep the sun out of his eyes. Does anyone else want sunglasses?"). This technique can provide structure enough for peers to adapt and include the child in the play.

Teaching strategies. To support children's earliest attempts at dramatic play, the following strategies are effective:

› Participate as a partner in children's dramatic play, and nurture the storyline. Child development and storytelling expert Vivian Paley (2004) notes that adults who join children's play are better observers, understand children more, and communicate with them more effectively during play interactions. However, to be a sensitive partner, observe first to understand children's intentions, then wait for an invitation or welcoming cues. Match your play level to theirs, and occasionally ask open-ended questions or suggest extensions while respecting their autonomy and ideas. For example, consider Mr. Jorje's actions:

> Four-year-old Sofonias and her family are indigenous people from the Yucatán in Mexico who attend Ms. Catalina's preschool. Sofonias's mother carries her infant in a Rebozo (short wraparound shawl worn over the shoulder). When Sofonias plays in the dramatic play kitchen center, she pretends to make dinner and wash dishes while carrying her doll wrapped in a piece of fabric, too. Four-year-old Andre notices this. He finds an additional piece of fabric and attempts to wrap his doll the same way, but he looks confused. Ms. Catalina then says, "Sofonias, Andre is trying to wrap his doll the way you have wrapped your baby. Will you show him how to do it?" Sofonias helps Andre wrap his doll, and the two children continue with their pretend kitchen play while caring for their babies.

ADULT-GUIDED experiences are especially important in learnings such as:

| Drama | Imagining characters and events |

Children imitate familiar people, animals, and actions on their own, but using their imaginations to create pretend-play scenarios often requires more active adult intervention. Encouraging young children to imagine and expand on characters and events helps them explore storytelling, empathy, and creative expression. "Suppose . . ." and "What if . . ." questions are good prompts that let children take the lead in an evolving scenario.

Teaching strategies. Use the following suggestions to encourage young children in imaginative play:

> Encourage dramatic play in the classroom and outdoors. Provide open space and materials, including real props collected from home, the community, or families.

> Allow play to flow between areas. For example, children in the "house" area may use blocks to create a backyard barbecue, a space station, or a leafy jungle.

> Engage in storytelling without a book. Tell a basic story using expressive gestures and movement so that children can join in, too. For example, when telling the story of King Midas and the Golden Touch, invite children to touch imaginary objects, turning them to gold.

> Invite families or professional storytellers to present folktales at large group time, highlighting how storytelling is prominent in many cultures.

| Drama | Pretending with two or more other people |

Cooperative dramatic play, which involves inventing stories with multiple characters, locations, and props, can lead to disagreements. These are excellent opportunities to teach conflict resolution skills to help children work through their challenges and continue their play. The adult's intervention varies based on children's ages and stages of play. For example, with toddlers engaging in parallel play, you might join in and offer additional props. For young preschoolers in associative play, you might narrate their plotlines and help them negotiate roles. Cooperative play, typically seen in 4- to 5-year-olds, involves more elaborate storylines and interactions. Adults in this scenario act as helpful narrators, facilitating the play and helping resolve conflicts that arise.

Teaching strategies. To expand the number of partners that older preschoolers can include in their pretend-play scenarios and to support more complex play, try the following ideas:

> Provide materials that encourage children to collaborate. Try large boards, boxes, blankets, rocking boats, or buses that several children can use together to develop play scenarios with multiple roles.

> Facilitate social problem solving. Encourage children to think of alternate roles or scenarios that will let them all participate in the play. For example, say, "It looks like you all have a problem. Bethany, Soo-yi, and Marta all want to be the oldest elephant, and you all look mad! How can we solve this problem?" or "I wonder if any other puppets can be good guys too?" This approach helps children learn compromise, emotional regulation, and creativity.

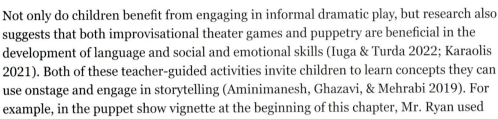

Drama | **Exploring improvisational theater games and puppetry**

Not only do children benefit from engaging in informal dramatic play, but research also suggests that both improvisational theater games and puppetry are beneficial in the development of language and social and emotional skills (Iuga & Turda 2022; Karaolis 2021). Both of these teacher-guided activities invite children to learn concepts they can use onstage and engage in storytelling (Aminimanesh, Ghazavi, & Mehrabi 2019). For example, in the puppet show vignette at the beginning of this chapter, Mr. Ryan used elements of improvisational theater by accepting play offerings of the children rather than leading the play, a concept called *yes, and* (O'Neill 2014). As Mr. Ryan participates, he subtly facilitates the play episode, responding as an audience, central to performance of the play.

Teaching strategies. Try these suggestions for improvisation and puppetry:

> Invite children to engage in character improvisation using simple costumes or props. Provide them with basic items like hats, scarves, or masks, and encourage them to adopt different characters, such as animals, community helpers, or imaginary creatures. Prompt children by asking questions such as "How does a firefighter act?" or "What would a friendly dragon say?" This allows children to explore various roles and personalities.

> Encourage children to create their own puppet characters and tell stories. Provide materials for making simple puppets, then prompt children to use their puppets to tell stories, either alone or in groups.

Dramatic Play

Throughout this book we have highlighted dramatic play and play in general as an effective and vital vehicle for children's learning across all developmental domains and content areas. As dramatic play is central to all types of learning, its inclusion in this chapter on creative arts is not intended to limit it to this area of learning. Dramatic play is both the means and the measure of the child's advancing cognitive growth—the beginning of symbolic and abstract thought. Providing opportunities for culturally rich dramatic play can foster children's sense of self and belonging in the classroom as well as expand their understanding of others and the world around them (Salinas-Gonzalez, Arreguin-Anderson, & Alanis 2017).

> Model puppet use during large group time (Karaolis 2021). Stay nearby to guide puppet play, and scaffold prosocial themes by asking questions such as "I wonder what his problem is?" or "Gee, she looks really excited. What happens next?"

> If older preschoolers show interest, they may enjoy creating and performing short plays they initiate and improvise. You can assist with writing down the plot and pose open-ended questions: "How could you build a stage?," "Will there be curtains?," "Where will the audience sit?," "Will they need tickets?" Each of these provocations invites the children to develop or refine skills across developmental domains.

Art Appreciation

Art appreciation provides opportunities for young children to notice and enjoy many kinds of art, letting them explore how art makes them feel on their own while also guiding them to understand the emotions, cultures, and times that inspire art.

Of the key knowledge and skills around art appreciation, child-guided experiences seem particularly important for the following:

> Developing aesthetic awareness and recognizing the feelings expressed through art

Adult-guided experiences are especially significant for the following:

> Developing aesthetic understanding and artistic expression

> Recognizing cultural and temporal influences on art

CHILD-GUIDED experiences are especially important for learnings such as:

Art Appreciation	Developing aesthetic awareness and recognizing the feelings expressed through art

Young preschoolers exhibit a deep fascination with specific aspects of a work of art. They tend to focus either on one dominant feature or on the work as a whole, providing an opportunity to explore these elements. Young children may sense the emotion in a work of art, expressing their understanding through body and facial gestures (a slump or frown to communicate sadness), a dance movement (hopping with glee), or a comparable representation in their own artwork (tight circles of energy drawn in red crayon).

Teaching strategies. Try these strategies to heighten children's aesthetic awareness and an understanding of the emotions behind art:

> Plan activities focused on a single art element, such as color or line, tempo, or a dramatic play role. For example, play recordings of two string instruments, such as a West African kora (harp) and an Indian sitar (and have photos of both), so that children can compare the sounds and move their bodies expressively to the music.

> Use games that support children to home in on one aspect of a work of art, such as I Spy with tools like magnifying glasses for hands-on exploration.

> When sharing storybook illustrations and art reproductions with children, discuss the aesthetic experience. Provide art materials, then invite children to create something that shows how the works make them feel or interpret the artist's feeling

ADULT-GUIDED experiences are especially important for learnings such as:

Art Appreciation > **Developing aesthetic understanding and artistic expression**

As children explore art, music, movement, and storytelling, they begin to develop a deeper understanding of the creative process. This includes learning specific vocabulary to describe art forms, elements, and techniques. Introduce this vocabulary, and encourage children to use it in conversations and art creations. Several publications include glossaries of art terms to use with young children (for example, the Ducksters Art and Artist Glossary and Terms for Kids at ducksters.com). Add to these published glossaries the vocabulary words, phrases, and definitions that teachers and children use while discussing their art interests, including those for the art prevalent in their home languages, cultures, and community.

Teaching strategy. Repeated exposure helps children grasp and use art language confidently. Use strategies like the following:

> Offer thoughtful comments and open-ended questions to invite children's ideas and discussions. "I wonder" is a good way to encourage reflection and conversation. Here are some examples: I wonder . . .

- How it feels, sounds, smells

- What it reminds you of or makes you think of

- How we could move like it or move to it

- How you will pretend to be that and what props you will use

- Why the artist did it this way/or did not _____

Sandy, Alberto, and Olivia (age 3) sit on the rug with Ms. Jeannette around a print of "The Starry Night" by Vincent van Gogh, each with magnifying glasses in their hands. "What do you notice in this painting?" Ms. Jeannette says.

Sandy leaps up and responds, "Look at those swirls!"

"Oh, I noticed those swirls, too, Sandy," Ms. Jeannette says, imitating his arm motions. Alberto uses his magnifying glass to focus in on the moon. "Look at that moon!" Ms. Jeannette prompts, "Tell me more about the moon, Alberto."

"It's yellow . . . bright yellow!"

Ms. Jeannette adds, "The bright yellow color contrasts with the dark background. It makes it stand out! And how does that make you feel?"

Olivia chimes in, "It makes me feel a little sleepy. When the moon is out, I am usually in bed."

Art Appreciation ▸ **Recognizing cultural and temporal influences on art**

Children learn how context—personal background, community, cultural beliefs, and geographic setting—shapes art experiences.

Teaching strategies. Support multicultural awareness by connecting children's backgrounds to their art experience. Try strategies like the following:

> Show art in various media types from other cultures and times, reflecting classroom diversity. For example, display Asian pottery, Middle Eastern music, South American dance, and African folktales. Make connections with the children's lives. For example, say, "I see a pattern in your sweater, and this textile has patterns, too."

> Invite families to share art from their home and culture in any media.

> Invite artists to the classroom or take a field trip to a studio or gallery. If that's not possible, arrange a virtual museum tour. At the time of the publication of this book, the Art Institute of Chicago (n.d.) has a free virtual tour of their collections. Stream performances (such as Warner Classics, n.d.) as families and their children move through an open part of the classroom with scarves.

● ● ●

When teachers give the creative arts the respect they deserve, they can enrich their classrooms and their explorations of diversity. It is easy to push aside art, music, dance, and drama in favor of a more academic curriculum, but the arts have the capacity to change children's lives for the better, providing new ways for children to see the world and express their ideas and feelings. In addition, engaging in artistic endeavors strengthens skills across the developmental domains. Although many early childhood programs provide limited opportunities to go beyond making adult-led crafts, listening to popular recorded children's music, and using simple or stereotyped props for dramatic play, the intentional teacher chooses to dig deeper, offering richer learning opportunities such as those explored in the chapter. Creative arts open the door to joyful learning and to opportunities to reflect children's and teachers' home cultures throughout the classroom. Take a risk, jump in, and try something—the adventure will be worth it!

For Further Consideration

1. What arguments can early childhood advocates use to preserve the creative arts in the face of budget allocations favoring academic disciplines at the expense of other content areas?

2. How could an early childhood educator convince their director to see the promise of developmentally appropriate early art experiences as a path for children's later academic success?

3. Reflect on your own practices around open-ended creative experiences versus product-focused art activities. Do you find yourself, or other teachers you know, continuing to plan and carry out craft activities in which the children all make or do the same thing? If so, are you prioritizing finished products to display in your room? Does this benefit adults? Is it easier? Are open-ended experiences more intimidating? Are the families' and directors' expectations a factor? Knowing the importance for children's development of richer art experience, what is something you can do to change your own practices and advocate for more open-ended experiences outside your classroom?

4. Why is it important to become more knowledgeable about art from a variety of cultures and traditions, including those represented by the children and families in your program? How can you acquire this knowledge?

CHAPTER 11

Reflections on Intentional Teaching

Amy Schmidtke

Three preschoolers—Marcus, Asia, and Zeke—ask their teacher, Miss Jolene, to help them make playdough. From the house area, Asia fetches a big bowl, and Marcus gets the recipe page from the class cookbook. As Miss Jolene reads aloud the ingredients and their amounts, the children take them out of the grocery bag Miss Jolene has brought and set them on the table: one cup of flour, one-half cup of salt, one package of unsweetened fruit juice powder, two teaspoons of cream of tartar, one cup of water, and one tablespoon of vegetable oil.

"What else do we need?" asks Miss Jolene.

"Measuring cups and spoons!" says Asia, and she returns to the house area to get them.

"Anything else?" asks Miss Jolene.

The children look at the recipe page, ingredients, and cooking utensils and decide they have everything they need.

These young children are about to engage in scientific discoveries during an everyday activity. As you read the rest of the vignette, note how Miss Jolene takes advantage of a cooking situation to help the children become aware of scientific properties (dry and wet, shiny and not shiny) and the transformation of materials while introducing concepts in mathematics (numerals, measuring) and literacy (reading, vocabulary, the alphabet).

Miss Jolene: (*Points to the words in the recipe.*) The recipe says to mix all the dry ingredients first.

Marcus: I want to put in the flour. (*Scoops out a heaping cupful and dumps it in the bowl.*)

Asia: I want to do the salt. Which spoon do I use?

Miss Jolene: (*Hands her the measuring spoons.*) We need the half teaspoon. See if you can find the spoon with the numerals one and two on the handle.

Asia: (*Looks and shakes her head.*)

Miss Jolene: It looks like this. (*Writes ½ on a piece of paper and hands it to Asia.*)

Asia: I found it! (*Scoops salt out of the salt dish and adds it to the bowl.*)

Miss Jolene: There are still two more dry ingredients.

Zeke: (*Picks up the oil.*) Not this!

Miss Jolene: How do you know the oil isn't dry?

Zeke: 'Cause it's gloopy.

Miss Jolene: The oil is gloopy and wet.

Marcus: This is dry! (*Holds up the package of juice powder.*)

Miss Jolene: (*Nods.*)

Marcus: (*Adds juice powder to the other dry ingredients*). And this. (*Holds up the dish of cream of tartar.*)

Miss Jolene: Now we have to stir the dry ingredients together. (*Looks expectantly at the children.*)

Zeke: Hey! We forgot the big wooden spoon! (*Gets it from the house area and takes a turn stirring the mixture.*)

Marcus: (*Peers into the bowl and points to the juice powder.*) The red dots are shiny!

Miss Jolene: Sometimes dots like that are called crystals. The pieces of salt are called crystals, too.

The children look at the mixture, commenting that they can't tell the difference between the flour and cream of tartar once they are mixed together because both are white and *not* shiny.

Zeke: Can we add the water and oil now?

Miss Jolene: (*Hands Zeke the cup to get very hot water with the help of her coteacher. Helps Asia measure the oil.*)

Zeke: (*Watches the mixed playdough drip off the wooden spoon.*) It's too gloopy!

Asia: Yeah, it's way too wet!

Miss Jolene: How can we make the playdough drier?

Asia: Add more crystals!

Miss Jolene: We only had one package. What else could we do?

Marcus: Add more flour. (*Adds another heaping cup.*)

Zeke: Now it's too dry! (*Refills the water cup.*)

Miss Jolene: How do you know that's the right amount of water to add?

Zeke: (*Hesitates.*) Maybe a little less? (*Pours off half and then pours off a little more.*)

The children again take turns stirring the mixture. They decide to add another one-half cup of flour and a "teensy, weensy bit" of cream of tartar. Then they announce that the playdough is just right—ready for them and the other children to use.

In the next vignette, Abdel uses trial and error to sort objects he has collected into piles labeled "sticky" (lifted by the magnet) and "not sticky" (not lifted by the magnet). When he discovers an object that falls under both categories, he solves the problem by replacing the object with a clear-cut choice.

Four-year-old Abdel sits in the toy area with a magnet and a basket filled with small objects he has gathered: plastic counting bears, nails and screws, wooden puzzle pieces, cardboard cubes, a jeweler's screwdriver, an assortment of cooking utensils, and pieces of twine. He tries to lift each item with the magnet, and then he sorts them into two piles, which he labels "sticky" and "not sticky." When Abdel gets to a can opener with a plastic handle and a metal tip, he goes back and forth between the two ends several times before finally putting the can opener back in the basket. He finishes sorting the other items and looks at the can opener again. Then, he returns it to the house area and finds a different, all-metal can opener, which he checks with the magnet and adds to the pile of other "sticky" objects. Abdel sits back, surveys the two piles, and smiles with satisfaction.

The children in both scenarios initiated the activity and were clearly involved in pursuing their interests. In Abdel's case, the teacher provided materials and time, whereas in the playdough example, the teacher offered thoughtful comments and questions to further the children's understanding of scientific concepts.

The teaching and learning principles illustrated in these examples apply to every area of learning addressed in this book—whether it is approaches to learning, social and emotional learning, physical development and health, language and literacy, mathematics, science, social studies, or the creative arts. In every domain and subject area, the most meaningful and lasting learning occurs when children are interested in the topic and actively engaged in mastering its specific knowledge and skills. As this book has illustrated, children can explore and understand some of this body of content through child-guided learning experiences, either on their own or through interactions with peers and older children. For children to acquire other information, concepts, and skills, adult-guided learning experiences are essential. Intentional teachers adeptly support all children, including multilingual learners and children with developmental delays or disabilities. They understand their own pivotal role in both child-led and teacher-guided experiences.

Guiding Principles of Intentional Teaching

The framework and examples in this book offer a starting point for you as you consider and choose appropriate teaching strategies. Although there will still be many instances in which you make your own decisions about whether child- or adult-guided learning experiences are more suited to a particular topic, setting, child, or group of children, the guiding principles that follow can help you decide which strategies to use across a range of learnings and situations.

The first set of principles describes the basic characteristics of all intentional *teachers*—that is, what they know and do. The remaining two sets list the conditions, respectively, under which intentional teachers either encourage child-guided experiences or engage in instruction that is more adult guided. The focus of all these principles is on *children* because it is in observing and being sensitive to those you teach that you can best determine the most effective instructional strategy to use to support each child.

Although these guiding principles are derived from the theory, research, and practices presented in this book, they are offered here as hypotheses rather than proven facts. You are invited to view them critically and think about how you can test them through further study and application. There is still much to learn from additional research and reflection as teachers strive to make intentionality a standard part of their professional development and daily work with children.

To teach with intention, teachers

> Create a learning environment rich in materials, experiences, and interactions

> Build meaningful relationships with each child

> Understand that all learning and development take place within children's social, cultural, and linguistic contexts, and value and build on each child's individual contexts and experiences

> Encourage children to explore materials, experiences, relationships, and ideas

> Talk respectfully, reciprocally, and frequently with children

> Consciously promote all areas of learning and development

> Know the content (concepts, vocabulary, facts, skills) that makes up each area of learning along with the learning progressions for each area

> Know and use general teaching strategies that are effective with most young children

> Use their knowledge of each child to individualize support, adjusting teaching strategies and using a strengths-based approach as they work with different individuals and groups

> Know and use specific teaching strategies that are effective in different content areas

> Match content with children's developmental levels and emerging abilities and interests

> Partner with each child's family to learn ways to connect home and school learning

> Are planful, purposeful, and thoughtful

> Take advantage of spontaneous, unexpected teaching and learning opportunities

> Carefully observe children to determine their interests and level of understanding and to plan next steps

> Neither underestimate nor overestimate what children can do and learn

> Provide challenges that encourage children to question their own thinking and conclusions

> Scaffold learning, with careful consideration for introducing new materials and ideas

> Reflect on and adjust teaching strategies based on children's responses

Intentional teachers support child-guided learning experiences when children are

> Exploring materials, actions, and ideas actively and making connections on their own
> Establishing interpersonal relationships and learning from one another
> Turning to one another for assistance
> Considering and investigating their own questions about materials, events, and ideas
> Motivated to solve problems on their own
> So focused on their enterprise that adult intervention would be an interruption
> Challenging themselves and each other to master new skills
> Applying and extending existing knowledge and skills in new ways

Although these behaviors and attitudes signal that child-guided experiences will be particularly fruitful, this does not exclude using other teaching strategies and planned activities. Even when you pick up on cues like these, you will likely want to make strategic use of adult-guided experiences to optimize children's learning.

Intentional teachers employ adult-guided learning experiences when children

> Have not yet encountered the material or experience at home or in other settings
> Cannot create established systems of knowledge (such as letter names) on their own
> Do not see, hear, or otherwise attend to something likely to interest them
> Have not reflected on how or why something has happened, or considered what might happen "if . . ."
> Do not engage with something teachers know they will need for further learning
> Ask for information or help explicitly
> Are bored or distracted and need help focusing
> Appear stalled, discouraged, or frustrated
> Appear ready for the next level of mastery but are not likely to attain it on their own
> Are not aware of the potentially unsafe or hurtful consequences of their actions
> Appear to use materials or actions very repetitively over time
> Are conscious of and upset about something they cannot yet do but wish to

Although these behaviors and attitudes suggest that children benefit from adult-guided learning experiences, this does not mean that child-guided experiences are not also an important part of the full learning picture.

Nurturing Your Own Professional Growth

To effectively nurture young children's learning and development, intentional teachers must also prioritize their own professional growth. By fostering habits of intentionality and continuous improvement, teachers not only enhance their effectiveness in their daily work with young children but also model lifelong learning as members of the early childhood profession (NAEYC 2019c). You can nurture your own growth and continuous improvement by doing the following:

- Participating in ongoing professional development to stay updated on effective practices, improve skills, and deepen knowledge of specific approaches and content areas

- Seeking feedback from peers and mentors to gain fresh perspectives and insights

- Sharing knowledge with colleagues and engaging in collaborative activities to build a supportive community of practice

- Reflecting regularly on your teaching practices to identify areas for growth improvement

- Applying new ideas and strategies learned from professional development or colleagues to enhance your teaching

- Gathering ideas from families, support staff, and children to discover innovative ways to encourage growth (Schmidtke 2022c)

Final Thoughts

Just as this book has presented a balanced approach to teaching and learning, so too are the following thoughts offered in the form of "on-the-one-hand" and "on-the-other-hand" propositions. These ideas reflect the complexity of intentional teaching in early childhood as a *both/and* endeavor. You may agree fully, partially, or not at all with these statements. The important thing is to consider these ideas and reflect on how they apply to you in your capacity as an early childhood practitioner, administrator, researcher, or advocate.

Valuing Teachers

> Early childhood educators have a wealth of wisdom. With proper training, mentoring, and supportive work environments (admittedly a significant "if") and a commitment to self-reflection and growth, teachers can develop the ability to be creative and thoughtful in the classroom. Prescriptive lesson plans are not necessary for working effectively with young children.

> On the other hand, meaningful learning cannot be left to chance. There is a body of knowledge that teachers should know regarding how children learn and how best to teach them. Each content area has a set of knowledge and skills that teachers should study and be familiar with to assess what children know and determine how to scaffold further learning.

Valuing Children

> Preschoolers are still young children, not small adults or even scaled-down elementary school students. They come to the early learning settings as individuals with their own personalities, languages, cultures, and background knowledge. The early childhood field should resist pressures for excessive testing that can label children, families, teachers, and schools as failures. Teachers need to follow developmentally appropriate, research-based practices. In that way, they can stop extending the early elementary curriculum into preschool and kindergarten and preserve young children's eagerness to learn throughout their childhood and adult lives.

> Nevertheless, teachers should respect young children's curiosity and eagerness to learn and not be afraid to introduce information, model and coach specific skills, use unusual vocabulary words, and challenge children to solve complex problems that are meaningful to them. If you observe children's thinking and actions, your attempts to scaffold their learning are likely to be on target. And if you occasionally introduce something beyond their grasp, the children will let you know. You can then back up a step or two, providing appropriate support and opportunities for practice.

Valuing Families

> Families are integral partners in children's development and learning. They serve as children's first teachers and hold a deep understanding of their child's unique needs, interests, and learning styles. Partnering with families gives teachers valuable insights to inform their teaching practices and contribute to a holistic approach to education. Collaborating with families strengthens the relationship between home and school, creating a supportive environment for children to thrive.

> However, there is no one-size-fits-all approach to partnering with families. Each family has its own values, beliefs, and expectations for their child's education. Effective teachers meet families where they are by listening to their perspectives and building trust. By adopting a strengths-based approach, teachers can honor and respect families while co-creating strategies that align with each family's circumstances. This flexible and individualized approach fosters meaningful partnerships and supports children's holistic development.

Valuing Content

> The knowledge and skills children need to acquire extend beyond language and literacy, mathematics, and science. School readiness involves social skills, dispositions for learning, physical health, and the arts, which are integral to fostering community and joy.

> However, because early childhood educators have traditionally emphasized the social and emotional domains, they must effectively communicate the value of play and playful learning to the public. When educators say that "learning happens through play" and that "play is a child's work," they must explain how and why purposeful play supports meaningful learning. The best play is purposeful and engages children's minds, bodies, and emotions; is meaningful; often involves others; is iterative; and is joyful (Zosh et al. 2022). In contrast, random activity neither satisfies nor enhances learning in a meaningful way.

> Inclusive and culturally responsive intentional teaching enhances content learning. Instruction should reflect children's backgrounds and experiences and incorporate materials and examples relevant to children's lives. By tailoring instruction to children, teachers can ensure access to meaningful and engaging learning opportunities.

From the research on child development and real classroom examples in this book, it is clear that teachers can help children learn—and enjoy learning—in all the content areas necessary for school readiness and lifelong success. A great deal is already known about what it means to teach with intention and the kinds of knowledge and skills educators can help young children acquire. Yet, there remains more for professionals to explore about fostering meaningful child- and adult-guided experiences in the early years—experiences that facilitate equitable opportunities for every child.

Advancing the concept of the intentional teacher will require ongoing efforts in theoretical work, research, curriculum development, staff training and mentoring, program evaluation, child observation, administrative leadership, and reflective practice. Each of these elements is essential to continually refine teaching approaches that respond to the diverse and evolving needs of children and families.

Every early childhood educator has one or more roles to play in this research and development process. If this third edition of *The Intentional Teacher* has encouraged you to reflect on your practice, deepen your professional growth, and actively contribute to the collective wisdom and advancement of the field, it has achieved its purpose.

Glossary

adult-guided learning: Experiences that proceed primarily along the lines of the teacher's goals, although that experience is also shaped by children's active engagement.

alphabet knowledge: Understanding that there is a systematic relationship between letters and sounds. Also known as the alphabetic principle.

approaches to learning: Dispositions toward responding to educational experiences in varying degrees of curiosity, creativity, confidence, independence, initiative, and persistence. Includes both a child's readiness for and response to learning experiences.

child-guided learning: Experiences that proceed primarily along the lines of children's interests and actions, although teachers provide materials and other support.

conflict resolution: Using appropriate, nonaggressive strategies to discuss and develop solutions to interpersonal differences with children; also known as social problem solving.

content: The substance or subject matter that is the object of children's learning and the knowledge (certain vocabulary and concepts) and skills in an area of learning, including literacy, mathematics, science, social studies, and creative arts.

decontextualized talk: Conversations about objects, people, and events that, while familiar to children, are not immediately present or occurring.

developmental domains: Important knowledge and skills that young children want and need to master in the areas traditionally associated with early childhood education: social and emotional, physical, linguistic, and cognitive.

developmentally appropriate practice: A framework of principles and guidelines for practice that promotes young children's optimal learning and development through a strengths-based, play-based approach to joyful, engaged learning.

emergent literacy: A gradual progression of literacy learning that begins in infancy and continues through formal reading and writing instruction in school.

emotional skills: Recognizing, expressing, and regulating one's own emotions and identifying the emotions of others.

executive function skills: The command-and-control abilities that allow one to manage and execute tasks. These skills play a crucial role in how individuals engage in and adapt to learning experiences.

information talk: Describes what children are doing when playing.

intentional teaching: Planful, thoughtful, and purposeful acts teachers implement to ensure that young children acquire the knowledge and skills (content) they need to succeed in school and in life. Intentional teachers use their knowledge, judgment, and expertise to act with specific outcomes or goals in mind for children's development and learning, and they integrate and promote meaningful learning in *all* domains.

intentionality: Interactions between children and teachers in which teachers purposefully challenge, scaffold, and extend children's skills and have an understanding of the expected outcomes of instruction.

movement concepts: The movement knowledge component of the early childhood curriculum relating to *where, how, and in relationship to what* the body moves.

movement skills: Fundamental physical/motor skills that young children need to develop and refine.

number sense: Intuition about numbers and their magnitude, their relationship to real quantities, and the kinds of operations that can be performed on them.

phonemic awareness: A subset of phonological awareness that involves the understanding that individual sounds make up words (blending) and that words can be separated into sounds (segmentation).

phonological awareness: The general ability to attend to the sounds of language as distinct from its meaning. Initial awareness of speech sounds and rhythms, rhyme awareness, recognition of sound similarities, and phonemic awareness are all elements of this ability.

planning *(child)*: Choosing with intentionality one's own course of action; an important component of executive functioning.

readiness for learning experiences: A child's initial willingness to explore materials, ideas, people, and events.

responding to learning experiences: How a child thinks about, relates to, and navigates the physical and interpersonal environment both during and after a learning experience.

scaffolding: Finding the right balance within a child's approach to learning and developmental level by first supporting the child's current level of understanding and then gently extending their learning.

social and emotional development: One of the primary domains of early childhood education; the process of developing social and emotional competence that includes self-awareness, self-management, social awareness, relationship skills, and decision making.

social concepts: Subject matter that forms the standard topics taught in school as social studies, including economics, history, geography, and ecology.

social skills: The range of appropriate strategies for interacting with others.

social systems: The norms, values, and procedures that affect human relationships in our day-to-day lives.

socialization: The acquisition of knowledge of social norms and customs.

subitizing: The immediate and accurate recognition of very small quantities (up to four or five) *without* counting.

Index

child-guided experiences in, 108–109
writing experiences, 156

F

families
building children's self-identity, 72
building partnerships with, 38–39
creating a variety of engagement opportunities for, 79
help from, in building emotional competence, 74
language use in, 132
of multilingual learners, 133–134, 140
roles within, 248
support in developing moral framework, 89
supporting children's planning, 56
supporting technology use for learning, 29
talking with, about outdoor play, 260
valuing of, in intentional teaching, 298
feedback versus praise. *See* encouragement versus praise
feeding and dressing oneself, 117
fine motor development, 96–97, 108–109, 111–112, 156
fitting the learning experience to the learning objective. *See* adult-guided learning experiences; child-guided learning experiences
following up, encouraging children in, 62
food and nutrition, 120–121
formative assessment, 40–41
functions. *See* patterns, functions, and algebra
funds of knowledge, 21

G

games
for expanding vocabulary, 145
improvisational, 287
with mathematical elements, 170
rethinking elimination games, 100
that promote phonological awareness, 143–144
geography, 258–259
geometry and spatial sense, 166, 178, 182–188
grammar, 159, 161
gross motor development, 28, 93, 95–96

grouping children in a variety of ways, 32
growth, children's, 218–219
guided play, 25, 26

H

healthy behavior. *See* personal care and healthy behavior
history, 256–257
hygiene. *See* personal care and healthy behavior

I

ideas, engaging with, 56–57
imagination. *See* pretending
imitation, 281–282, 284
inclusion. *See* diversity, equity, and inclusion
independent problem solving, 37, 58–59
individualized support for children with developmental delays or disabilities, 23
information. *See* data analysis; obtaining, evaluating, and communicating information; representing gathered information
information talk, 136, 137
initiative, encouraging, 35, 52–53
integrated learning through science, 210
intentional teaching
child-guided/adult-guided learning balance, 4–9, 15–16
general principles of, 294–296
listening and speaking, 135–147
social contexts of, 14–15
terminology, 9–14
valuing teachers, children, families, and content, 297–299
vignettes, 1–2, 3–4, 292–294
interest areas in the classroom, 27–28, 30
interpersonal hygiene, 119–120
intuiting number and its properties, 175, 176

L

language and literacy
children's development in, 127–129
conversations with multilingual learners, 132–133
expressing science investigation questions using, 215
five dimensions of language knowledge, 125–126

57, 61, 138, 197, 275